To:

Derek

RIFLE GREEN
IN
THE CRIMEA

with our best wishes

from

Bob Cooper

&

G. Caldwell

£35.00

This book is dedicated to the memory of Sir William H. Cope, Bart. and Colonel Willoughby Verner, the Historians of the 95th Rifles, The Rifle Brigade. Their research and books have been invaluable in enabling us to continue the history of the regiment in our Rifle Green series, to the benefit of all past and present Riflemen.

JAMES DANN

Rifle Brigade Officers' Shako Badge Crimean War period.

Rifle Green
in
The Crimea

AN ACCOUNT OF THE RIFLE BRIGADE
IN THE CRIMEAN WAR OF 1854–56.
WITH A FULL MEDAL AND CASUALTY ROLL
AND DETAILS OF WEAPONS, CLOTHES AND EQUIPMENT
USED IN THE CAMPAIGN.

by

George Caldwell and Robert Cooper

BUGLE HORN PUBLICATIONS

By the same authors

RIFLE GREEN AT WATERLOO

In preparation

RIFLE GREEN IN THE PENINSULA (4 volumes)

© Copyright G. J. Caldwell and R. B. E. Cooper
1994

All rights reserved

Published by
BUGLE HORN PUBLICATIONS
in a
LIMITED EDITION OF 1,000 COPIES
of which this is Number

101.

British Library Cataloguing in Publication Data
A. A catalogue record for this book is available from the British Library

ISBN 0 9516600 1 2

Contents

FOREWORD	13
INTRODUCTION	15
ACKNOWLEDGEMENTS	18
1. 2ND BATTALION RIFLE BRIGADE IN THE CRIMEA	**27**
To the East	29
The Landing	40
The Advance to the Alma	44
The Battle of the Alma	47
To Sebastopol	62
Little Inkerman	70
2nd Battalion at the Battle of Inkerman	74
Winter 1854–1855	77
The Band in Constantinople	80
Draft arrives from England	82
18th June: Storming of the Redan	97
The Final attack on the Redan	105
2. 1ST BATTALION RIFLE BRIGADE IN THE CRIMEA	**115**
The Voyage East	117
Landing in the Crimea	124
The advance to the Alma	127
After the Battle	131
Advance to Sebastopol	133
Siege of Sebastopol begins	136
The Battle of Balaclava	143
Battle of Inkerman	146
The Capture of the Rifle-pits	157

Winter in the Crimea	164
The First Attack on the Redan	171
The Second Attack on the Redan	176
Explosion in the French Magazine	179
Return to England	181

3. **RIFLE BRIGADE CRIMEAN UNIFORM, ARMS AND EQUIPMENT IN 1854** — 185

Uniform	187
Equipment	191
Arms and weapons	196
Additional clothing, unofficial and official	200

4. **CRIMEA MEDALS AND AWARDS TO THE RIFLE BRIGADE** — 205

Distinguished Conduct Medal	213
Companion of the Order of the Bath	214
Victoria Cross	214
Legion of Honour	215
Turkish Crimea Medal	215
The Sardinian War Medal	215
The Reserve Force for the Crimea	218
Distribution of the Victoria Cross, Hyde Park 1857	219
Medal Rolls, Remarks Columns	222

5. **1ST BATTALION RIFLE BRIGADE MEDAL ROLL FOR THE CRIMEA** — 225

6. **2ND BATTALION RIFLE BRIGADE MEDAL ROLL FOR THE CRIMEA** — 277

NOTES ON THE ILLUSTRATIONS — 337

BIBLIOGRAPHY — 348

Plates

Death of Lieutenant Tryon, attack on the Rifle-pits	Plate 1
Lt-Colonel Alfred Horsford	Plate 2
Major Lord Alexander Russell	Plate 2
Lt-Colonel Edward Somerset	Plate 2
Captain Henry Clifford, V.C.	Plate 2
Captain John P. C. Glyn	Plate 3
Captain Hercules Walker	Plate 3
Captain Frederick Morgan	Plate 3
Lieutenant Hore Ruthven	Plate 3
Lieutenant William J. M. Cuninghame, V.C.	Plate 4
Lieutenant H. Tryon	Plate 4
Lieutenant Claude Thomas Bourchier, V.C.	Plate 4
Lieutenant George R. Saunders	Plate 4
Colour-Sergeant John Fisher	Plate 5
Bugle-Major David Peachey	Plate 5
Rifleman James Hawksford	Plate 5
Bugle-Major David Peachey in later life	Plate 5
Rifleman Francis Wheatley, V.C., D.C.M.	Plate 6
1st Bn. Rifle Brigade officers in various forms of dress on return from the Crimea	Plate 6
Rifleman William Reith	Plate 6
Record of Service of William Reith	Plate 7
Officers and other ranks of 'K' Company, 1st Bn. Rifle Brigade	Plate 8
Colour-Sergeant, Sergeant and Rifleman	Plate 8
Riflemen Hannan and Ferguson, the affair in the trenches	Plate 9
General Sir George Brown	Plate 10
Lieutenant Colonel A. MacDonell	Plate 10

Colonel A. J. Lawrence	Plate 10
Major William Norcott	Plate 10
Captain and Adjutant John Ross	Plate 11
Captain H. Colville	Plate 11
Assistant Surgeon J. B. C. Reade	Plate 11
Captain F. R. Elrington	Plate 11
Captain The Earl of Erroll	Plate 12
Captain E. Newdigate	Plate 12
Captain W. A. Fyers	Plate 12
Lieutenant John Knox, V.C.	Plate 12
Major J. R. Glyn	Plate 13
Lieutenant F. E. Sotheby	Plate 13
2nd Lieutenant C. R. NIcholl	Plate 13
Lieutenant Henry Newdigate	Plate 13
Rifleman Joseph Bradshaw, V.C.	Plate 14
Rifleman Roderick MacGregor, V.C.	Plate 14
Rifleman Robert Humpston, V.C.	Plate 14
Colour-Sergeant James Winchcombe	Plate 14
Colour-Sergeant Daniel Fisher	Plate 15
Rifleman George Evernden	Plate 15
Provost Sergeant Mills	Plate 15
Rifleman William Salter	Plate 15
Corporal Edward Morley	Plate 16
Crimean veterans of the 2nd Bn. Rifle Brigade	Plate 16
Bugler Tobin, Rifleman Hill and Cpl Wiseman, D.C.M.	Plate 16
Crimean War Medal 1854 with unofficial clasp for Balaclava	Plate 17
Turkish Crimean Medal with unofficial fixing suspension	Plate 17
Medals of Rifleman Francis Wheatley, V.C., D.C.M. 1st Bn.	Plate 18
Medals of Captain the Earl of Erroll, 2nd Bn.	Plate 18
Medals of Colour-Sergeant George Evernden, 2nd Bn.	Plate 19
Medals of Colour-Sergeant Daniel Fisher 2nd Bn.	Plate 19
Other Ranks' shako badge for the Crimea period	Plate 20
Part of Bugle-Major's cloth rank badge, 1st Bn.	Plate 20
Minié Rifle shooting badge	Plate 21
Colour-Sergeant Daniel Fisher's cloth rank badge for tunic	Plate 21

Short Enfield shooting badge .... Plate 21
George Evernden's Colour-Sergeant's rank badge
  for greatcoat .... Plate 21
Enfield Rifle. Detail of Lock .... Plate 22
Enfield Rifle muzzle and ram rod, showing front
  band and sling fastener .... Plate 22
Combination tool for Enfield Rifle .... Plate 23
Plaque from Russian Bass drum captured by 1st Bn.
  at Inkerman .... Plate 23
Albert Shako 1844–1855 .... Plate 24
Officers' shako badge of the Crimean period .... Plate 24
The Marshal and a Rifleman, c.1857–1860 .... Plate 24

Illustrations in the Text

Officers' shako badge, Crimean War period	*Frontispiece*
Two Private Riflemen, c.1850	31
Scutari hospital and cemetery	36
Lady Errol's tent, Monastere	37
The Alma. Print after Dupray	49
The transport for the Light Division	61
Sebastopol being viewed by the British General Staff	67
In the trenches before Sebastopol	68
Sebastopol: view from the sea	69
The Battle of Inkerman. Print after Dupray	75
Old sentry and young sentry before Sebastopol	76
On sentry duty in the trenches, winter 1854/5	78
All that remains of the transport for the Light Division, December 1854	79
Balaclava town	83
The French conveying the British sick to Balaclava	85
The trenches at night	87
Rifle Brigade guarding the advanced trench	88
Storming of the Redan. Engraving after W. Paley	99
Camp of the Light Division, about July 1855	102
The attack on the Redan	109
The trench in front of the Redan the morning after the attack, 9th September 1855	110
Balaclava harbour	113
Encampment of the 1st Bn. at Constantinople, 1854	119
The Battle of the Alma	129
Balaclava harbour, one or two days after its capture	134
Scutari hospital: in the wards	138
Bird's-eye view of Sebastopol, showing Allied siege lines	140

Lord Raglan conferring with General Canrobert at the Battle of Inkerman	146
Russian attack at the Battle of Inkerman	150
Battle of Inkerman. Engraving by J. J. Crow	152
Firing from the advanced trench at the Quarries and Rifle-pits	159
Transporting supplies from Balaclava	165
Burying the dead, January 1855	168
68-pounder gun in the 8-Gun Battery	170
Bullets brought back from the Crimea by Colour-Sergeant John Fisher	172
Camp of the 4th Division, 15th July 1855	173
Storming of the Redan. Print after Dupray	176
Veterans of the 1st Bn. Rifle Brigade, Hamilton, Canada, 1911	184
Pouch	193
Other Ranks' ammunition pouch viewed from underneath	194
The Minié Rifle	197
The Long Enfield Rifle and Bayonet	198
The Short Enfield Rifle	199
Style of Royal Mint impressed naming	206
Styles of Depot naming	207
Privately engraved naming styles	207
2nd Battalion engraved naming styles	208
Privately engraved	208

Maps

1	The theatre of war in the Crimean campaign, 1854–55	19
2	The main area of the siege of Sebastopol	20
3	The Alma, 20th September 1854	21
4	The general area of the battle of Balaclava, 25th October 1854	22
5	1st Battalion Rifle Brigade at Balaclava, 25th October 1854	23
6	Main positions of the battle of Inkerman, 5th November 1854, showing the main areas for the Rifle Brigade companies	24
7	Attack on the Rifle Pits ('Ovens') by Lieutenant Tryon 1st Battalion Rifle Brigade, 20th November 1854	25
8	British Right attacks on the Redan, 18th June and 8th September 1855	26

Foreword

by
General Sir James Glover K.C.B., M.B.E.
Colonel Commandant The Royal Green Jackets 1984-1988

MANY RIflEMEN over the years have proved to be powerful chroniclers of The Rifle Brigade's history. The exploits of the 'Bloody fighting Ninety Fifth' in the Peninsula and at Waterloo as described by its officers and men, the likes of Henry Smith, Johnny Kincaid and Rifleman Harris, are well published. But such has not been so of the regiment's proud record in the Crimean War despite the excellence of Henry Clifford's letters, William Norcott's journals and the contemporary accounts of Colour Sergeant Fisher and others. George Caldwell and Robert Cooper have now set the record straight. They have skilfully drawn on a rich array of sources to produce a telling story—the triumph of courage and endurance over hardship and mismanagement.

The Crimean War was a watershed in the history of the British Army. Many of the old lessons of the Peninsula had to be discarded. Many new lessons were painfully learnt and these were to have a profound effect. They precipitated fundamental changes in the Army's structure. Yet the intrinsic characteristics of the Regiment remained largely unaltered, indeed they were strengthened by the Crimean experience.

The authors take us through the separate stories of 1st and 2nd Battalions The Rifle Brigade—the 3rd Battalion was formed in 1856 as a direct consequence of the Crimean War. After vivid descriptions of their departure from England and the voyage to the Black Sea we are given a graphic insight into the battles of the Alma, Balaclava, Inkerman and of the siege of Sevastopol. These abound with anecdotes of the cheerfulness of the riflemen fighting under appalling conditions, of cheeky disdain for higher authority, of proud professionalism, of the bonds between officers and men and perhaps above all of inimitable bravery. Time and again we are reminded of one of the oldest lessons of battle, that ultimate success depends upon the quality of leadership at the contact point. Witness the actions of William Norcott, Lieutenants Knox and Bourchier, Corporal Winchcombe and others. The Rifle Brigade was awarded eight of the newly instituted Victoria Crosses—4 to officers and 4 to riflemen—more than to any other regiment. But at high cost; roughly half of those who embarked at Southampton and Portsmouth in 1854 did not return—some 11 officers and 931 men.

An intriguing social commentary of the time underpins much of the detailed narrative. There are glimpses of wives accompanying husbands onto the field of battle, of travelling gentlemen *alias* tourists assembling as spectators above Sevastopol, of the Regimental Band playing amidst the splendour of the Ambassador's residence in Constantinople in stark contrast to the chaotic inadequacies of the hospitals and the supply system.

The book will have special appeal to the dedicated military historian. The detailed descriptions of weapons, equipment, clothing, payrolls and medal lists are most comprehensive. They underline the authenticity of the text. Indeed the authors have produced a fine record of a glowing period in the history of The Rifle Brigade.

James Glover.

Introduction
by
Michael Barthorp

IT HAS been observed, with some truth, that the British Army has never really been a homogeneous army at all, but rather a collection of regiments, each with its own separate identity, traditions and character. This, of course, has applied particularly to the British Cavalry and Infantry. Some have argued that this has been one of the great strengths of the Army. When, in 1968, a Corps of Infantry was being mooted in some circles, the late Field-Marshal Sir Gerald Templer forcefully pointed out that 'the regimental system of the British Army is and always has been the envy of the world.' Certainly an infantryman's loyalty to his particular regiment has more than proved its worth on the battlefields of three centuries.

Before the old regiments began to be tampered with in the second half of this century, on the grounds of economy, administrative convenience and suchlike, in none of them was this individuality more marked than in the Rifle Brigade, once the 95th Rifles, and now incorporated into the Royal Green Jackets. The Rifle Brigade was the only infantry regiment never to have worn the red coat, nor fired the smoothbore musket; the first entire regiment to have been clad in 'rifle-green' and raised initially as an Experimental Corps, to perform a new mode of fighting; and the only regiment ever to have been removed from the Infantry of the Line and constituted as a corps on its own, no longer 95th but Rifle Brigade, separate from Guards and Line. This singular distinction, conferred upon one of the youngest regiments then in the Army, raised only sixteen years earlier, was in recognition of its outstanding services in the Peninsula and at Waterloo.

The regiment's part in the great battle of 1815, at which all three of its battalions were present, has been most comprehensively recorded by the authors of this present work, in their 'Rifle Green at Waterloo.' After the defeat of Napoleon, and reduced to two battalions, the Rifle Brigade was to encounter no European foe for nearly 40 years. Those years were peaceful for the 2nd Battalion, at home and in various overseas stations, but the 1st Battalion, ordered to South Africa in 1846, found itself engaged in the Seventh Kaffir War, and against the Boers in 1848. Three years later, after a brief spell at home, it returned to the Cape for the Eighth Kaffir War. When it next arrived home, war with Russia was looming and the 2nd Battalion was already under orders to join what was to be called the Army of the East. Before long the 1st Battalion, too, received orders to sail and, with its operations in South Africa to its credit, was the only one of the expeditionary force's 32 infantry battalions with recent active service experience. Thus both battalions of the Rifle Brigade were committed to the first war against a European power since the defeat of France, which was now to be their ally against Russia.

Despite the passage of time the Rifles' outward appearance had not altered greatly since Waterloo. The buttons of their rifle-green uniforms had changed from silver to black, matching the leather of their equipment, the cut of their coats was somewhat different, and they, like all the Line Infantry, sported a new shako, designed by the Prince Consort. Their old Baker rifle, which had wreaked such destruction among the French, had been superseded by the Brunswick, used by the 1st Battalion in South Africa, but now this too had given way to a new weapon, the Minié rifle. As this had also been issued to most of the red-coated battalions of the Army of the East, the Rifles were no longer the only rifle-armed infantry. The Minié was to give the British Infantry great fire superiority over the musket-armed Russians in the battles of the Crimea, but, when first issued to the 1st Battalion, its long barrel and outward similarity to the percussion musket failed to impress their Colonel Buller who, used to the short rifles of the past, called it, with some disgust, 'a red soldier's gun.'

Although their weapon had changed, the spirit and character of the Rifle Brigade, not to mention the competence of its officers and the skill-at-arms of the Riflemen, were all as they had been in the

Napoleonic War. How the two battalions in the Crimea lived up to the reputation of their forbears, displaying the same dash, marksmanship and quick tactical thinking, not forgetting their stoical endurance in the first dreadful Crimean winter, all is brought out in this most detailed account, compiled with great diligence and enthusiasm for the subject by its authors.

By 1854 the function of the Rifles on the battlefield, in relation to other Infantry, had undergone a slight change of emphasis. By then all companies of well-conducted Line battalions, not merely their Light Companies, were trained to skirmish and provide piquets at the outposts, in addition to their close-order manoeuvres in line or column; in these roles they were greatly assisted by the issue of the rifle with its longer range and greater accuracy. This meant that such roles were no longer the sole preserve of the Rifles and Light Infantry, as they had been in the Peninsular War. Even so, despite the once-special tactical expertise, which they had pioneered, being now spread more widely over the Infantry, if not always so competently performed, when the Army of the East first advanced against the Russians in the Crimea, it was the two battalions of the Rifle Brigade that covered its front and open flank.

As they began, so they continued. In the Peninsula they had drunk the old toast, 'To the bloody, fighting Ninety-Fifth, the first in the field and the last out of it.' So too, at the end of the Crimean War, was a journalist inspired to write: 'The Rifles are always foremost in battle, and the last in retreat.'

Michael Barthorp

Acknowledgements

OUR SPECIAL THANKS go to Michael Barthorp, Philip Haythornthwaite, Derek Haighton, Jim Balmer, Barbara Caldwell, Diane Catlow and Carol Cooper for all their outstanding patience, help, encouragement and understanding, but for which this book could not have achieved the finished standard.

Our thanks are also extended to all friends and relatives who have given freely of their time and help:—

Major June Anderson (Rtd), QARANC, Alison Barnard (Assistant, Photographic Services, Windsor), David Boniface, Ms. Gwynedd Campling (Head of Photographic Services, Windsor Castle), Major Ron Cassidy, MBE (Rtd) (RGJ Museum), David Cliff (CWRS), Bob Courtney (Australia), James Cooper (book photography), Crimea War Research Society, James Dann (artist), Ron Debenham (Australia), John Darwent, G. P. Dyer (Librarian & Curator Royal Mint), The Rev. E. J. A. Easten, Dr. Peter English, Judith Farrington (researcher), Nicholas FitzHerbert, Glen Urquhart British Legion, General Sir James Glover, KCB, MBE, Ernest S. C. Glynn (CWRS), Miss C. A. Goodfellow (Librarian, Inverness), Jason Grovier, Brian Hagen, Michael Haines, Alan Hankinson (author), Canon Arthur Hawes, Bill Hibbard, The Rev. Paul Kelly, Ian Laidler, Barry Langridge, Major H. R. MacDonald-Haig, MC (Rtd), Alan McLeod, John D. O'Malley (USA), A. L. T. Mullen, Les Nicoll, David Paterson, Peter Poulain (CWRS), Eric Price, Rifle Brigade Trustees, Rifle Brigade Club, Rod Robinson (CWRS), Royal Green Jackets Museum, Alan Seldon (CWRS), Ms. Alice Sheridan, CBE, John Sly (researcher), Ivor Snooke (RGJ Museum), Andrew Solars (photographer), Keith Webster.

Crown copyright material in the Public Record Office is reproduced by permission of the Controller of Her Majesty's Stationery Office.

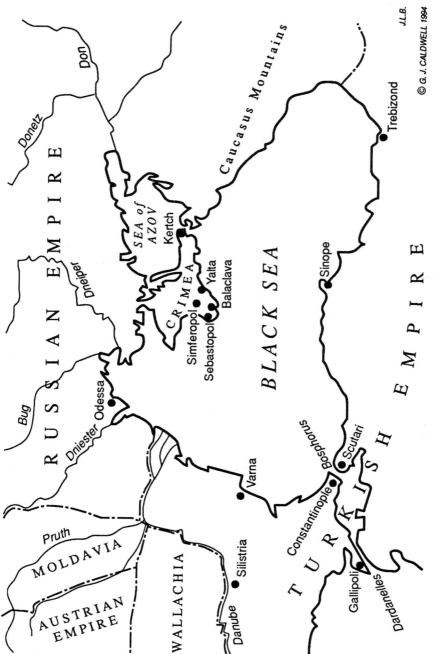

Map 1—The theatre of war in the Crimean campaign, 1854–55

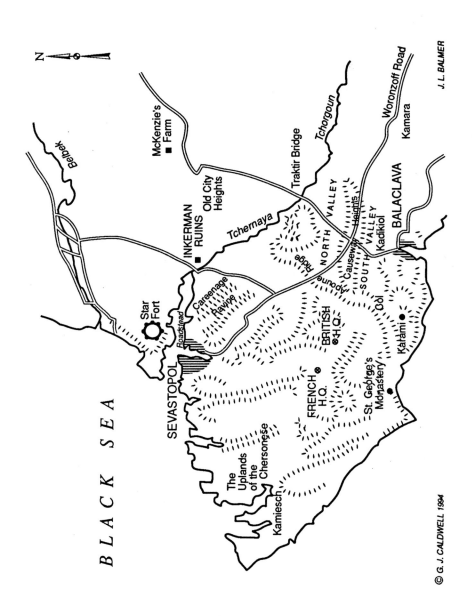

Map 2—The main area of the siege of Sebastopol

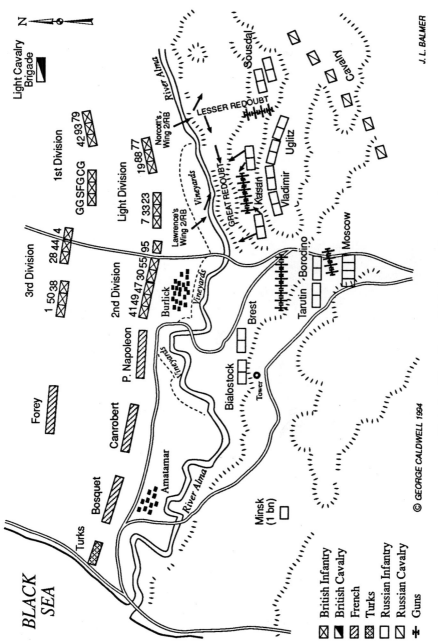

Map 3—The Alma, 20th September 1854

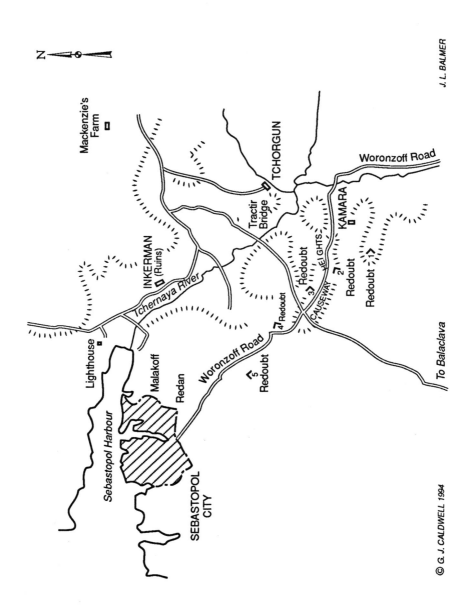

*Map 4—The general area of the battle of Balaclava,
25th October 1854*

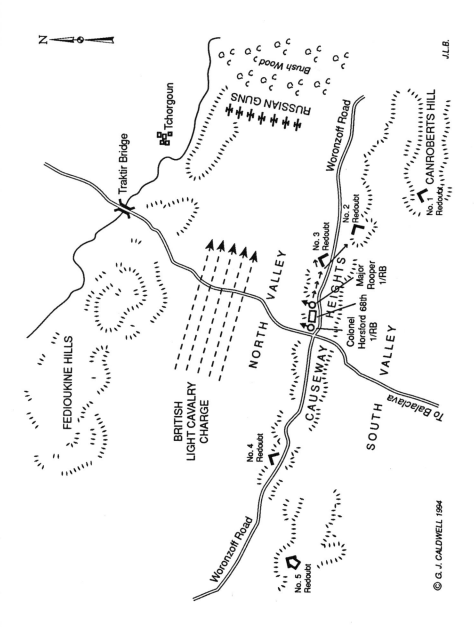

Map 5—1st Battalion Rifle Brigade at Balaclava, 25th October 1854

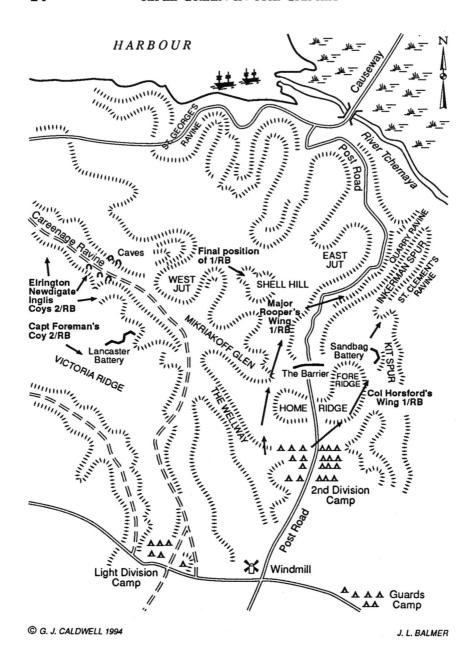

Map 6—Main positions of the battle of Inkerman, 5th November 1854, showing the main areas for the Rifle Brigade companies

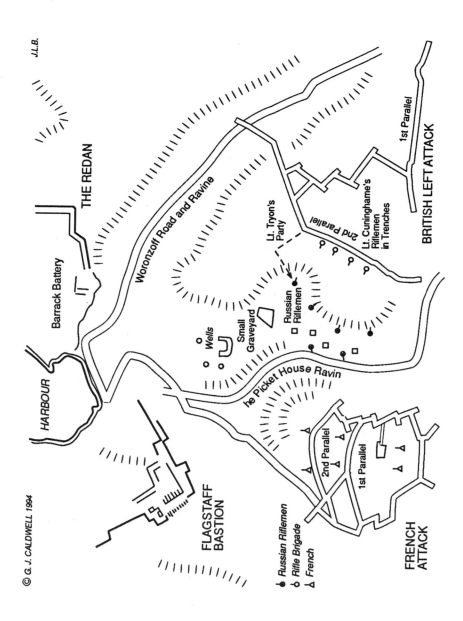

Map 7—Attack on the Rifle Pits ('Ovens') by Lieutenant Tryon, 1st Battalion Rifle Brigade, 20th November 1854

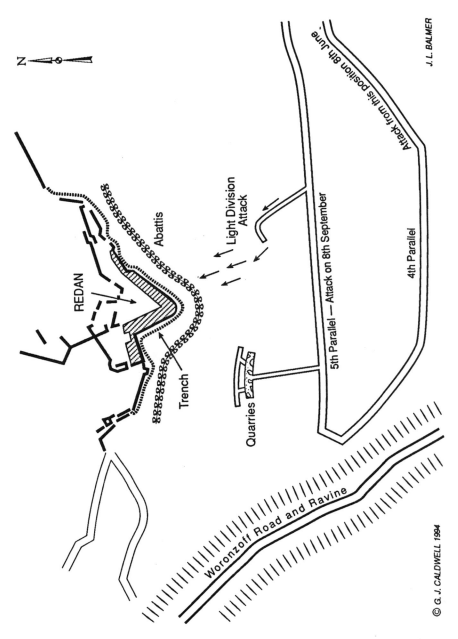

Map 8—British Right attacks on the Redan, 18th June and 8th September 1855

PART ONE

2nd Battalion Rifle Brigade in the Crimea

To the East

ON the 26th May 1852 the 2nd Battalion of the Rifle Brigade disembarked at Portsmouth after an absence of ten years overseas service, nine of which had been spent in Canada. They went by rail to Canterbury where they occupied barracks. Lieutenant-Colonel Sir George Brown, then Adjutant-General of the Forces, inspected the Battalion on the 13th July.

The Duke of Wellington died at Walmer Castle on the 14th September 1852 and, as he had been Colonel-in-Chief of the Rifle Brigade since 1820, the 2nd Battalion Rifle Brigade were to represent the Regiment at his State Funeral to be held in London on the 18th November. On the 17th November they proceeded to London and were billeted at Chelsea. On the day of the funeral the 2nd Battalion Rifle Brigade led the procession from Chelsea Hospital to St. Paul's and returned to Canterbury the following day, where they remained until June 1853. They travelled by rail to Guildford on the 13th and marched to Chobham where they camped and formed part of a Brigade under the command of Major-General Sir De Lacy Evans for the recently-established Camp of Exercise. After a month's training, they proceeded to Portsmouth where they were quartered at Clarence Barracks.

At the beginning of 1854 war fever gripped the country over possible hostilities with Russia in support of Turkey, with the result that an expeditionary force was organised to be sent somewhere in Turkish territory! The exact destination was unknown at this time.

The war's immediate cause had arisen over a petty dispute over the custody of the Holy Places and guardianship of various churches and shrines in Jerusalem and Bethlehem, then Turkish territory, between the Catholic and Greek Orthodox clergy. The former looked to the Emperor of the French, Louis Napoleon, to plead their cause, while the latter appealed to the Czar of Russia.

The Czar used the dispute to bring himself in direct conflict with Louis Napoleon whom he detested. Prince Mentshikoff presented an ultimatum, demanding the acknowledgement of a Russian protectorate covering all the Christian subjects of the Turkish Empire. When this was refused by the Sultan, Russia occupied Turkish territory along the Danube. Turkey then declared war on Russia. Austria became concerned for its Danubian trade, France for its prestige and influence in the Near East, while as for Britain, the prospect of a Russian fleet entering the Mediterranean via Constantinople meant a threat to her communications with her eastern possessions, particularly India, which was already threatened by the Russian presence in Central Asia.

On the 27th of March 1854 Queen Victoria, in a message to both Houses of Parliament, stated that she felt bound to afford active assistance to her ally, the Sultan, against unprovoked aggression, and on the following day war was declared, in alliance with France, against Russia.

The 2nd Battalion Rifle Brigade were to be part of this initial force and received orders to make themselves ready for active service. At this time the Battalion contained many long service soldiers, but they had little or no campaign experience. To rectify this deficiency and give the Battalion a bit of veteran backbone, one hundred volunteers were transferred from the 1st Battalion Rifle Brigade: these men having all seen active service in the Kaffir Wars of 1846–47 or 1850–53.

On February 23rd 1854, prior to its embarkation, the 2nd Battalion Rifle Brigade was inspected at Portsmouth by Major-General Simpson on the Governor's Field. The General gave them a brief address in which he stated that they were going out to defend the interests of their Sovereign and Country and succour the oppressed; he hoped they would not flinch in the performance of their duty, or allow the honour and renown of their Corps to suffer any diminution. That same afternoon the baggage of the Battalion was placed on board the *Vulcan*, screw troopship. The following day, Headquarters with six companies led by the Regimental Band marched through the streets of Portsmouth to the docks for embarkation on board H.M.S. *Vulcan*.

The strength of these companies was 20 Officers, 6 Staff, 37 Senior N.C.O.'S and Sergeants, 12 Buglers and 703 Rank & File under the command of Lieutenant Colonel Lawrence. Meanwhile the two remaining companies had proceeded to Southampton by rail and embarked on board H.M.S.S. *Himalaya*, with a strength of 6 Officers, 1 Staff, 9 Sergeants, 3 Buglers, and 195 Rank & File.

Behind the main party of the Battalion marching through the streets of Portsmouth was a small group of women struggling to keep up with the swift marching pace of the Riflemen. These were the on-strength wives of the Battalion chosen by ballot to accompany their husbands on campaign. Each carried a variety of treasured possessions tied into bundles, whilst others had hung around them a spare blanket or various kitchen utensils.

These wives were followed by another larger group of women and children also belonging to the Battalion but who had to remain in England. This forlorn band kept up as best they could with the Battalion, eager to grab a final glimpse of their husbands and fathers. For many it would be for the last time.

Two Private Riflemen, c.1850

Queen's Regulations made provision for only six women per company to be allowed on a Regiment's strength when going on active service. Those chosen to go were decided the night before by the drawing of lots in order of seniority, beginning with the wives of sergeants. Mothers were not allowed to take part in the ballot as children were ruled out, so some women would be disappointed from the start. The thought of being parted from wives and children for some of the men was a great strain. For one, Colour Sergeant John Wager, a fine soldier with fifteen years' impeccable service, it was to prove too much. The day before sailing he cut his throat, unable to endure the knowledge that his wife and child would be left behind without support.

John Pine of the 1st Battalion the Rifle Brigade writing to his father from Portsmouth on the 1st May 1854 says, 'I never heard anything more about Sergeant Wager, his brother has left us, discharged last month. I must inform you that one of our Sergeants has ended his days by cutting his throat. He was on detachment at Hythe, at target practice and it appeared had fallen in love with some young woman who did not feel disposed to have anything to do with him, that is I understand the reason why he did it.' From the letter by John Pine it would appear that Wager was not the Sergeant who committed suicide, but the casualty roll for the second battalion clearly states Colour Sergeant John Wager as the soldier. Could it be that Wager was a friend of Pine's father and he wanted to hide the true identity of the suicide from him?

For the men of the 2nd Battalion Rifle Brigade the trauma of being parted from wives and children was far greater than in any other Regiment at this time. Having just returned from service in Canada many of the wives were Canadian, which meant that they could not rely on the parish for assistance.

The Rifles' departure created a problem for the people and Borough of Portsmouth. 'We believe' wrote one of the residents, 'that about two hundred wives and children are left destitute and the subject has caused a deep impression on the inhabitants. Many of the Rifles' wives being Canadian have no parish to be sent to and must all become chargeable to the local union, or starve.'

The union or workhouse had very little to offer in the way of assistance; the minimum was often reduced to a pathetic fraction. An illustration of this can be given in the treatment of the wife of a Guardsman who, having not been told of her husband's imminent departure, was left penniless, with several children and expecting another. The sudden news of his departure caused her to go into labour and be delivered of a dead child in the street. The union's response was to send her a shilling and a loaf of bread!

A correspondent to *The Times* however, expressed confidence that the people of England would do their duty by looking after the soldiers' wives during the war. 'If not,' he declared, 'we deserved to be knocked into a cocked hat'!

However, not all wives took the situation lying down or trusted in the system. One Rifleman and his wife hatched a remarkable plan to get her to the war; possibly with the aid of a number of the men. With close cropped hair and dressed in full uniform, rifle at the shoulder, she marched with the Rifles through the streets of Portsmouth, having been drilled into the part by her husband, an officer's servant, who was not with the main party. She had spent the previous night in barracks, having mustered and answered the roll call in the early morning, no doubt with the help of a trusted friend. She held her own with the seasoned Riflemen through the necessary small-arms movements and went unnoticed as the Rifles lined up at the dockside and filed up the gangway. She was actually on board ship before her presence as a stranger in the ranks was detected. Though this 'Romantic attempt,' as the *Morning Post* called it, was nipped in the bud and she was ordered off the transport, her daring impersonation was rewarded. Lady Erroll the wife of Captain the Earl of Erroll, a Company Commander with the Rifles, was also on board going with her husband to the Crimea. To see her off were the Duchess of Sutherland and the Marchioness of Stafford. This distinguished trio of Ladies showed some concern as the female Rifleman bereft of belt and accoutrements prepared to go ashore. The order was suddenly quashed and she was allowed to remain on board. Lady Erroll had no such problems as regards her allowed passage to the Crimea having her own cabin and personal maid.

The *Vulcan* now set sail and anchored off Spithead where she waited for the powder to be shipped out and placed on board.

Headquarters reached Malta on March 11th, and the men all turned out before breakfast to have a look at their destination which was a novelty to so many of them. The ship made straight for the docks and the men walked on shore as soon as they had had dinner. The Rifles occupied quarters in the Ropewalk Barracks, where they found the two companies from the 'Himalaya,' who had arrived just ahead of them. The Battalion were quartered below one of the Batteries, each man being issued with a piece of matting, a straw mattress and a blanket.

Major-General Ferguson inspected the 2nd Battalion Rifle Brigade on the 17th, and it paraded in review order on the 23rd for inspection by the French General, Canrobert and his Staff. The Guards, 33rd and 93rd Regiments also took part. Canrobert seemed especially pleased with the Rifle Battalion.

On the 30th March the Battalion embarked this time on board the S.S. *Golden Fleece* with the exception of Captain Newdigate's

Company, which (for want of room) proceeded in the *Sir George Pollock*, sailing transport, plus some sixty horses a number of which also belonged to the Rifles. The commander of the expedition, Sir George Brown and his staff also travelled on board the *Golden Fleece* much to the displeasure of the Officers and men of the Rifles. They had originally attempted to embark the day before but the arrangements were so blundered that only Newdigate's Company got on board while the rest had to march back to barracks for the night. Those in charge had attempted to put all the stores on board plus a month's provisions for 3,000 men, camp equipage, ammunition, engineering tools, etc., twenty five horses and 1,200 men all at the same time!

The Battalion arrived at Gallipoli on the 6th April where two days were then taken up in reconnoitring the ground for their camp. The Rifles eventually disembarked on the 8th. As soon as each company was assembled on shore, they were marched off eight miles to a Turkish village about two miles from Balahar, near the Gulf of Xeros, where they encamped. The Riflemen were kept employed until the 21st in making roads and digging wells. A Rifleman committed suicide in camp and died about the 10th April, but no reason could be found for his action. The Rifles' camp was on the left of the position which was being fortified by a continuous line of field works across the isthmus. The ground was undulating and rose to a height of approximately five hundred feet. The supply of drinking water was very poor and could only be obtained by hard labour, digging wells and making reservoirs. Every stick of fire wood which was required for cooking had to be brought up on bullock-waggons. Green coffee was the staple drink. Those who ventured to visit Gallipoli found the town, built on the side of a hill, a mass of low built houses with tile roofs. Here and there minarets pointed upwards above the houses from the top of which the priests called the faithful to prayer. In the centre of the town was a fine ruin of an old Byzantine castle which was being used to deposit all the filth of the town.

Two regiments came up from Gallipoli on the 18th and formed a Brigade with the 2nd Battalion Rifle Brigade, with Colonel Lawrence taking command.

From the 21st the Riflemen were employed in the construction of the English half of the lines, from the Gulf of Xeros to the centre of the position. On one of the return marches to camp a Rifleman collapsed, falling senseless to the ground. The cause was found to be the tightness of the leather stock around his neck. The simple remedy for his recovery was the opening of the stock, but it took until June for an order to be issued that stocks would no longer be worn during the hot weather.

Towards the end of April, in a violent gale, the pegs of the Errolls' marquee were torn out from the soft soil and this caused it to collapse. The men who rushed to help were rewarded by the sight of the otherwise remote Lady Erroll, in her nightwear, crawling about on hands and knees from under the flapping canvas, with streaming face and dishevelled hair. His Lordship, Captain the Earl of Erroll, was spared the rush of muddy water by being elevated on his bed.

On the 6th May the 2nd Battalion Rifle Brigade, after loading the mules with the baggage, marched to Gallipoli. Captains were allowed one animal for their own luggage, tent and camp kettle; Field Officers were allowed the same, while subalterns had one animal and a tent between them. It would seem that some officers did not stick to this allowance as Captain Hammond had at least two mules and a horse. Here the Rifles were inspected by Sir George Brown, General Canrobert and Prince Napoleon. The morning was excessively hot and, with the men being over-weighted, many collapsed. They re-embarked on board the *Golden Fleece*, arriving on the 7th April at Scutari, on the Asiatic side of the Bosphorus facing Constantinople. They disembarked on the 9th. Scutari had once been a Turkish garrison town dominated by a now deserted barracks and this was to become the headquarters of the Guards and Light Divisions.

The barracks was a magnificent structure of three storeys, standing in a courtyard with a tower at each corner and was most imposing from a distance. The Rifles on entering were horrified by the sights they encountered: the courtyard was covered with floating filth and after making their way through this they found that the interior was no better. The floors and corridors were full of decaying refuse, with their walls steaming with damp that had soaked through the plaster. Dead animals, rats and vermin of all sorts mingled with the litter. The rotting carcass of a horse was later found to be a sort of filter through which the water ran to supply the building. Sewers from under the building were choked, and the stench from these added to the poisonous air carried far beyond the building.

It was decided that this building would be the principal hospital, yet there were no beds or medical supplies and no means of treatment. But there was at least space for sick and wounded in the big rooms and corridors, once they had been cleared and as far as possible cleansed. The medical provisions for the expedition can at best be described as pathetic! The medical necessities for the five Infantry Divisions and one Cavalry Division-some 30,000 men comprised 1,000 pounds each of lint, adhesive plaster and tow, with 200 old sheets, which had all been supplied by a Bond Street firm.

Scutari hospital and cemetery

Because of the squalid conditions and being overrun with fleas, the Rifles moved out of the barracks and pitched camp between the hospital and the barracks. Lady Erroll caused some curiosity amongst the Turks when she rode up from the beach to the Rifles camp. Here she found she was to share a green Marquee with her husband, which again had been erected in the centre of the Rifles' lines. This marquee became the obvious object of interest to the men, who made every excuse for passing it, especially at night. The interior, being lit by a single paper lantern which hung from the centre pole, caused parts of the canvas to become almost transparent. While the occupants felt screened from those outside, they were in fact on display to all who ventured near the area. There was only one room in the marquee which contained a single small bed, Captain Erroll occupied this, while his lady slept on the floor!

The Rifles received orders on the 18th May to increase the strength of the Battalion from eight to twelve companies, four Depot and eight service. It was about this time that the Light Division was formed under the command of Sir George Brown.

The Division consisted of:—

> Brigadier Buller's 1st Brigade: 19th, 77th and 88th Regiments.
> Brigadier Codrington's 2nd Brigade: 7th, 23rd, and 33rd Regiments.
> Four companies of Rifles attached to each brigade.

The irony in the creation of a Light Division was that it did not contain one single Light Infantry Regiment! Its creation was made purely out of sentiment to the Peninsula Light Division.

There was a lot of drunkenness in the British and French Armies at this time at Gallipoli and Scutari, which was due to the cheapness and availability of the local spirits and the only cure was found to be the flogging of a number of offenders. A serious scuffling fight took place at Gallipoli between the 1st Royals and the 30th Regiment which resulted in a number of broken heads, but they were all soon good friends again.

The 25th May being the Queen's Birthday, there was a grand review of all the troops. At midday Lord Raglan and his immense staff arrived at the ground; they were greeted by three cheers from the

Lady Errol's tent, Monastere

troops. Then all the bands started to play 'God save the Queen,' but as they were all playing in different keys it spoilt the fine effect it would otherwise have had. There were about 16,000 men on parade. That same evening at the Guards camp they erected a monument made of wood and covered it with evergreens and variegated lamps, which when lit had really a very handsome effect. By the 29th the 2nd Battalion had re-embarked on board the *Golden Fleece* and proceeded to Varna, arriving the following day.

The Brigade encamped outside the town near the Shumla gate, the Rifles being placed nearest to the town. They remained here until all the horses and troops had been landed. On June 5th, the Battalion marched to Aladyn, nine miles along the road to Shumla, and on the 30th marched to Devna, seven miles further inland. When the Rifles entered Devna Lady Erroll was at their head. She made quite a dashing figure, dressed in a well-cut, swallow-tailed coatee with rows of shining buttons, her trailing skirts bunched about her knees as she rode side-saddle, wearing a plumed hat and a brace of pistols in her belt.

On July 23 the Battalion received a draft of 1 Officer (Lieutenant Churchill), 2 Sergeants and 150 Rank and File, who arrived from England. Cholera had now appeared in the Division and the Rifles marched four miles further to Monastir and camped on an elevated plateau in the hope of finding healthier quarters. But this was to no avail for on the 27th the scourge broke out in the Battalion. Corporal Thomas Singer and Rifleman Richard Brown both died on this day and many more men were ill. A curious incident took place here when a Rifleman was ordered to take a Bulgarian and his cart to the Rifles' Surgeon for use in conveying the sick. He was confronted by the driver who had other plans and pulled a knife on the Rifleman. However the driver was soon disarmed, but later out of pure spite he broke up the cart and burnt it.

Paymaster Newberry of the Rifles, an old officer who had seen much service, died at Varna on the 1st August. Lieutenants Balfour and Alexander being sick, were invalided to Varna. In order to help divert their attention from the cholera, the men were instructed in the making of fascines and gabions. A large amount of unripe fruit was growing in the area, such as plums and apricots, which the men ate even though the act was punishable if caught.

On August 17, Sir George Brown came up from Varna for an inspection of the troops. The Rifles marched to Yuksarood on the

26th and, after a days halt, proceeded to Kara Gola, marching into Varna on the 29th and embarked for the Crimea that same afternoon.

During July and August the 2nd Battalion Rifle Brigade lost 30 men from cholera.

The cholera epidemic, which had originally started in the French camp, had made the district around Devna into a hot-bed of disease and the casualties were mounting daily. In the Guards Brigade they suffered some four hundred dead and sick, whilst the Light Division lost four officers and a hundred men. The medical staff worked overtime, but a man could be stricken, dead and buried in a couple of hours. Corpses were everywhere putrefying in the heat. The soldiers who had marched away so proudly a few months before now moved about looking like ghosts, hollow-eyed, some mere skeletons who carried with them an atmosphere of doom. The cholera, with its fever and dysentery, had also started to spread through the ranks of the women who had accompanied the army. The first of those afflicted was the mother of a young Artillery officer. The men thought it indecent to bury a woman, like a soldier, stitched in a blanket, so when a second woman died they set about making a coffin. Wood was scarce, but enough was obtained from boxes in the camp stores which were broken up, then fashioned in the shape of a coffin. On the day of the burial a solemn procession formed, the bearers shouldered the coffin and moved off slowly. Though the occasion was one of sadness, as the coffin was borne past, the onlookers there could hardly repress a smile. They read, standing out on one side of the coffin in bold black letters, the words, 'Bass's Superior Pale Ale.'

For transportation to the Crimea the 2nd Battalion Rifle Brigade was broken up into companies.

The Headquarters and Colonel Lawrence went with Captain Hammond's Company in the *Pride of the Ocean.*
Captain Elrington's Company in the *Monarchy.*
Captain Earl of Erroll's in the *Echunga.*
Captain Inglis's in the *Caliope.*
Captain Fyers's in the *Marianne.*
Captain Newdigate's in the *Harkaway.*
Captain Forman's in the *Lord Raglan.*
Captain Hon. W. J. Colville's in the *Talavera.*

The Landing

SOME of the transports sailed on September 7 for Batchick Bay and the rest followed on the 9th for the rendezvous at Cape Tarkan. On the 13th the whole fleet anchored in Kalamita Bay and started to disembark on the 14th September. After receiving a pre-arranged signal, the boats pushed off from the different ships in no set order of attack. The landing was unopposed, a company of the 23rd Regiment being the first to reach the beach. Sir George Brown sent them at once to lie down behind the brow of a hill in skirmishing order to cover the landing from any imminent attack. Captain Colville landed with his company just after the company of the 23rd; he also had Major Norcott with him who was in command of the left wing of the Rifles. Sir George then ordered Major Norcott to send a company in support of the 23rd. Norcott at once sent Colville's as they had already formed, although they in fact belonged to Colonel Lawrence's right wing and not Norcott's wing. The landing was still unopposed but about half a dozen Cossacks were watching from a distance, taking note.

By eleven o'clock the 2nd Battalion Rifle Brigade had disembarked and formed into its two wings of companies: Colonel Lawrence and Major Bradford with the right wing of Inglis, Elrington, Markham and Colville; the left wing of Erroll, Fyers, Newdigate and Forman under the command of Major Norcott. The men had been ordered to leave their knapsacks on board ship and told to carry only the greatcoat, a blanket, a pair of spare boots, mess-tins and the cumbersome water canteen. Officers were desired to take only such things as they could carry. Eventually some Brigades became formed and then the whole Light Division was ready to move.

A number of men became ill whilst on board the transports and amongst these was Captain Hammond who was too ill to land with his Company and had to return to Scutari on board the *Kangaroo*.

Lieutenant Markham now took over the command of the Company until Captain Hammond's return later the following year.

Sir George Brown, on landing, spotted some of the locals coming along on their country carts and sent the Company of the 23rd Regiment to bring them in, which they did. One of the retiring Cossacks who had previously been monitoring the landing, took a pot shot at them and succeeded in hitting one of the drivers severely in the foot.

The Light Division by this time had pushed on at a fair rate and soon covered about six miles before halting. The Rifles, still in their separate wings, had advanced considerably ahead of the Division. Colonel Lawrence and the right wing, having moved in an easterly direction, came upon a convoy of seventy country carts drawn by oxen and laden for the most part with flour, which they captured. Lawrence kept back two camels from the convoy as part of the spoil for the use of his own wing, where they did good service as baggage animals until the drivers eventually ran off with them in the winter. Colonel Lawrence continued with his wing to the village of Kentugan which he then occupied. Major Norcott and his left wing had been ordered to occupy and barricade themselves into the village of Kamishli. As they approached the village the inhabitants came out to greet them, each bearing a pumpkin or fowl, and made signs of submission and welcome. It now began to rain, but by ten o' clock Norcott had the village securely barricaded with the use of carts, gates, barrels, stones and anything else that could be found to serve the purpose. Norcott sheltered with his officers in the headman's house while the Riflemen found what shelter they could, mostly by making room inside haystacks. The wing of Riflemen settled down for the night, which proved quite comfortable except for the changing of the sentries. A Cossack did make his way down to the village at one point to see if it was occupied. The advance sentries tried to get a shot at him but because of the heavy rain they had not recapped their rifles and he was able to make good his escape.

That first morning, in the half light, a stray horse and bullock thought to be Cossacks were shot by mistake. The animals' misfortune was the Rifles' gain and they soon cut up and cooked the bullock, Major Norcott being presented with the animal's heart.

For the next couple of days Norcott had the unenviable task of keeping the village intact by preventing the French and English troops from plundering it. At the same time the Riflemen were continually harassed day and night by Cossacks. When learning that the village held by Colonel Lawrence's wing had been gutted, Norcott was determined that his should not suffer the same fate. The want of wood was severe in the army; the men were desperate to cook their rations and Norcott even had a note sent to him from the Colonel of one of the Guards' regiments asking for a few sticks for which he would pay. The villagers were thankful to their protectors and they became quite friendly. The Riflemen were even willing to help in the everyday tasks of village life. This pleased the women who proudly detailed the men to helping with their various tasks. An interpreter was eventually found who could translate the women's eager jabberings; the men were amused to find out that they were being hailed as heroes more strong than lions and more gentle than lambs.

It was while they were stationed at this village that the Riflemen were to make the acquaintance of Sergeant John Knox of the Scots Fusilier Guards, who later in the campaign would become an officer in their ranks and a true hero, winning the Victoria Cross. Sergeant Knox visited the village with some men of his Regiment and they obtained some poultry by payment and barter.

Norcott's protection of the village gained the approval of Sir George Brown and Lord Raglan and supplies were bought from the village for the army which encouraged the people to bring forth even more grain. Norcott was also able to provide the Commissariat with 35 bullocks and 25 carts, making the village a place of great value to the British. The Riflemen still had hard work in protecting the village and at times Norcott had to have 200 men on sentry duty round the area with the rest ready as a reserve. They caught at one time some Highlanders about to carry off the crossbeams of the bridge over a low marsh which was their only link with the army. On a number of occasions Norcott had to resort to his knowledge of the French language to defuse what could have been some tricky moments, especially when French officers asked to enter the village for water backed by hundreds of Zouaves! On the 17th September Captain Cresswell of the 11th Hussars with twenty-five men arrived at the village to be placed under Norcott's command and were a welcome reinforcement. Captain Cresswell, however, was not a well man, cholera having started to take a hold of him which proved to be fatal.

Colonel Lawrence's wing did not have the good fortune of Norcott's. They did, however, occupy the residence of a person of some substance whose property they were able to protect. Sadly the French pillaged the rest of the village, and it was totally gutted.

An Aide-de-Camp from the commander of the cavalry entered Lawrence's village with a demand for immediate assistance. The Colonel at once put his four companies under arms and they were soon off at the double to give the required aid. They were met on the way by another officer with a note of thanks and told that their help was not required after all, as the advanced vedettes had mistaken a body of their own force as the enemy. Lawrence and his men returned to the village of Kentugan where they stayed until the advance on the 19th.

Norcott's wing of Rifles left the village of Kamishli with the thanks of the inhabitants and their cheers ringing in their ears. However, in a short time the Zouaves had marched in and treated the villagers to some horrible cruelty and spoliation and in no time a terrible change had come over the village and it was left a ruin.

The Advance to the Alma

At daybreak on the 19th the whole army began their march forward, the British on the landward flank, with the French nearer the sea. Norcott's left wing covered the front of the Light Division, while Lawrence's wing protected the flank. They continued in this formation up to the Bulganak, a small swampy muddy stream with a small bridge and post-house. Here the men procured such water as they could. Unfortunately the cavalry, having been in advance of the infantry, reached the stream first and turned it into mud.

It was at this time, whilst endeavouring to get a drop of water to drink, that the alarm was sounded. The enemy's cavalry was in sight. The British guns with fifty Riflemen to each battery and the cavalry went instantly to the front. Once the divisions resumed their order of march they followed this advance party.

The Cossacks now began to show in some force to the front and the British cavalry extended to skirmish with them. A squadron drew up across the road and almost immediately the flash of a Russian gun sent a shot right into their midst which actually burst in a horse. In spite of this, the whole squadron remained as steady as rocks although three or four horses had been wounded. Lord Raglan ordered the artillery to reply, but, finding that the troop of horse artillery of 6-pounders attached to the cavalry did not reach with good effect, he ordered up the troop of horse artillery and the battery attached to the Light Division, both of which had 9-pounders. 'C' Troop had also taken with them a section of thirty-six Riflemen to act as sharpshooters. These were stationed on the axletree boxes, one on each trail, with three more on each limber box.

The Russian shot continued to bound through the ranks of skirmishers, but fortunately the British guns now un-limbered and returned the fire. These opened with considerable effect, so much so, that the Cossacks soon broke from their close order and covered the plain about a mile off, then retired. The Russian artillery wisely limbered up and retired in a hurry, having fired 16 shot, while the British fired altogether 80 rounds, 55 round shot and 25 shrapnel shells. Besides the casualties to the horses, the cavalry had five men wounded, two requiring amputation. Of these, one was the Paymaster-Sergeant of the 13th, who had no right to be under fire and Trooper Williamson of the 11th, who came riding out of the ranks with his leg shot off and hanging by his overall. Both of these men were claimed by their respective Regiments as to being the first British field casualties of the campaign, forgetting the few casualties received on landing by the 23rd Regiment! The Russian casualties were about 25 men killed and wounded.

With this affair now over the British and Allies bivouacked for the night. The men who had not replenished their water at the Bulganak now had to go without or return some two miles or more to the stream. Many of the men in the British force who did not bother were to regret this decision the following day, as the next water would not be until they reached the Alma.

At daybreak on the 20th September the Allies began to prepare for the advance, but for security reasons no bugles or trumpets were sounded for rouse. The 2nd Battalion Rifle Brigade was ordered to move off at seven o'clock; Colonel Lawrence extended two companies to cover the front, but having done this the final order to move did not come until some hours later.

Instead of breaking camp at the allotted time a delay had been caused by the British ammunition train being brought up and the troops guarding the rear and flanks being wheeled into line. At about ten o'clock the army was ordered to advance, not to the front but to incline to the right front so as to close the gap which had developed between the British and French Armies whilst on the march the previous day.

Colonel Lawrence advanced with his right wing of Rifles, covering the front of the division, while Norcott protected the flank. Both wings continued following the Sebastopol Road, which crossed vast undulating plains. Cossacks could be seen hovering all around together with their regular cavalry units out on the flank.

At last the combined armies moved forward still inclining to the right but in parallel lines. Because of the late start the heat was overpowering and the men had to make frequent halts. Towards midday the march was flagging. Drum taps had replaced the music from those bands like the Rifles who had retained their instruments and men were gasping for water, many weakened by disease were struggling in the rear or falling out unable to carry their rifles or even bear the weight of their shakos.

The Rifles, out in front, moving at their distinctive Rifle pace were also suffering. They did, however, have two guardian angels watching over them in the shape of Lady Erroll and her French maid. Being mounted on mules they both followed close behind the Rifles' skirmishing line. They continually stopped and collected the rifles from the men who were in the worst condition. Towards noon a rise in the ground was topped and the heights beyond the Alma were now visible; a halt was called and the men ordered to eat their midday meal.

The Battle of the Alma

BETWEEN one o'clock and one thirty the bugles sounded for the British and French to reform, then advance. However, because of the closeness of the two armies, the French inclined to their left, which in turn pushed the 2nd Division into the Light Division causing the 95th Regiment to overlap the front of Sir George Brown's right-hand regiment, the 7th Royal Fusiliers. The two leading Divisions were now halted and ordered to lie down. The Russians had opened up an artillery barrage as soon as the Allies formed to advance and the two front Divisions found themselves in a most intolerable position, being shelled without being able to reply or take shelter. The 1st and 3rd Divisions were halted and stood at ease out of effective range of the Russian guns. For well over an hour the men were kept in this position until the outcome of the French attack was known. Lord Raglan, having received a request from the French, who had just anticipated his own orders to join the attack, then gave the long awaited order to advance.

Colonel Lawrence extended two companies of his right wing to cover the advance in skirmishing order and placed his remaining two companies in support. As they descended towards the Alma the British columns were now formed into line with the 2nd Battalion Rifle Brigade extended some three hundred yards in front across the front and flank of the Light Division with four companies in advance and four in support. They were soon in contact with the Russian skirmishers who were concealed in the vineyards on their side of the river.

The Russian General had picked his defensive position well, placing his troops to their greatest advantage. On the heights of the south bank in defence of the river and in command of its crossing points, Menschikoff had under his control some 39,000 men and 96 guns. On the slopes of the Kourgane and about halfway down was a ridge on which he had constructed a battery of 12 powerful guns known as the Great Redoubt. This in turn was protected by a low breastwork about three feet high; on either side of the Redoubt ran a protective ditch to accommodate infantry. Shallow trenches had been made between each gun in which sharpshooters could be placed as cover for the guns. To its right on the same ridge, but about a half a mile distant, was a second redoubt of nine guns, set at an angle so that it was able to cover any flank attack made by the British left. To the left of the Great Redoubt and at a similar elevation stood a battery of eighteen guns which dominated the road north and south and the bridge over the Alma. Along the top of the Kourgane, placed at tactically advantageous points, were a number of field batteries which could fire into the Great Redoubt if it was captured. In the redoubts, batteries and the valleys and folds of the ground, unseen by the advancing British and French troops, were five regiments of Russian infantry some fifteen thousand men. Also on the extreme right and rear of his defensive line was the Russian Cavalry five thousand strong.

Only the River Alma divided the two Armies, the British and Allies advancing from the north bank, with the Russians defending its much higher southern bank.

The Alma at this time was nothing more than a gorge or gully running serpentine down to the sea, with precipitous banks which made it very difficult to ascend in places. The gorge was between two and three hundred yards in breadth, with the actual river varying from forty to fifty yards wide, some parts deep and others quite shallow. Both banks had had extensive trees and copses which the enemy had cleared to give a free field of fire for the defenders. Vineyards and gardens were also on either bank but more so on the Russian side. The holes around the vine roots formed natural rifle positions, while the garden embankments had been heightened to leave a small ditch on the attackers' side. What buildings there were had also been made into strong defensive positions.

At first the Russian round shot fell short doing little damage 'Great ponderous shot' wrote Lieutenant Tipping 'came bounding along the ground like cricket balls. As the men saw them approaching they opened their ranks and the balls went hissing past. They even caused some merriment, amongst the men when a greyhound belonging to Captain Forman in Norcott's wing of Riflemen pursued them barking furiously. But when a man put his boot out to stop a cannon ball and his foot was carried away the laughter ceased abruptly.'

Colonel Lawrence continued with his right wing companies in skirmishing order covering the front. They had advanced so far ahead of the Light Division that they were treated to a deadly fire from the Russian skirmishers who were swarming through the vineyards along the river. Major Norcott's wing, also moving swiftly forward, were getting ahead of the division which left the flank without any cover. Both wings continued to advance in front of the Light Division with Lawrence and his wing in the most advanced position.

With the divisions finally in motion there would be no further halts for the living until the battle was over. The British Lion was at last starting to stir.

As the Rifles advanced a sudden burst of flame and smoke issued out of a fold in the ground on their right which turned out to be a sunken road some six to seven feet in depth. This road ran up to the Russian right centre. It was thought at first that this fire came from a retiring Russian piquet having set fire to some straw or hay to prevent it falling into the hands of the British. As they neared the source of the fire they could see that the smoke and flame, which had hitherto obscured the Rifles' view, came from the village of Bourliouk. This the Russians had set alight to hamper further the

The Alma. Print after Dupray

British and Allied advance. The French who had advanced ahead of the British came upon a similar problem when the village of Almatamak was also set on fire.

The blinding smoke from the village made it impossible for the Rifles to return any fire and to skirt this obstacle both wings had to incline to their left. By altering their course, they gained some welcome shelter from a natural dip in the ground. This change of position, however, left Codrington's Brigade without any cover. Colonel Lawrence had in fact advanced his wing so far to the left that they now covered the front of the 19th Regiment, the right hand battalion of Buller's Brigade. Lawrence ordered his men to fix swords* and rush a small group of houses to their front which they found had already been evacuated. The Russian skirmishers who had originally been opposed to them, had made their escape to the southern bank of the Alma. The Riflemen, however, were grateful for some much needed shelter behind these smoking ruins. From the shelter of these houses the bugles sounded the advance and the Riflemen rushed into the vineyards which lined a large part of the north bank and passed on into the river Alma. They forded it with little difficulty as the river in most parts only came up to their thighs, but all around them the water was peppered by showers of bullets from the Russian skirmishers on the south bank.

Rifleman William Salter of Captain Newdigate's Company tells us that on crossing the Alma the younger brother of Hugh Hannon shouted out that he had a snake around his legs, which turned out to be the chain from a gold watch. He also further states that the Riflemen threw away their shakos and a number of the soldiers from the other regiments did the same, but after the battle were ordered to return and collect them. The Riflemen, however, did not bother to go back for theirs! Salter's comrade, Michael McBride, was hit by a round shot which broke both of his legs and from these horrific wounds he died.

Major Norcott, moving even further to the left with his wing, led his Riflemen towards the walls of more of these vineyards; Fyers Company was extended on the extreme left with Erroll's Company followed by the support companies. The Riflemen of the two advanced companies were anxious to push on, but Norcott kept

---

* The Rifles always referred to the bayonet as a sword from the early days in the Regiment when the sword-bayonet was part of their equipment.

them at a walking pace until within forty yards of the walls, then allowed them to make their rush, gaining the cover they longed for. Although the shot and grape was tearing up the ground all about them and Norcott was most conspicuous on his black horse. Up to this point not a man of his wing of skirmishers had been hit.

Norcott's continued movement to the left brought his wing to a part of the river that was very shallow and much more fordable, making their crossing easier than expected. Once they reached the opposite bank and the two support companies of Forman and Newdigate arrived, Norcott sent Fyers and Erroll's companies over the walls into the vineyards and the companies of Forman and Newdigate down a track which ran through the vineyards to a farmhouse. Once through these, the Riflemen halted at a low wall which separated the cultivated land from the slope beyond. Here Norcott moved up Erroll's Company and extended it on the right of Fyers. The whole wing now ascended the slope with great speed pushing the enemy before them; the Rifles' extended order saved them from severe casualties.

Meanwhile, with Colonel Lawrence's wing firmly positioned on the opposite bank, the 19th Regiment started to cross the river and were soon finding shelter under the slope of its southern bank. Much of the shot and musketry which the enemy were pouring down from the Redoubt passed over them, but they were still receiving severe casualties from a flanking fire, for the Russians had a battery on their right, which was firing into their packed ranks.

The burning village, the cause of the Rifles' movement to the left, had become an even bigger problem for the following Regiments of the Light Division. Advancing in their closely packed formations, detours had to be made around the burning buildings. This broke up their rigid formations, further delaying the crossing of the river with the much-needed support for the Rifles. The result of the delay and their rapid advance meant that the Rifles were some twenty minutes ahead of the division; a position the Russians were slow to exploit!

The consequence of this delay was that Norcott's wing reached a point where they expected to be supported by their Brigade, but on looking round found they were completely isolated. The Russians eventually made a movement of their own to counter the British advance. The Rifles saw at this moment some sixty or seventy Cossacks followed by a column of infantry coming down a road.

Norcott's isolation made the position of his Riflemen critical and, as they were about to be cut off from the rest of the army, he had to act very quickly. At the same time a retreat in full view of the advancing army might have discouraged the troops. Added to this was the knowledge that their rapid movement to the front had left the left flank of the Light Division without any protection and open to attack.

Major Norcott had little choice but to retire and ordered the Bugles to sound the recall. The Riflemen moved reluctantly back from their positions to the lower ridge from where they had earlier driven the enemy. This would place them closer to their supporting Regiments and also give them the added protection of the farm buildings. At the farm, he placed Fyers's and Erroll's Companies about its walls and moved Forman's and Newdigate's into the vineyards. By chance, at this point Norcott was joined by a fifth Company of Rifles in the form of Captain Colville from Lawrence's Wing. As the furthest left flank Company of this wing he had entered Norcott's part of the field due to their continued movement to the left. By chance Norcott's need was greater than Lawrence's at this point and he ordered Colville to place his Company in line across the road, leading down to the farm, by which the enemy were still progressing. With the added strength of Colville's Company and the defensive position he had made of the farm, Norcott was determined he could now make a stand until supported by the Light Division.

To try and make his position even stronger, Norcott ordered Captain Erroll's Company to move from the left flank of Fyers' Company and take up position on his right, in the hope they would join forces with more of Lawrence's wing. This movement to the right made no difference to Norcott's position as Erroll's Company made no contact with any of the companies of Colonel Lawrence's wing. The Russians continued to descend from the plateau on their left and still in their direction.

Leaving his Riflemen waiting for the Russian attack Major Norcott galloped from Colville's position back to the previous ridge to see what progress the advancing enemy column had made. On reaching the ridge he was surprised to find that the Russian column was in fact retiring! Turning to look behind him Norcott could see the reason for this: the line of the 2nd Brigade was crossing the river and looking further to his left he could also see the 1st Brigade crossing the river. Both Brigades, however, were receiving a heavy artillery bombardment from the Russian 24- and 32-pounder batteries; their accurate and deadly fire was carving out huge gaps in the ranks of the advancing Regiments of the Light Division. A fresh threat also faced the Regiments of the Light Division: the Russians, seeing the effect of their heavy guns, had advanced two large columns of infantry from behind the batteries in the Great Redoubt.

Norcott returned to his wing and immediately put his Companies in motion. The original danger having passed, he set off in the direction of the 1st Brigade who, in great confusion, were still crossing the river. Norcott's Riflemen edged their way gradually to the right keeping under cover of the ridge, only showing their heads to return an accurate and telling fire obliquely into the advancing Russian columns.

Once the Riflemen reached the front of the battery he ordered them to halt and lay down while he galloped off about fifty yards to the 1st Brigade.

At the same time Colonel Lawrence, with his three Companies of Riflemen, had entered this part of the field and halted a short way behind and a little to the right of Norcott's men, who were now pouring a telling fire into the advancing Russian Columns from the cover of the ridge which was also a little in advance of the bank of the river.

With the 19th Regiment forming in preparation to advance, Colonel Lawrence moved on with his Companies and rode up the bank with his Adjutant, Lieutenant Ross, followed by his faithful Riflemen. They advanced through part of Captain Fyers' Company from Major Norcott's Wing who were lying down closest to them. Lawrence's Riflemen were then treated to a tremendous fire in all directions from the Russian front line, but they continued to advance up the slope.

Norcott, on riding down to the 1st Brigade, found that the Regiments having passed the river in line would stop in groups of up to thirty or more men to drink or fill their canteens. Norcott shouted to these men to get into line two deep, 'By Heavens they are only 150 yards from you. You will annihilate them. Only get into two deep.' It was impossible. The men, almost dead beat, sat down some to drink and others literally pulling out bread and meat to start eating! At length the enemy columns came within one hundred yards of the bank under which the Brigade lay and three or four Russian skirmishers rushed up to the edge of the bank and fired into the men below. The men, as if stung by this fire, rose some twenty deep and ascended the steep bank, firing at the enemy columns and the battery beyond, causing the Russians to retire from their advancing fire.

With the Brigade at last in motion and following Lawrence's Riflemen, Major Norcott returned to his own men and ordered up his whole line of skirmishers, who poured in a flanking fire while advancing rapidly at the same time. Colonel Lawrence's movement to the left combined with Norcott's to the right had in effect reversed their original positions.

The Regiments of the Light Division had also been joined by the 95th Regiment from the 2nd Division who also advanced against the Great Redoubt.

The enemy guns, seeing their columns in full retreat and the 2nd Brigade moving towards the rear of their right, moved off but not before firing a parting shot from their deadly 32 pounders. The Russian Infantry however, halted at the Redoubt to make a fight of it and protect the retreating guns.

Colonel Lawrence, riding in advance of his Riflemen with his Adjutant, was within a few yards of the Redoubt when a discharge of grapeshot fired by a field-battery on the higher slope of the Kourgane Hill killed both Lawrence's and Ross's horses. They were both sent crashing to the ground, Lawrence being lucky to avoid having his dead horse roll on him. After freeing himself from the harness he scrambled for shelter under the walls of the Redoubt.

Sir George Brown meanwhile, was at the head of the 2nd Brigade urging them on. Hugh Hannan, the tallest and most right hand skirmisher of the Rifles, was alongside the General, when Major Norcott rode up to Sir George and asked if he could be allowed to storm the position, to which he agreed. Norcott, drawing his sword, galloped forward calling out to his men, 'Come on my hearties' and rode right up to within five yards of the battery. The Russians were just turning to retire when General Codrington came up and entered the Redoubt to prove that it was empty.* His A.D.C., Campbell of the Rifles, joined Norcott and they both rode into the Redoubt, quickly

---

* Major Norcott in his diary states that he was the first man up to the embrasures of the Battery but he was too busy with the positioning of his men which gave him no time to write his name on the gun. Kinglake in his 4th edition of 'Invasion of the Crimea' gives the honour of entering the

followed by the Rifle Companies of his wing. Colonel Lawrence's Riflemen had also reached the Redoubt and were entering it from the opposite side. The Rifles' Officers were so intent on deploying their forces to defend the captured position and send a telling fire into the retreating Russians, that they missed the opportunity to mark the only captured gun which had been limbered up ready to escape just before the soldiers of the Light Division came pouring into the Redoubt. Hugh Hannan, however, did not miss this opportunity and marked it for the Rifles, but being ordered to man the works, had to leave it to Colonel Chester's men, who had just come up and they marked it '23rd Fusiliers' The mass of men now just stood and fired into the retreating enemy who were marching off in quite an orderly and calm manner. The Regimental Colours were being waved to the sound of the men's cheering, while to the Brigades still waiting to cross the river and ascend the slopes the Battle must have looked all but over.

When the 2nd Brigade advanced against the Redoubt, General Sir George Brown, moving at its head, was most conspicuous on his grey horse. As he neared the works he had just shouted out, 'Hurrah for the Royal Welch, I shall remember you!,' when he fell amid a cloud of smoke and dust, his horse having been killed by a round shot. It was thought at first that he had also been killed and a number of men came to a halt, but Sir George jumped to his feet with his face red with anger shouting,' I'm all right' and he continued on foot up to the Redoubt. Once inside, a fresh horse was brought up and Rifleman Hugh Hannan assisted the General to mount under a murderous fire from the enemy that was knocking the regiments to pieces. Hannan coolly saluted him and said 'Are your stirrups the right length Sir?'

The Russians, meanwhile, having descended a small slope about one hundred and fifty yards away stopped and returned a deadly rifle fire. They were assisted by two guns which commanded the position from a height about four hundred yards off. Standing hidden in the hollow of the slope was a third body of two battalions of Russians whose existence had previously been concealed. The

---

Redoubt to Sergeant Luke O'Connor of the 23rd Royal Welch Fusiliers. As O'Connor was wounded, on foot and carrying a heavy colour the odds would be in favour of the officers mentioned, being on horseback, gaining the Redoubt ahead of the brave sergeant!

massed battalions of the Russian Columns, covered by their skirmishers, now advanced against the Light Division with an eerie wailing sound. The exhilaration, felt only moments before by the greater part of the soldiers in gaining the Redoubt, soon changed as these massed columns of Russians counter-attacked.

The massed ranks in the Redoubt were easy targets for the Russian riflemen whose deadly fire soon caused a severe loss in officers and men. At one point in the action an officer of the Staff came galloping along the ranks shouting to the men not to fire! 'Don't fire'! Don't fire! The column's French!' He shouted. The buglers were ordered to sound the 'cease fire' which took place for a little while until the mistake was realised. Few had stopped to ask themselves how the French could have moved to the British front from having been not half an hour earlier on the right flank, or how they became to be dressed in long grey overcoats! The Russians were gradually regaining the Redoubt. The counter-attack was too strong for the mixed up and disordered regiments to hold off without support, and the Guards were still formed up in the plateau below on the other side of the Alma as if they were on parade at St. James, when they should have been up in support of the Light Division.

Major Norcott, seeing that the situation had become desperate rode down to the Guards who, having at last been put in motion, were starting to lose their formation because of the obstacles which had earlier disrupted the line of the Light Division. Riding past the three Regiments he called out, 'Steady gentlemen and for God's sake preserve your two deep, they are not half your numbers.'

The resistance of the Light Division had now begun to waver from the severe fire of the Russian Artillery and Infantry. Groups of men started to fall back until a retreat was in full cry, with the Russians regaining the Redoubt. As the men fell back some of the Rifles continued to engage the Russian skirmishers but in the end had to give way. Two of the last men to retire from a small party of Norcott's men were Hugh Hannan and Charles Dencer.

The Guards Brigade at last started to cross the Alma and the Scots Fusilier Guards, being first over, received a request from Codrington's ADC to support his Brigade. Because of the urgency of the request they advanced at once though they were in a ragged formation, having had no time to reform. The tide of retreating men was so great that they ploughed into the advancing Scots Fusilier Guards, forcing them back down the hill.

The two remaining Guards Regiments, having taken time to reform their ranks, waited until the mass of retreating men passed them and until the Scots Guards had rallied and formed up; then the whole line of Guards advanced as one with the Highland Brigade formed on their left. The Light Division also regained some form of order and once again ascended the slope in rear of the Guards as support.

Norcott's wing of Riflemen having first taken off their packs fell in ready to advance in front of the Guards as a skirmishing line; but at this moment an A.D.C. came galloping down and reported to Norcott that the Brigadier desired him to instantly form a reserve and act as support. At the same time Colonel Lawrence came up with his wing of three Companies, Colville's still being with Norcott.

The Russians having been successful in their counter attack sent the Vladimir Regiment out from behind the Redoubt covered by their skirmishers and started to descend the slope to meet the advancing Guards Regiments.

Again the frantic figure of a Staff Officer on horseback was seen riding from right to left across the front of the Guards proclaiming; 'Retire! You're firing on the French! Retire!' This time he was ignored and the Guards prepared to meet the advancing Russians.

With the Buglers sounding the Regimental call the Rifle Companies rallied ready to advance behind the Guards, who stood waiting for the Russian Column to come closer. At about eighty to a hundred yards distance the Guards Brigade sent a crashing volley of deadly Minié balls into the front ranks of the Russians while the Highland Brigade advanced against the lesser Redoubt on their left. The Russians were falling in great numbers under this telling fire, while the Guards continued to advance, only stopping to fire or load, each rank firing in turn. By the time they had reached the Redoubt they had expended about sixteen rounds of ammunition per man. This advancing wall of scarlet topped with bearskin was too much for the Russians who started to leave the position in droves. The Russians discarded their accoutrements in a bid to make their escape easier. A great cheer rent the air as the Guards entered the captured Redoubt, and bearskins and shakos were soon being waved on bayonet-topped rifles.

The Rifles continued with the artillery and cavalry in pursuit of the retreating Russians. The ground was being strewn with muskets, knapsacks, cartouche-boxes, greatcoats and helmets long after the killed and wounded had ceased to fall. After proceeding about a mile the Rifles were recalled, and on returning, the Battalion bivouacked on the heights above the Alma on the ground they had won. With the withdrawal of the last of the Russian troops the Battle of the Alma ended. The failure to follow up the defeated Russian Army and take Sebastopol was to prove a costly error of judgement for the rest of the Campaign.

Having gained the victory it was now time to count the cost. The Regimental Bandsmen moved amongst the mounds of bodies and extricated the wounded for the surgeons. The rest of the day the troops spent preparing for the night, placing pickets all round the position and finding comfortable quarters and cooking their rations. Throughout the night the bandsmen and others worked like slaves to bring in the wounded, those who could not be moved being covered with blankets and left on the battlefield for the night. For the Surgeons there was no respite and they worked on through the night. One Doctor passing along the battlefield checking the wounded was almost killed; a Russian soldier was just about to take aim and fire but was checked by a man of the 21st Regiment. Throughout the night those men on outlying picket duty had to listen to the moans, groans and cries of despair, suffering and agony which had a terrible effect on them.

In the morning the men were allowed to wander over the battlefield for a short time until the order that ten men per company were to be employed in burying the dead. The Pioneers of all the Regiments were set to work digging long trenches about seven feet wide for the internment of the Russian dead. Men were sent out in all directions to collect the bodies, which were brought in on stretchers and laid out like sardines in a box, in about three layers. Once the earth was filled in on them a large mound was made over the pits composed of fifteen or sixteen gigantic graves at a distance of about five hundred yards from the river.

While the army was burying the dead, the Navy were also on hand to carry the wounded in blankets the three miles to the seashore to await being put on board ship. Those men not on burying detail were set to collecting the arms and they also made a good collection of money from the dead. As no pay had been received, with the military chest being still on board ship, the money went into the canteens: the French being the receivers of most of it, the commonest drink obtained from them was Brandy which soon had an effect on the men as they had had very little food.

The total British losses were 362 all ranks killed, with 1,621 wounded; of this latter number many would also die. The Russians had severe losses estimated to be 5,500 of which 1,800 were killed. The French losses were given as 1,343. It is thought that these figures were deliberately exaggerated or included their cholera victims and a truer figure would be around 500.

The only officer casualty in the Rifles was Captain Erroll, who had been wounded in the right hand when advancing with his Company. This resulted in the fore-finger being amputated and his middle fingers being paralysed.

The full casualty list was:—

KILLED

Sergeants
  W. Simpson.
  James Swallow.
Corporal
  John Robinson.
Riflemen
  Cornelius Finnucane
  Edward Hexter
  William Kennedy
  Michael McBride
  Thomas Pine
  Charles Rason
  George Robinson

WOUNDED

Sergeant
  Lucas Lucas
Buglers
  John Davis
  Isaac Dyre
  George Ebethurte
Riflemen
  Thomas Allen
  Augustus Beeton
  James Bennett
  Jesse Burchill
  John Cooley
  George Coombes
  Henry Cooper
  Elijah Coston
  William Farrar
  Thomas Ford
  James Gray
  John Griffiths
  Richard Hawkins
  Joseph Hicks
  Charles Howell
  Patrick Howley
  William Illman
  David Jones
  Thomas Kally/Nally
  Richard Lloyd
  William Long

Richard Marton	John Sand
William Mills	Alexander Stewart
Morris Naillon	Richard Summers
John Owen	William Taylor
Henry Price	George Warren
Charles Rhodes	Samuel Woolf

Major Norcott must have led a charmed life throughout the battle, 'Inkyboy' his fine black horse being struck in eleven places, three times clean through the body, in the chest by grape shot and in the off fore leg by a round shot. The horse was unable to proceed the final one hundred yards to the Rifles' bivouac, his service and pension days sadly over.

The captured position was also visited by those who had taken no part in the action as well as the curious, but by far the saddest sight was the Regimental wives looking for the familiar facings worn by their husbands' Regiments hoping to find their loved ones safe and uninjured. The Russian wounded were also being treated in the same manner as the British but all had not been so ready to thank their saviours.

Lord Raglan in his despatch praised the conduct of the Regiment and stated that the capture of the Great Redoubt was 'materially aided by the advance of four companies of the Rifle Brigade under Major Norcott.'

He was also recommended for the Victoria Cross by Sir George Brown, who added: 'Major Norcott's conduct on that occasion was not only conspicuous to the whole Division, but attracted the notice of the enemy; for the Officer in command of the Russian Battery, who was subsequently made prisoner, informed Lord Raglan, that he had laid a gun specially for 'the daring officer in the dark uniform on the black horse.'

Sir George Brown's report to Lord Raglan was worded in such a way that no provision was made for the part played by Colonel Lawrence or Major Bradford and his wing of the Rifles in the capture of the redoubt.

The 2nd Bn. Rifle Brigade spent the 21st and 22nd September on the Alma position burying the dead, assisting the wounded and generally observing the captured position. How confident the Russians were in holding the heights was evident by the wooden enclosures specially built by the order of Menshikoff for his lady friends, in which they could sit and enjoy a picnic, while at the same time witness the defeat and destruction of the British and Allied Armies. It was quite evident however, that they had made a hurried flight, leaving bottles of wine, baskets of food and even some delicate reminders of their persons, in the shape of parasols, bonnets, shawls and, most suggestive of all the mementoes, a petticoat. This latter piece of clothing was fingered and lingered over by many of the curious soldiers.

On the advance of the Army to Sebastopol on the 22nd there were still hundreds of Russian wounded out on the ground. Doctor Thompson of the 44th Regiment attended by John Macgrath, an Irish soldier of the same corps, volunteered to remain on the field and attend to some 750 wounded Russians who had been lying in their own blood for up to sixty hours. The only protection for the Doctor and his orderly against the Cossacks, that hovered on the heights above the scene of slaughter, was a white flag of truce. Doctor Thomas toiled without ceasing to relieve the suffering of these men and after many risks rejoined his regiment at Balaclava, only to perish of cholera a few days after his return.

The transport for the Light Division

To Sebastopol

ON the 23rd September, the 2nd Battalion Rifle Brigade, having been under arms from seven o'clock, finally left the Alma Heights and advanced towards the River Katchka which they reached at sunset. The Rifles, in front of the army, passed through vineyards and a village, and crossing the river, approached the position with caution. It was found to be evacuated and so they decided to bivouac here for the night. On the 24th the 2nd Battalion was once again under arms at seven o'clock, but was delayed until near twelve o'clock while a reconnaissance was made. On finally moving off the Rifles covered the advance of the army; ascending the ridge they moved on over a level plateau which then descended to the valley of the Belbek.

Pushing on through vineyards and gardens they forded the river and formed a protective skirmish screen to cover the crossing of the River Belbek by the army. The Rifles ascended the opposite heights where they stayed until dusk when their skirmishers were brought in. The Battalion bivouacked on these heights, but also had to provide a picket of two companies.

On the 25th September the army was to make a further advance, Colonel Lawrence and his 2nd Battalion Riflemen were ordered to keep themselves ready so as to be at the disposal of Lord Lucan. They were to cover the flank of the cavalry on the advance march from the Belbek towards Mackenzie's Farm. The men were ordered to put their spare shirts and boots, wrapped in their greatcoats, on the limbers of the artillery's guns. Four Companies moved off on the flank of the cavalry, while the other four companies brought up the rear.

The Rifles had been moving through wooded countryside which now became too dense for the files to continue in skirmishing order and remain in contact. As they approached Mackenzie's Farm, Lord

Lucan, Lord William Paulet and the Deputy Adjutant-General dismounted to look at a map; as they did so, a gun fired which startled the party and soon after a second shot followed. The cavalry hurried forward, followed by the Rifles who soon quickened their pace, having received a message from Lord Raglan to push on as quickly as they could. It was quite by chance that the advance guard of the British Army had come upon the baggage train of Menshikoff's forces which had marched out of Sebastopol with the intention to operate in the field in a free role but in ignorance of the allied forces' movements and intentions.

The Rifles, having doubled for a short distance, cleared the woods and came to the road where they fell upon the baggage of Menchikoff's column. They pursued the rear-guard for a short distance but the temptation of the baggage carts was too great. The Riflemen were soon amongst the carts helping themselves to provisions, wine and whatever they could lay their hands on; ladies underwear and improper French novels were part of the loot. While the former might have sent the men's pulses racing, the latter would have had little effect on the men who would have found them difficult enough to read in English! However they did not go to waste as the officers claimed them.

Some prisoners were taken, including an Artillery Captain too full of drink to escape, while the horses and carts were all a welcome addition to the allies' poor transport stock. The Riflemen, however, released a piebald from a cart's team and gave it to Major Norcott to replace his charger 'Inkyboy,' disabled at the Alma.

The Rifles crossed the River Tchernaya by a stone bridge and bivouacked on the heights beyond. The men were almost exhausted by this time, having been on the move since early morning until after dark without anything to eat, unless they had been amongst the lucky ones to find something in the captured baggage train. On the 26th the army advanced on Balaclava, with the 21st Regiment leading. The approach was by a narrow gorge, which had high bare hills on each side.

Colonel Lawrence detached Major Norcott and three Companies to the right and Major Bradford with another three Companies to the left, while he moved with two Companies in the centre. They now approached Balaclava having sent out their skirmishers, but met with no opposition until they had advanced a considerable distance. Here, they were greeted by some musketry fire from the heights by a few men who were soon dislodged and driven in, and the advance continued.

A Staff Officer reported to Lord Raglan that the road was clear. He rode forward and was about to enter the gorge when Colonel Lawrence brought his attention to a party of the enemy still on the hills and asked permission to send a Company in advance. This was granted and Major Norcott took Captain Fyers and his Company towards the town. As they approached it, and with the Battalion appearing on the heights behind them, a couple of token shots were fired from the Genoese Fort which fell harmlessly in their direction. With the Rifles still continuing to advance and nearing the position, a white flag was raised.

Captain Fyers, an old and wily soldier, was not fooled by this ploy and halted his Subaltern, Egerton, with half the Company, while he with the other half advanced on the fort by a narrow road engineered between the high ground and the sea. When Captain Fyers and his Riflemen entered the fort the governor left it by another side door, but ran into Lieutenant Egerton and Adjutant Ross with the other half Company. He surrendered and handed his sword to Egerton.

Captain Fyers now took his Company down into the town of Balaclava, which name derived from the Italian 'Bella Clava' (beautiful port). A baker came out and looked in terror upon being confronted by this force of men dressed in dark uniforms. Going back into his house he returned with a roast turkey which he offered to Fyers along with a number of loaves. These he desired him to break in two and give half to each man.

The Battalion under Lawrence came up and subsequently occupied Balaclava, posting sentries that night for the protection of the inhabitants. Some spoil was found in the fort. Colonel Lawrence became the owner of a fur coat, a gift from one of the Riflemen, and Adjutant Ross obtained a remount to replace his horse killed at the Alma.

The following day the 2nd Battalion Rifle Brigade was moved about a mile nearer to Sebastopol and encamped for some days. The main army now converged on Balaclava and were greeted by the friendly inhabitants, who emerged from their green-tiled cottages to welcome them with fruit, flowers and bread sprinkled with salt. The port of Balaclava had been a thriving hive of activity in its day but now was little more than a single street, both port and town being overlooked by a menacing range of cliffs.

Some of the regimental wives of the army had been left behind when the army marched inland towards the Alma, while others simply vanished. Some, having lost their men at the Alma, gave up and returned in the ships to Scutari.

Lady Erroll was no longer with the Rifles, having returned to England with Lord Erroll. But one dogged wife had kept up with the Rifles' quick pace and joined the Battalion on these heights and we can be sure it gladdened Rifleman Crangle's heart to be re-united with his wife!

On the 29th the 2nd Battalion Rifles, leaving their bivouac near Balaclava, advanced on Sebastopol, and took up ground on the left of the position towards Kamiesh. On the 1st October they moved their position to the right on the Woronzow Road and shortly after to near the windmill, having a wing on each flank of the Light Division.

The next day, the Battalion being still exposed to the Russian fire and many shells falling into the position, they moved to the rear and east of the stone quarries, and took up the position which it occupied during the remainder of the siege. On the 3rd they were kept on the alert all day by shot and shell coming from the enemy lines. The 4th October the 2nd Battalion Rifles were issued with tents and brought them up from Balaclava harbour. They had bivouacked every night since the 18th September without proper shelter.

The Battalion furnished a picket under Colonel Lawrence, consisting of two Companies, to cover the working parties at the five-gun battery on 8th October. These companies remained on this duty for twenty-four hours under a constant fire without a man being touched. Major Norcott also furnished a covering party at Gordon's battery.

The Light Division sent out a small working party on the 10th October but because the working party arrived late Captain Gordon could not find his trace in the dark and they returned. The covering party of a wing of the 2nd Battalion still remained in advance.

The 13th October a remarkable shot was made by a Rifleman while on outlying picket. Rifleman Herbert noticed a Russian Officer on a white horse quite some distance off. Fixing the sights of his rifle at its extreme range he took a shot at him. The officer fell, while the horse moved on. The distance was estimated from one thousand three hundred yards downwards. Rifleman Herbert's own estimate on the distance was that he thought he was about one thousand yards from the Russian.

On October 14th Captain Fyers and his Company were in the field gun battery, when he observed a column of Russian infantry advancing towards them. Taking a rifle from one of his men, he put the sight at what he considered their distance and fired, carefully watching the effect of the shot. When he perceived that it struck the ground a little in front of the column, he ordered his men to fix their sights to 750 yards, to stand up on the parapet and 'give it them.' They had not been long firing when he found that he was under fire from the rear.

Some Russians had moved unseen up the ravine towards a house which was occupied by a picket from another Regiment, under the command of a Sergeant. Having retreated on their approach, the Russians had taken possession of the house and were able to fire on Fyers' men. Captain Fyers now positioned his men for an attack and charged out of the battery and drove the Russians back, but the Russians did not give up the captured position until they had eaten the dinners of the former occupants of the picket house; they also carried off their greatcoats and blankets. Most of these they dropped in their escape which probably impeded their retreat, pressed as they were by Fyers and his men.

Hugh Hannan, of the 2nd Battalion was on this duty. He fired at a retreating Russian but missed him and the Russian fired back and also missed. Hannan chased after him and, after overtaking the Russian, hit him with a tremendous blow, knocking him over a small wall and leapt after him. On dropping his rifle and sword-bayonet he grappled with his prize but Hannan's opponent was as large and as powerful as himself. The Russian seized hold of the blue neckerchief which all the Riflemen wore and screwed it up on Hannan's throat, while at the same time drawing his short sword, was about to stab him in the thigh, when Rifleman Ferguson, Hannan's comrade and rear-rank man, shot the Russian dead. Hannan's pride was hurt by this act and to the end of his career he stoutly maintained that the charge he had made with Captain Fyers, combined with the fact that he had greatcoat and blanket rolled horse-collar fashion round his body, had blown him and prevented him using his full strength.

Fyers and his men captured a sergeant and made some men prisoners, three of these being wounded; several others were carried off by their companions and many were killed. Fyers had two men wounded.

On the alarm Sir de Lacy Evans moved up two Regiments and some of the 1st Division. The rest of the 2nd Battalion were brought up and halted in rear of Gordon's battery; some guns were also ordered up. Before any of these troops could go into action Fyers had repulsed and effectually disposed of the Russian attack.

Preparations had been taking place for the bombardment of Sebastopol and the spade was in the hands of the soldier more than his rifle, in order to dig out the trenches and gun emplacements which had been scheduled for the 17th of October. The men of the Naval Brigade had been bringing up their ships' guns which dwarfed the nine-pounders of the field artillery. These guns had to be man-handled from the ships in Balaclava to their final placings above Sebastopol. There were no horses available and it took around seventy to eighty sailors per gun to achieve. At the same time the Russians could be seen making their own preparations for the defence of the town, women and children all helping through the day and during the night by the aid of lamps, torches and flares.

The war in the Crimea had also become a point of interest for those who liked to travel. These tourists, or travelling gentlemen as

Sebastopol being viewed by the British General Staff

they were called, gathered on the morning of the 17th, along with many of the officers' wives, to witness what was to be the most intense artillery fire ever known. Many men not on duty also clambered to gain positions which would give them a view of the action which would have Sebastopol's defence collapse in eight to twenty four hours or three days at the most! At the sound of the first gun the air was rent with the cheers of the spectators and soon the whole Allied line erupted with a crescendo of exploding guns. They continued throughout the morning and it was intensified in the afternoon by the addition of the British and French fleets' broadside bombardment of Sebastopol.

However, a cheering could also be heard in Sebastopol, the Russian guns having replied. Their shot crashed down onto the batteries and trenches along the heights and into the line of ships that provided easy targets for the Russian gunners. The damage received to the defences of Sebastopol during the bombardment was soon repaired under the cover of darkness. It became evident the following morning that the town would not be bombed into submission and an all-out assault would be necessary, but no plans had been made and when they finally were the British and French could not agree.

The troops had been led to believe that the war would not be prolonged, but now had to face the possibility of a harsh Russian winter for which they were ill-prepared. Their clothes had already

In the trenches before Sebastopol

started to deteriorate in the short time they had been in action and their boots were falling to pieces. The bombardment now became the daily routine and gradually was of less interest to those who had come out from England at their own expense.

The 2nd Battalion Rifle Brigade, during this time, was furnishing the usual round of pickets, covering parties and general duties, but they were lucky in the fact that they still had a functioning band who played for their entertainment whenever the occasion permitted.

A detachment of two Sergeants, two Corporals and forty-four Riflemen made up from the eight Companies of the Battalion had been sent to Balaclava on duty. These men were the only members of the 2nd Battalion still present at Balaclava on the 25th October, when the Heavy Cavalry Brigade and 93rd Highlanders were in action and the ill-fated charge by the Light Cavalry Brigade took place. Whether these men took any part in the action that day is not recorded but they remained on this duty into November, missing the Battle of Inkerman.

Sebastopol: view from the sea

Little Inkerman

THE MORNING of the 26th was quiet and all aspects of the weather predicted a most pleasant one. The only sounds of note came from the distant tolling of bells and cheering from the general direction of Sebastopol. All remained peaceful until just after one o'clock when a sharp fire came from the advanced pickets and soon after artillery and columns of Russian Infantry came over the crest of Shell Hill. This was in fact six Battalions of Federoff's force who had marched out of Sebastopol at midday and crossed the northern slopes of the Inkerman Heights, then having wheeled right so as to advance southwards over Shell Hill.

The advancing Russian columns were preceded by skirmishers and were coming up the northern slopes of Shell Hill. They were dressed in long grey coats and cloth caps with a red band. They were confronted by the most advance picket of the 49th Regiment who were gradually being pushed back by the weight of numbers employed against them. This force was about 4,300 strong, but the 49th contested every inch of ground until they were in danger of being surrounded. To avoid this they fell back onto other pickets of the 2nd Brigade positioned on their left. Two pickets of the 30th Regiment advanced from the Barrier to join another of the 30th and formed a skirmishing line on the southern slope. This line, about three Companies in strength, was able to delay the enemy advance, buying valuable time for the remaining pickets to collect in force. At the same time the 30th Regiment's skirmishers were picking off the Russian Artillery Gunners and lessening the deadly fire they could produce on the small force opposed to them.

Captain Goodlake and his roving band of Guards sharpshooters had moved down to the bottom of the Careenage ravine some half a mile forward of the West Jut. Goodlake and Sergeant Ashton had advanced ahead of the men to inspect some caves and at this point a flanking battalion of the Russian force came upon them unseen; they surged up the ravine and engaged with the sharpshooters. Unknown to them they had isolated Captain Goodlake and his Sergeant, who seeing the tight spot they were in and knowing that detection would be certain death, they made a brave rush out from the caves. Advancing with the Russians at first undetected because of the similarity in colour of their greatcoats, they then fought their way to the front and dashed in amongst their men escaping from a desperate situation. The Guards Sharpshooters had halted at a ditch across the gorge, below and between West Jut and the Lancaster Battery. This Battery was being defended by Lieutenant Markham and his Company of Riflemen. The 95th Regiment's right-hand picket had also advanced to the Barrier and joined the three 30th Companies, which gave a combined strength of four Companies defending that part of the battlefield.

Meanwhile, Sir de Lacy Evans commanding the 2nd Division had called the rest of the Division to arms and ordered his two batteries to align their guns along Home Ridge while the infantry moved into cover behind it. The Guards Brigade was already advancing to their aid, having sent its H Battery forward, which was soon to be joined by the Light Division's E Battery. Evans strengthened his forward Companies by sending a further Company of the 30th to join the other three and the single 95th Company with the Light Company of the 41st to assist those of the 49th. The eighteen guns on Home Ridge, added to the extra rifle fire began to take effect on the advancing Russians, causing the eastern most column of the 2nd Line to break into some disorder and seek shelter in the Quarry ravine.

Lieutenant Markham, seeing Goodlake's sharpshooters hard pressed by the Russian column, brought his Rifle picket out from the Lancaster Battery and joined him in the Careenage ravine. The fighting had become quite intense, but they were soon joined by some men of the 30th and 41st Regiments. This party was able to hold off the Russian force opposed to them and later the Riflemen helped to clear the enemy from the caves in the ravine known as the Magazine Grotto, where a Russian officer and a number of men were taken prisoner. The Rifles' detachment had five men wounded during the action. The 2nd Line of the Russian attack was in a confused situation, their 1st Line being still engaged with the British at the Barrier. Federoff now ordered a retreat; having tested the

British defences there was little more he could achieve. His 1st Line fell back in good order and at the same time kept up a controlled musketry fire which enabled them to hold off the advancing Companies of the 30th Regiment, who were coming at them with the bayonet.

At the beginning of the action a fatigue party of the 7th Fusiliers had been cutting wood down in the ravine below the Rifles' position. One of the men, having nothing to defend himself with, had to make a hasty retreat leaving his red coatee behind. This was seized upon by the advancing Russians and one of them picked it up and started to make his way back towards Sebastopol with it placed on his rifle as a trophy. One of Lieutenant Markham's Riflemen at once darted from the position and chased after the Russian carrying his prize shouting,' the coatee will not enter the town.' As the Rifleman came up to the Russian, the latter turned and aimed his rifle at him and the Rifleman did the same. As luck would have it, neither of them were capped. They both threw down their weapons and the Rifleman closed on the Russian with raised fists and began to get the better of his opponent; with some telling blows he knocked the Russian to the ground. At which point the Rifleman jumped on top of his antagonist, but the Russian proved the stronger in this position and soon had the upper hand. The Fusiliers and Rifle picket looked on unable to fire in case they shot their own man. The Russian, having drawn a short sword, plunged it at the Rifleman and was just about to make a telling second strike, when a Corporal, who had run out from the Battery as fast as he could, dropped to one knee and taking a steady aim fired, killing the Russian instantly. The men cheered them heartily from the Heights until the Riflemen and Corporal were made prisoner by a British Officer! In due course he had them brought before the Commander who having made inquiries into the case, made the officer aware of his displeasure and presented five pounds to the Rifleman for his courage in not allowing the red coat to be carried into Sebastopol, while he had the Corporal promoted to Sergeant for his presence of mind in saving the life of his comrade.

The Russian Batteries opened up an early cannonade against the British Lines on the 2nd November and some of the 2nd Battalion going on trench duty were wounded. (Sergeant Joseph Lassad wounded/died, Rifleman James White wounded, Riflemen John Wilson, George Birch, Daniel Sutton, David Webster killed) Captain

H. Clifford of the Rifles reports that four men of the Second Battalion were killed by a single cannon ball in the trenches.

On the 4th November four Companies of the 2nd Battalion Rifle Brigade, Erroll's, (now under the command of a junior officer) Fyers,' Markham's and Colville's, under the command of Major Bradford (Major Norcott being sick), proceeded to the heights of Balaclava to annoy the enemy. The Russians had mounted a number of guns on the very top of the mountain overlooking the Marines and Batteries. Luckily their shells had fallen short in spite of the commanding position they held. In the remaining wing two Companies, Captains Inglis's and Newdigate's, were in camp; Captain Forman's were on duty in the five gun Battery with Captain Elrington's on picket duty in the trenches.

2nd Battalion at the Battle of Inkerman

JUST before dawn on Sunday the 5th November General Codrington had visited his advance pickets supplied by Captain Elrington's Company of Riflemen and was now riding back to the Light Division camp at a leisurely pace when two shots fell close by. He at once galloped back to the picket and found Elrington's Riflemen on the alert in good defensive positions ready to receive the enemy. They were already putting such a telling fire into the advancing Russians that the latter were reluctant to rush the pickets. Aided by the thick fog and misty rain, the strength of Elrington's small command was not known to the enemy and caused them to hang back. The Buglers at the picket sounded the general alarm while General Codrington returned to the Light Division camp to call the Division to arms and organise the immediate defence of the position. Amongst these troops were the two remaining Rifle Companies, who came at the double from the camp and joined Elrington at the picket. By now it was known that the attack was a general offensive against the right of the British lines and all the pickets were engaged. Codrington advanced his Brigade and positioned them along the Victoria Ridge with the three Rifle Companies extended along the Careenage ravine on the extreme left of the line. Soon after they took up their position a column of Russians, part of Soimonoff's force, advanced up the Careenage ravine and, after opening fire on the Riflemen, attempted to ascend its south bank. Captain Elrington advanced against them with two of his Companies and at once attacked them, driving them back down the ravine at the point of the bayonet. Having retreated to the bottom of the ravine, they did not make another appearance in that part of the field.

In this attack a Rifleman named Lewis, having put on a greatcoat and cap taken from a dead Russian soldier, followed the retreating

The Battle of Inkerman. Print after Dupray

Muscovites down the ravine, and managed to pick off a number of them undetected. He narrowly escaped being shot however by his own comrades. Lewis was recommended for the Distinguished Conduct Medal. He also had a brother serving in the Battalion; both of them were to die in the Crimea.

The repulse by Elrington's Riflemen occurred at the very beginning of the Russian attack and the casualties were five men killed and ten wounded in this gallant affair.*

After Elrington's exploit in the morning, the three 2nd Battalion Companies were kept posted on the left of Codrington's force on the Victoria Heights. While Captain Forman's Company remained in the Lancaster Battery, Elrington's men kept up an accurate fire on the Russians positioned on the opposite height (Mount Inkerman) whenever they came within range. Some Russian riflemen crept into the Careenage ravine and advanced as far as the Magazine caves,

---

* For his distinguished service Captain Elrington was recommended for the Victoria Cross; but Sir George Brown turned it down on the grounds that the 2nd Battalion as a whole had not been engaged in the battle of Inkerman!

General Codrington said many years later that he always believed that it was mainly due to Elrington's energy and having deployed his pickets so well that the Russians were prevented from rushing through the British weak lines of outposts and perhaps from driving them into the sea.

where they took shelter while the Companies on the hill kept up a constant fire at them, which prevented them from showing themselves or making good their escape. A party of the Battalion descended into the ravine and made them prisoners.

The three Companies remained in this position until the end of the battle, receiving further casualties of one Officer and eight rank and file killed (Lieutenant Malcom was shot through the head) and Captain Newdigate and twenty seven rank and file wounded.

After the battle the Riflemen were employed in burying the dead.

Old sentry and young sentry before Sebastopol

Winter 1854–1855

ON the 14th November occurred the memorable gale which caused so much havoc and destruction. The tents of the four Companies of the 2nd Battalion, who were stationed at Balaclava, and all of their belongings except what they were standing up in, were blown clean away, never to be seen or heard of again. The other four Companies of the Battalion were on duty in the trenches at this time and, because of the chaos caused by the storm, they remained in the trenches and were not relieved for 48 hours; due to the cold and severe storm one man died from exposure.

Of the ships lost in this gale none was mourned more than the *Prince*, which sank with all the winter clothing on board, which included the following items:—

53,000 woollen coats,
33,000 pairs worsted stockings,
2,700 lambswool socks,
17,000 pairs of woollen drawers,
16,000 blankets,
10,000 palliasses for the hospitals,
3,700 rugs,
2,500 cloaks,
12,880 pairs of boots,
1,000 pairs of hospital shoes.

We can see from this list the reason why the men had to resort to using biscuit bags and any discarded rags to keep warm.

Rifleman MacNeal, servant to Colonel George Evelyn, had to go on a Court Martial on the 17th November to give evidence against a man of the 57th Regiment who had stolen Evelyn's horse. He was caught in the act by Rifleman Dowsell when stripping the horse of all its furnishings in order to sell them.

The men of the 2nd Battalion Rifle Brigade were now called upon for some very hard work. The right wing had been on duty on the 22nd November for three consecutive nights, while from the 26th the men were on duty for five nights out of six. The exposure to the weather combined with the lack of food because rations were sometimes wanting for two or three days at a time, all began to tell heavily on the Riflemen. Added to this, cholera and dysentery was also ravaging the Battalion.

Around the 22nd or 23rd of November an Officer and a party of Rifles of the 2nd Battalion were in the rifle pits near the Greenhill trenches between the 2nd and 3rd Parallels and a number of them had been wounded by the enemy. Two Bandsmen of the 68th Regiment advanced to their position amidst a furious fire and collected the most severely wounded man of the Rifles' casualties. They picked him up and rushed back to the rear with him, but before they could reach safety, Bandsman James Sims was knocked over by a shot which hit him in the heels.

On sentry duty in the trenches, winter 1854/5

At one stage during this month the men only had a quarter of a pound of salt pork and a pound of biscuit for some days, owing to the difficulty of getting up supplies from Balaclava. During the month of November the 2nd Battalion Rifles had 13 men killed and 1 officer and 33 men wounded; of these three suffered amputation.

The clothing in which the Riflemen had come out from England had been worn day in and day out for fatigue duty, working in the trenches, fighting and sleeping, and was just about on its last legs. The men now presented a strange and sorry sight as sheer necessity took over from regulations to conform; the greatcoat was always worn and the blanket, with a hole cut through it for the head, was put on under it, sandbags, pieces of knapsacks, anything that would bend, were wrapped round the legs by way of gaiters. Some had loose Russian boots, which were worn over the trousers, for the cold was intense and food and fuel scarce and everything that could give warmth, for comfort it could not be called, was pressed into service.

The suffering of the men was now very severe. During the whole month of December fresh meat was only served out two or three times and they received no fresh vegetables of any kind.

All that remains of the transport for the Light Division, December 1854

The Band in Constantinople

WITH the war continuing as a siege, the 2nd Battalion Rifle Brigade Band were able to revert at times to their original role as musicians, which gave some light relief from the harsh conditions of the campaign. The band had in fact become quite accomplished once again and at some time during December they were ordered to Constantinople and the British Ambassador's residence.

With the British and Allied Armies shivering out an existence around Sebastopol and the sick and wounded trying to survive the conditions of Scutari, Christmas Day was much the same as any other day. Things however were quite different for Lord Stratford de Redcliffe, the British Ambassador at Constantinople, a man of immense influence and wealth. His magnificent residence overlooked the Bosphorus and he loved the grandeur of his position and lived up to it by keeping an army of servants. He also took his own plate with him wherever he went, reported to weigh some seventy tons!

It was to this beautiful palace with its terraced gardens of luxurious flowers and shrubs that the Rifles' Band made their way to play at a grand ball held that Christmas. The many guests made their way through the dark streets guided by the lanterns of the local population and passed guards of Turkish soldiers who lined and patrolled the surrounding streets. Crowds of onlookers thronged the entrance to the Embassy, its white stone corridors decorated with branches of holly and shining leaves of scented flowers of myrtle and orange decorations.

In a recess off the main ballroom the Bandsmen of the Rifle Brigade played softly the popular tunes of the day. Suddenly the music changed to 'God save the Queen.' The doors were flung open and Lady Stratford made a grand entrance, followed by her two daughters, to join their guests. It seems that not only the Rifles' Band were pleased to be away from the war for a short time, as amongst those enjoying themselves were. Lords Lucan and Cardigan, Lord and Lady Paget, Admiral Sir Houston-Stewart and the French General Pelissier, even Miss Nightingale took time off from her duties in the hospital. The band provided the dance music for the rest of the evening's entertainment which made a welcome change from that played back at the Division's camp in the Crimea. How long the band remained in Constantinople is uncertain but we know they were back in the Crimea in the spring, being once again in great demand for all the functions that were being arranged for visitors from England and the Officers of the Army.

Draft arrives from England

ON the 23rd December Lieutenant Markham was promoted to Captain in the Coldstream Guards.

Meanwhile, on the 25th December 1854, a draft arrived at Balaclava from the Depot of the 2nd Battalion Rifle Brigade in England. Rifleman George Evernden was amongst this draft and it is from him we get a graphic description of the journey out to the Crimea, the conditions he encountered on landing and what tasks fell to the lot of this detachment on joining his Battalion.

Once on board ship for the Crimea the men were told off into three watches; the first watch remained on deck for twenty-four hours while the other two were kept below until it was time for the second watch to take their turn on deck. This they continued around the clock until landing at Balaclava. Meals for the journey lacked variety and consisted of:—

Breakfast: Cocoa and biscuit.
Dinner: Pork and pea soup on one day followed by, Beef and pudding the next.
Tea: Pint of tea and biscuit.

Besides this each man was issued a dram of rum per day

However scant and mundane these meals seemed on the outset, far worse was to follow in the Crimea before regular rations would be seen in plenty and on a daily basis.

On reaching Gibraltar the men lined the ship and were amazed by the small flotilla of boats that met them selling cheese, bread, oranges, figs and tobacco all at a quarter of the prices back in England. After another six or seven days at sea they reached Malta and the novelty here was the white houses, which to the men looked from a distance as if they were carved out of the rocks. The water was so clear in the harbour that young boys would dive after coins thrown by the troops into the water and could be seen chasing them to great depths.

During the voyage out the ship hit a tremendous storm, the top of the main mast broke and smashed to the deck. Everything below deck was thrown all over the place. Evernden, who was on watch at the time, went down below deck after the storm. It looked as if all the men had been pelting one another with all the contents of the ship.

They arrived at Balaclava on Christmas Day, but only a small detachment went ashore with a party from the Battalion to collect their tents and take them up to the camp. The main body landed the following day after being issued with three days allowance of biscuit, salt pork and grog, the latter made up with three parts water.

Balaclava town

The main draft was met by another group of Riflemen from the Battalion and they could not believe the condition they had been reduced to, looking quite ragged and half starved. These men told them they could not get boots or any clothes, the coats they wore were patched and covered in mud. Their legs were bound with old pieces of sacks and their boots were almost in pieces! They laughed and told the new draft it would not be long before they were in the same condition. After the six mile march through the seas of mud the start of their transformation had begun.

On arrival they were told off into groups of sixteen and their first task was to put up a bell tent which was to be their home for some time. The inside of the tents was much the same as the ground outside so a party of men from each tent went off to cut down some brush wood to place on the ground so that the men could lay their blankets on it. The knapsacks were placed around the tent and when the men went to sleep they used them as a head rest with their feet to the centre pole.

The following day the draft was told off into pairs and placed into their respective Companies, but for the first weeks they were employed as fatigue parties for the Battalion. Each day they went down to Balaclava where they brought up stores by hand to the Regimental Hospital or carried sacks of biscuit to the Headquarters of the Army a distance of about six miles. This was real hard work for the men: besides the weight of their loads over considerable distances, the conditions of the roads, or lack of them, made it almost impossible for them to keep their feet on the steep parts of the journey.

The fine clean uniforms of the draft were now beginning to take on a different appearance, having been slept in and covered in mud. Water, the basic need, had to be brought in from quite a distance and was only used for drinking or cooking. Personal hygiene was the last of their priorities. The cold and severe frost was so intense that in the mornings the water bottles were frozen. Only being issued with two blankets, they lay on one and used the other to cover themselves which meant that it was necessary to sleep with their clothes on at all times. Cooking was also proving a difficulty: wood was very scarce, meat was seldom properly cooked, and coffee was issued as raw green beans. The men attempted to roast these but only ended up burning them which when ground with a round shot and boiled with water, gave them nothing more than a sooty mixture!

On the morning of December 30th the four Companies of the 2nd Battalion who were stationed on the Heights near Balaclava, were ordered by Sir Colin Campbell to be under arms at half past six. They paraded accordingly under Major Bradford, waiting until about eight o'clock, when they proceeded with a Regiment of Highlanders to cover the flank of a considerable French force which was to make a reconnaissance. The Riflemen marched in skirmishing order through the woods and ravines as they advanced on the village of

The French conveying the British sick to Balaclava

Kamara, from which the Cossacks slowly retreated. The French troops pushed on to the village of Tchorgun which they burned. The Riflemen were not actively engaged but remained under arms until the afternoon, when they received orders to return to their camp.

The hard work and poor conditions had started to take effect on the men of the draft and a number were taken ill. Rifleman George Evernden had contracted Typhus and was taken down to Balaclava, where he went into one of the General hospitals on the 8th January 1855 just two weeks after landing in the Crimea. From his experiences we are given a true insight into the harsh conditions of the general and regimental hospitals which the sick and wounded men had to face. On reaching the hospital, as all the beds were full, Evernden was laid on the floor with a number of others and remained there for some time until a bed became available. He had now become quite delirious and was almost down to a skeleton, having taken very little food. Once the fever had passed the provision made for regaining his strength was dry hard biscuit and meat, boiled with rice. He did, however, receive plenty of port wine of which there seemed to be an abundance and this aided his recovery. Although all around him men were dying at the rate of two or three a day, he remained in the hospital for a month and could just about walk when they discharged him to the convalescent depot in another part of Balaclava!

This place was about a mile from the hospital and was nothing more than a run-down old building with no beds and just the bare floor to lie on, even all the windows were broken. It did have a fire place, but the men who had been sent there had to find the fuel for themselves. When Evernden was discharged from the hospital he still had the two blankets with which he had been issued but the man discharged with him had lost his. At the convalescent building they spent the first night by laying one blanket on the floor and lay together with the other over them, still wearing their greatcoats. As the building was full the only space left was by a window, which kept the men from gaining any warmth from their shelter, as the snow blew in on them all night. The next day, in agony from the bed sores on his back and hips gained in hospital, and the bitter cold, Evernden was grateful for the daylight. Some of the men went for rations which consisted of salt meat, rice, biscuit, coffee, tea and sugar, a meagre ration for sickly men. Later they had to attend the hospital to see the doctor and receive their medicine and when Evernden complained of being so weak the doctor told him he was better off out of the hospital.

Evernden dragged out an existence with the other men for about two weeks. Still weak, dirty and full of vermin, he decided to make his way back to the Rifles stationed on the Heights above Sebastopol, some six miles from his position at Balaclava. In this condition he set off early in the morning in full marching order of knapsack, containing one pair of trousers, one jacket, pair of boots, two cotton shirts, one flannel shirt, one jersey, one pair of drawers, two pairs of socks, saveall* complete, two blankets and a greatcoat strapped to his back. Across his shoulders he carried his belts with sixty rounds of ammunition in a pouch, his sword bayonet and a haversack containing his cleaning things, a water bottle and his rifle. After frequent stops and with the aid of two men from the 34th Regiment, who gave him a drop of rum and carried his kit, he reached the Rifles' camp and reported to the Sergeant of his Company. His comrades now came to his aid and the Pay Sergeant gave him some money, with which he bought a loaf of bread for three shillings and six pence and paid one shilling for a piece of cheese.

---

* The saveall mentioned in Evernden's account we can only assume was a kind of bag for keeping washing and shaving equipment etc.

Next morning he reported to the regimental hospital and was excused duty that day, but had to go with others in similar condition to scrape up some roots from the Inkerman Hills to cook the hospital rations. It took the men some time before they had managed to dig up enough to take back; at the same time the Russian gunners sent them the odd round shot to keep them moving. Some of the men were suffering terribly from dysentery but it was not until this weak and sickly band had collected enough to fill their bags that they returned to the camp. Evernden remained at the regimental hospital for about a week until he had recovered enough to take his turn in the trenches.

This duty consisted of going down to the trenches at four o'clock in the morning and returning at eight o'clock that same evening, then at ten o'clock having to carry up shot or powder to the front until twelve o'clock. After which the men went to sleep until four o'clock, when they were up again for trench duty. It is easy to see how men fell asleep at their posts under such trying conditions. A Sergeant in the 21st Regiment was found asleep on duty and received a Court Martial at which the sentence was, 'to be shot to death by musketry.' However, the men of his Company and all the officers of the Regiment signed a petition, as he was so well liked

The trenches at night

and had been exhausted from being continually in the trenches. Lord Raglan gave way to their request and he was pardoned.

While working in the trenches the men were fired on continuously by shot, shell and bullets. The larger shells made a peculiar sound as they passed over; the sailors who were also doing their share of trench duty called them 'Whistling Dicks.' When the firing slackened, the men would go back to digging, while one man kept watch for the tell-tale puff of smoke from the enemy battery. He would then shout 'down' in the hope it went over them, doing no harm.

On the 12th January a sentry of the 2nd Battalion Rifles posted on the mountain tops above Balaclava, reported that there was a fire below in a ravine in the direction of Cossack pickets. A small party of Riflemen was despatched in the direction of the light and discovered four men in the uniform of French soldiers seated round a fire. On being challenged they made a dash for it; two of them made good their escape while the Riflemen captured the other two. They were handed over to the French authorities and found to be deserters and were both shot the next morning.

The months of January, February and March were the most severe in the Crimea and the Russian Emperor called these his three best Generals. The trenches would fill with snow and have to be constantly cleared, while most of the time the men stood in knee-high frozen water and many men suffered from frostbite.

Rifle Brigade guarding the advanced trench

It was about this time that the army was incensed by the news that the five mortars in the old fort at Balaclava, which surrendered to Captain Fyers of the Rifles, had been taken on board the British ship *Agamemnon*, and that they now had brass plates on them with the inscription,

'AGAMEMNON BALACLAVA 1854.'

On the 19th February a party of the 2nd Battalion Rifles, under the command of Major Bradford, formed part of a reconnaissance in force under Sir Colin Campbell. They were under arms soon after midnight and at about four in the morning moved down towards the plain and marched in the direction of Kamara and Tchorgoun. It was snowing heavily when they started and by daybreak the storm had increased. The Riflemen preceded the advance in skirmishing order. Orders were given not to fire if they came on the enemy and it was hoped that they might be surprised; but the density of the snowstorm only allowed the men to see a few feet in front of them.

However, the skirmishers made prisoners of three sentries, who were probably part of the picket at Kamara. It seemed that the alarm had been given as the vedettes fell back firing their carbines into the darkness. The drums were heard beating to arms and through the snow their Battalions were dimly seen assembling on the Heights over the Tchernaya. The snow began to fall even more thickly than before and the men could scarcely hold their rifles; with the position and strength of the enemy unknown, Sir Colin gave the order to return. The Riflemen arrived in camp about eleven in the morning, having suffered severely from cold and fatigue.

On the 7th March 1855, Major Macdonell took command of the four Companies of the 2nd Battalion at Balaclava. Major Bradford had been promoted to Colonel and to the command of the newly raised 3rd Battalion Rifle Brigade in England. During the month of March the work in the trenches was most severe and harassing to the men, many sank under it, mainly because of the small number of men now fit and effective for duty. Although the work was hard, the weather was starting to improve and provisions and further comforts from government and private sources began to reach the men. Wooden huts had been brought up to the camp by the Battalion and the men started to erect them on the 22nd. This month the Rifles also lost the services of Captain Colville, who had been appointed as A.D.C. to General Simpson, serving in that capacity throughout the remainder of the campaign and fall of Sebastopol.

On March 23rd the Russians made a great attack on the whole length of the Allied line. It was particularly severe on the right attack, where Captain Forman's company formed part of the trench guard and was actively engaged. This attack was led by a Greek in full dress who rushed at the magazine and fired his musket into it, but it was empty and he was immediately bayonetted by the men in the trench. George Evernden and another Rifleman were out on sentry duty behind some stones when the Russians began their attack. They could hear the Russians coming before they actually attacked, but both being young soldiers did not know what to do. Their orders had been to fire and retire only when they could seen the enemy, but with it being quite dark the Russians had come close up to their right and were fighting with the troops there. The position of the Rifles was between the fire of both forces and they were receiving it from both sides. At last the bugles sounded the retire and they fell back but one of the Rifles had been caught and taken prisoner. He was being led away by the Russians but in the confusion they were bringing him into the British lines. He repeatedly shouted out and a party of the 34th Regiment attacked them and he was able to escape. During the attack the Russians had entered the eight gun battery and turned over the mortars and guns. The Rifles party now reformed and attacked the enemy again. The Russians retired and left a good many dead behind them.

During March seven men of the 2nd Battalion Rifle Brigade were wounded in the trenches and on the 19th March the Battalion had been augmented to sixteen companies, but with only the eight service companies in the Crimea.

On the 22nd April a party of the 2nd Battalion were on duty in the advanced trenches near the Quarries. The Russians had established themselves in rifle pits, situated amongst the rocks over-hanging the Woronzoff Road, between the third parallel, right attack and the Quarries. (The latter at this time were still in possession of the enemy.) The Russian riflemen held this position every night and commanded a portion of the left attack, which impeded the work on a new battery which the British were erecting on the extreme right front of the second parallel, left attack.

Captain Forman of the Rifle Brigade, was in command of the Rifles' covering party. No plans had been made to deal with this troublesome position although action was badly needed. On the morning of the 22nd April, Corporal James Winchcombe decided to take matters into his own hands and gathered together an Acting Corporal and five Riflemen from various Companies who were on duty with the picket. The men with Corporal Winchcombe were, Acting Corporal Joseph Rowe, Riflemen Henry Arnitt, Joseph Bradshaw, Robert Humpston, Roderick MacGregor and William Perkins. This group crept down amongst the rocks by the Woronzoff Road, then charged the Russian position. As soon as they crossed the open they received a galling fire from the enemy riflemen. The men's determination carried them on and they soon reached the rifle pit. Winchcombe was the first to reach it and set about attacking the Russians at the stone wall of the breastwork. This enabled Bradshaw, Humpston and MacGregor who had now reached him, to enter the rifle pit. The Russians, who were too late to make good their escape, were attacked by these three Riflemen and killed. Acting Corporal Rowe and Riflemen Perkins and Arnitt had all been slightly wounded. Rifleman Humpston also received a slight wound whilst fighting in the rifle pit. Captain Forman, having witnessed the action, recommended Corporal Winchcombe, Riflemen Bradshaw, Humpston and MacGregor for the Distinguished Conduct Medal. The Commander-in-Chief, Lord Raglan however, refused this on the grounds that the men had acted on their own initiative and without orders from superior authority. He marked his appreciation of their gallantry and the importance of their services by giving them four pounds each. It was only when the regiment returned to England and names were being asked to be put forward for the Victoria Cross that Humpston, MacGregor and Bradshaw received their just rewards. However, Winchcombe always stated forever afterwards that because of the death of Captain Forman there was no one in Aldershot at the time to vouch for his part in the action which gained the others lasting fame.*

---

* Sir William Cope in his *History of the Rifle Brigade* says that the reason for this attack on the rifle pits was due to the death of a Bandsman of the 2nd Battalion by the name of Wright, who was killed by the Russians while drawing water from a well in front of the position. No man of this name can be found in the Battalion as being killed on this day. A Rifleman Flinn was wounded the day before and died from his wounds the day of the attack, but there is no knowing if he was a member of the Band.

During the months of April and May the Battalion Band was in great demand at all kinds of functions. They gave numerous concerts for the growing bands of ladies and gentlemen arriving at Balaclava who spent the cool evenings listening to them playing the music of Verdi, Rossini and the then popular Lanner.

About this time the new pattern tunic was issued to replace the old coatee for the men, whilst it also took the place of the jacket and pelisse for the officers.

On the 3rd May, the left wing of the 2nd Battalion Rifles embarked as part of the expedition destined for Kertch at the eastern end of the Crimea so as to cut off the Russian supply routes. The force was to consist of the Highland Brigade, four Companies of the Rifles, two of Sappers and Miners, 700 Royal Marines, one battery of artillery and one troop of Light Cavalry (50 horses) a total of 3,000 men. The French force for the expedition consisted of 8,500 with two batteries of artillery all under the command of Sir George Brown. The expedition sailed from Kamiesch Bay and Balaclava Harbour, taking the northerly direction past Sebastopol to act as a feint to the true direction of the force. After about six hours at sea, following a change of mind by the French the order was received for them to return and after landing, the Rifle Companies joined Headquarters before Sebastopol on 8th May.

Meanwhile, back in England on the 18th May 1855 on Horse Guards parade Queen Victoria distributed the Crimea War Medal in person to the following Officers and men of the Rifle Brigade who received their medals from Her Majesty's hands:—

Lieutenant Colonel Bradford, Lieutenant Colonel Horsford,

Major Elrington, Major the Earl of Erroll, Major the Hon. G. Elliott,

Captain Inglis, Captain Newdigate, Captain Ross, Captain Drummond, Captain Nixon, Captain Coote Buller, Captain Warren, Captain Rowles, Captain Lindsay, Captain Bourchier, Captain Deedes,

Corporal William Muggridge, 2nd Battalion (wounded),

Rifleman Thomas Palmer (wounded), Rifleman William Careless (wounded), Rifleman T. Dulahan, all 2nd Battalion,

Colour Sergeant Andrew Holdaway, 3rd Battalion,

Sergeant James Johnson, Sergeant John Titcombe, both 3rd Battalion,

—these latter three men having transferred into the newly raised 3rd Battalion.

Casualties for the 2nd Battalion Rifle Brigade for the month of May were one Rifleman killed and one Officer and twelve Riflemen wounded in the trenches, of whom three died. One man is also listed as killed in action. During the month the 2nd Battalion provided the usual trench work duty and covering parties; however their conditions were starting to improve. Bread was being issued about three times a week and the cold weather was no longer a problem, but cholera had broken out in the Battalion and many men died from it. The Allies continued their bombardments on Sebastopol and advanced the trenches and works closer to the Quarries in preparation for an assault. The Quarries, a Russian Battery in front of the Redan, was given the name by the men on account of it being built mainly of stone. It also gained another name, that of the slaughter house, because of the number of men that were killed in it!

The force that made up the expedition to Kertch was reformed on the 22nd May. They sailed that evening from Kazatch Bay, arriving off Theodosia on the morning of the 23rd, where they remained the whole day so as to mislead the Russians into the belief that a landing was to be made there. The French Navy and Royal Navy opened up on the batteries of Kertch and the Allied force landed with no resistance. Only one man was injured by an accident and the whole objective achieved with no loss and the total destruction of the enemy fleet and supplies.

The General after-order for the Kertch expedition 4th June 1855 stated:

'The Field Marshal announces to the army the further gallant exploits of the Allies (with the Kertch expedition), which this time have chiefly been accomplished by the ships of the French and English Navies. Berdiansk has been destroyed, with four war-steamers. Arabat, a fortress mounting 30 guns, after resisting an hour and a half, had its magazine blown up by the fire of our ships. Genit-Chesk refused to capitulate, and was set fire to by shells. Ninety ships in its harbour were destroyed, with corn and stores.

In these operations, the loss of the enemy during four days has amounted to four war-steamers, 246 merchant-vessels, and corn and magazines. Upwards of 100 guns have been taken.

It is estimated that four months' rations for 100,000 men of the Russian army have been destroyed.

On the Circassian coast, the enemy evacuated Soujak-Kaleh on May 28th, after destroying all the principal buildings and 60 guns and six mortars.

The fort on the road between Soujak-Kaleh and Anapa is also evacuated.'

William Russell of *The Times* who accompanied the expedition says that though a success, it was poorly led and marred by looting and vandalism. He was also outraged by the smashing of fine houses and a classical museum. The man he held responsible was Sir George Brown the Commander of the British force, but no blame could be 'attached' to any of the British contingent.

At Sebastopol Rifleman George Evernden was doing duty in the trenches on the 4th of June, standing as look out behind some gabions. (These were not unlike large wicker baskets about five or six feet tall but made of twigs and filled with earth to form a wall and provide cover from the enemies' shot.) When a gun was fired from the enemy position, Evernden saw the flash and taking cover, shouted to warn his comrades, but before he could complete the cry he was knocked off his feet. The round shot had hit the very spot he had been leaning against, but on getting up he found he was not injured and only Sergeant Joseph Cook had been slightly wounded by a piece of flying stone, which caught him in the side of the face cutting it open.

The British and French Commanders had made plans for the storming of the Quarries and Mamelon on the 7th June but for some days previous to this they had ordered a fierce bombardment of the town. The British Batteries consisted of 155 guns and mortars all of a heavy calibre, while the French had about 100 guns engaged in the same duty. The effect of this fire was that by the afternoon of the 7th the Russian Batteries had been almost silenced. As it was, to every twenty or thirty rounds from the Allies the Russians had only been able to return one round. They still managed to inflict some severe casualties in the British lines. On the morning of the attack a shell landed in the powder magazine of the advanced batteries which put them out of action for some time.

The order of attack was for the British to attack the Quarries while the French did the same on the Mamelon; the stormers of the British were drawn from the Light and 2nd Divisions. The 2nd Battalion Rifles supplied the usual covering parties and a number of men for the assault. The plan was for two parties of two hundred men each, made up from the 7th Fusiliers, 31st, 34th and 88th Regiments, to attack from the advance trench of the right attack in two separate divisions against the flanks of the Quarries, thus avoiding the central area which was known to be heavily mined. Eight hundred men of the 62nd Regiment would follow them as a working party as soon as the works were taken. Two further bodies of troops of five hundred men each were ready as support if needed in the Woronzoff Road ravine. There were also the usual covering parties in the trenches defending the Artillerymen serving the guns, amounting to a further three thousand men.

By six o'clock, a large crowd of spectators had gathered to watch from the heights around the position and at just after six o'clock three rockets were fired to signal the attack. The guns stopped firing and the storming party came dashing forward in two equal divisions led by Colonel Campbell, 90th Light Infantry, and Major Armstrong, 49th Regiment. The swiftness of the attack took the Russians by surprise although they had been expecting it. In a short time the stormers cleared the Russians from the Quarries at the point of the bayonet. They retreated to the Redan with the loss of one hundred officers and men. The stormers were now joined by the working party of the 62nd Regiment, who started reversing the defences in favour of the British and at the same time digging a trench to connect with the most advanced parallel. The stormers carried on after the retreating Russians to within a short distance of the Redan and poured in an accurate covering fire to shield the working parties behind them.

During the night the Russians tried to retake the Quarries six times, but the British troops made an heroic defence although receiving a severe bombardment from close range from the Redan and Barrack Batteries. At times the working parties had to throw down their tools and defend the position. The 2nd Battalion Rifles aided in its capture and defence having one man killed and eleven wounded, these being:—

3859	Rifleman	Joseph	Wilkinson	killed
2127	"	John	Booth	wounded slightly
3648	"	Fredk. J.	Hillier	" "
3289	"	Charles	Jacobs	" "
1617	"	Thomas	Jones	" "
4199	"	Robert	King	" "

3086	Rifleman	Henry	Longmire	wounded severely
4190	"	John	Moriarty	" slightly
3105	"	Edward	Nutty	" severely
3776	"	John	Reilly	" "
3727	"	Edward	Tench	" slightly
3770	"	Robert	Wiseman	" "

The total casualties for the action amounted to 671 killed and wounded.

On the morning of 9th June the enemy sent a flag of truce out to propose a suspension of hostilities to bury the dead and it was decided that after midday all firing should cease on both sides.

18th June: Storming of the Redan

WITH the capture of the Quarries and Mamelon the next objectives for the Allies were the Redan and Malakoff. Preparations were now in progress for an assault to be made on the 18th June, the anniversary of the Battle of Waterloo.

The Redan was built on what was once a vineyard. It was 306 feet above sea-level and it had two faces, each seventy yards long, meeting at an angle of sixty five degrees. The base from which it jutted out was a fortified line of earthworks spanning the ridge. A ditch had been dug in front of it roughly twenty feet wide and fourteen in depth, above which the Redan rose a further fifteen feet, making a total height of nearly thirty feet. From the Redan to the new parallels, which had been advanced since the capture of the Quarries, about 450 yards of open ground, much of it uphill, all of it exposed to either the Barrack and Garden Batteries on the Gervais and Malakoff guns on the right. The Redan itself was full of guns, some two tiers all behind well managed and shielded defences. The Russians also had a concealed battery in the rear of the Redan should it fall to the Allies; they were also able to rush reinforcements unseen to its defence. Fifty yards in advance of the ditch was an abattis made out of a mass of tangled branches around eight feet high.

At daylight on the 17th June the Allied batteries opened up a furious cannonade, and it was felt that the Redan and Malakoff could not resist such an intensive bombardment. It was hoped that this would also reduce whatever repairs had been made during the night. The assault was timed for five or six on the morning of the 18th, with the French making the first attack. However, they made their attack sooner than expected because of mistaking a shot from the Russians as the signal for the assault.

The British were to attack in two separate offensives. The first was to be against the Redan by three columns at its right and left faces and salient angle. This force was the proper assault, made up of men from the Light, 2nd and 4th Divisions. The second offensive, provided by the 3rd Division, was to be a diversionary tactic against the various works at the head of the Dockyard Creek by Eyre's Brigade. Barnard's Brigade was to assemble in the Woronzoff Ravine where they were to wait for the signal that indicated that the Redan had been taken. Their job was to then take the Barrack battery in reverse.

With the French attack floundering on the Malakoff, Raglan gave the order, against all logic, for the British to make their attack on the Redan for which the Russians had been patiently waiting. The 4th Division made up the left attack and the Light Division the right. The centre attack was never made and played no part in the action. Each attacking force was made up of the same strength. One hundred men of the 1st and 2nd Battalions Rifle Brigade went out first as skirmishers for their respective Divisions, followed by ten sappers, a ladder party, half of which was comprised of sailors, and fifty men with woolbags to throw into the ditch beyond the abattis. Behind these came the storming party 400 strong, backed up by 800 reserves. The left column was under the command of Sir John Campbell, the right of Colonel Lacy Yea.

Captain Forman of the 2nd Battalion Rifle Brigade and his Riflemen advanced from the right-hand trenches on the signal and at once were hit by a storm of grapeshot from the Russian guns. Still they continued to cross the open ground, though many of their number fell, and reached the abattis, where they fired at the defenders of the Redan. The Riflemen who formed the woolbag party under Lieutenant Freemantle and those in the ladder party under Captain Blackett advanced, also Colonel MacDonald with a working and gabion party.

Captain Blackett had hardly left the shelter of the trench when he was at once knocked to the ground having suffered a smashed leg. As he was dragging himself back to shelter, Lieutenant Knox, his second-in-command of the ladder party (who had been promoted from Sergeant in the Scots Fusilier Guards), was just leaving the trench with the last of the men. Knox now continued with those men still uninjured, reaching the abattis where they joined Captain Forman's skirmishers. Taking up the rifle of a dead Rifleman, Lieutenant Knox aided the skirmishers in trying to reduce the storm of lead raining down on them from the Redan. The Russians had

*Storming of the Redan.
Engraving after W. Paley*

placed their guns at a steep angle and were able to command all the open land in front of them, even that of the Rifles who were almost directly below them. Any men of the storming parties who ventured from the cover of the trenches were at once swept away.

Sir John Campbell's force on the British left attack was also in much the same position as the Light Division. Very few of the eighteen-foot ladders carried by the ladder parties reached the abattis. As men were shot down, so the ladders became too heavy for those still standing. The woolbag party fared little better. George Evernden had his woolbag knocked from his hands by the shot from a Russian gun. Those who reached the abattis with their woolbags had no chance of reaching the ditch on its other side; the situation was becoming desperate. Lieutenant Knox, after firing a number of shots from his rifle, then made for the position of Captain Forman, to ask for instructions as to what to do for the best. They both agreed they should hold their position until no one was left standing. Knox was just about to take aim once more with his rifle when he was hit in the left arm knocking the weapon from his grasp. Forman cried out to him from his position, 'You are wounded?' Knox replied 'I fancy I am.' Captain Forman at once made his way to his stricken comrade and offered him some brandy which he declined. Then, taking a large handkerchief from his pocket, he placed himself in front of Knox and bound up his wound. Just as he had finished, a shower of grape shot peppered the ground about them and he fell lifeless at the feet of Knox, who was still standing uninjured from this last blast. At some time during the attack the commander of the woolbag party, Lieutenant Freemantle, was also dangerously wounded. There was nothing Knox could do so he started to make his way back to the trenches. Before he reached safety, another burst of grapeshot caught his already broken arm, which splintered the bone and lodged in his arm. Still able to keep on his feet, he reached the shelter of the trench and then collapsed through the loss of blood. Four men of the 23rd Regiment placed Lieutenant Knox on a stretcher and took him to the rear. On the way they were stopped by Lord Raglan who inquired if he was seriously hurt. At the same time one of his Lordship's staff offered him some brandy, which he declined. With further journeys by stretcher and mule ambulance he was brought out of the action ahead of other casualties. This enabled him to be treated by the doctors, who straightaway removed the shattered limb from its socket with the aid of chloroform.

The attack having failed, the Rifles, being supported only by the 34th Regiment, made their way as best they could back to the trenches. The total casualties for the 2nd Battalion Rifle Brigade were:—

Captain Forman, two Sergeants, twenty three Rank and File killed: Captain Blackett (lost leg) Lieut. Knox (lost arm) and Freemantle severely wounded, three Sergeants and seventy five wounded.

For his gallantry on this occasion, added to that at the Alma when a Sergeant in the Scots Fusilier Guards, Knox was later awarded the Victoria Cross.

That night the Russians made a general attack on the English lines but they were repulsed without any loss to the Rifles.

For some days after the attack the heat of the sun made the position in the advance trenches almost unbearable as the dead bodies lying out in the open began to decompose. A flag of truce was eventually hoisted and the Allies and Russians went out with fatigue parties to collect and bury the dead.

On June 30th Lieutenant Woodford, 2nd Rifle Brigade, was wounded when on duty in the trenches and died the same day. This night another man was killed, Rifleman William King. When the Russians were shelling the trenches, one of these landed on his head and blew it away. After the men went to his aid, they found his head completely missing with only a cotton handkerchief round his neck, burning.

On the 3rd July Captain Fyers was coming off picket duty in the advanced work, with about 400 men, and retiring by a zig-zag, (trench system) which, by some oversight of the engineers, was directly enfiladed by a Russian gun. The Quarries were under constant bombardment from the guns of the Redan, and as soon as the men were seen into the trenches, a round shot was fired, which, bounding along, knocked down thirteen men of whom eight were killed or died of their wounds.

3525 Rifleman	John Bates	killed	
3946 "	James Martin	"	
4070 "	William Mitchell	"	
4332 "	James Burns	wounded slightly	
4164 "	James Childs	wounded slightly	
4033 "	Joseph Clarke	"	severely
3338 "	Daniel Cox	"	"
4586 "	Thomas Cumbert	"	"
4269 "	Samuel Green	"	slightly
3633 "	Charles Howe	"	severely
3366 "	John Lawn	"	"
3572 "	James Long	"	slightly
3626 "	Henry Reeves	"	severely
4598 "	John Watkins	"	slightly
4355 "	Henry White	"	"

Three Riflemen of the 2nd Battalion are returned in the *Gazette* as killed and 13 wounded for the 3rd July.

The wounded were removed by Captain Fyers, Colour Sergeant Kemp* and some men of another Regiment who came to their assistance. The rest of the Riflemen turned into another zig-zag not exposed to this fire. The ball, after its destructive course, ran along the trenches and stopped against the bank of the parallel.

This same day, the body of Lord Raglan, who had died on 28th June, was conveyed on a gun-carriage to Kazatch Bay and was embarked on board the *Caradoc* to be taken to England. A party of 100 men of 2nd Battalion accompanied his remains to the place of embarkation.

George Evernden relates that at this time they had spent about four months without taking their clothes off and that they were paid ten pence for a night's work in the trenches and five pence for day work. This extra money was well needed for the cost of a large

---

* Captain Fyers recommended Colour Sergeant Kemp for his bravery on this occasion for the Victoria Cross, but it was refused.

brown loaf from the French was four shillings and two pence, with cheese selling for two shillings a pound.

With the siege continuing during the months of July–August, the duties in the trenches were constant and the Riflemen were engaged either in working parties or in covering them, almost nightly attacks being made on these parties, and they were vigorously plied with shot and shell. Three men of the Battalion were killed and 43 wounded during the month of July. Of these, six proved fatal and four men who had been wounded in June died in this month. In August two men were killed and out of more than eighty wounded, six died.

Rifleman George Evernden had a narrow escape one evening when on duty in the trenches during this time. He had been firing at the Russians from a position he had made out of three sandbags. Having made a number of shots from this spot, he was about to take aim again when a man from another Regiment asked if he could have a shot, to which he told him he was welcome. This man then placed his rifle in the same spot and was taking aim when a bullet came from the Russians and passed through the sandbag into his cheek. This was extracted by one of the old soldiers and then treated by the doctor.

Camp of the Light Division, about July 1855

On the evening of September 1st a party of 2nd Battalion Rifle Brigade was ordered to cover a sap which was in the course of construction from the fifth parallel towards the flank of the Redan. At half-past seven this party, which consisted of Captain Balfour, Lieutenant Cary, two Sergeants and forty eight Rank and File, who were volunteers from all the Companies of the Battalion, left the camp for that duty.

The Russians had erected a screen at about eighty yards in front of the head of the sap, as a protection to their sentries and reserves who occupied a pit behind this screen and a ravine on their left in which there was a cave. They had, in the latter part of August, inflicted severe losses on the British working parties, which had made the men reluctant to carry out this duty. Captain Balfour detached Lieutenant Cary, one Sergeant and twenty three men to proceed down the ravine and turn the Russian left near the cave. He himself, with the remainder of the party, made a rush at the screen of stones which the Russian riflemen occupied. The Russians came rushing out to man the ground being attacked, then stopped and poured a heavy fire into Lieutenant Cary's party, wounding Cary severely and Sergeant Harrywood. The Russians now abandoned the screen of stones and the pit and retired towards the ditch of the Redan and to a small graveyard in the Karabelnaia Ravine. The Riflemen occupied the stone screens and altered them to their advantage and protection. This gave them some cover from rifle fire, but not from the shot and shells which knocked over some of the screens. The Russians tried to surprise the Riflemen during the night, but found them on the alert and left them alone. Lieutenant Cary had received a bullet wound in his right hand which caused him to have the little finger amputated at the second joint with the finger next to it. One man was killed and fourteen or fifteen were wounded, some in the assault and some in the night attack.

A few days after this affair, on the 5th of September, at the same sap near the ravine, Captain Balfour with two Sergeants and fifty Rank and File were once again the covering party. On this occasion the Riflemen were able to reach the stone screens before the Russians, who came out from the left of the Redan in some force. After exchanging shots they left the Riflemen alone until daylight. Sergeant Cherry, a most valuable non-commissioned officer, was wounded, with one man killed and seven or eight wounded. Some of the latter were wounded by splinters of shell from the British guns but this was unavoidable, being so close to the enemy lines.

Captain A. Cooke of the Royal Engineers praises this action; 'I partly attribute this success to the very judicious manner in which Captain Balfour of the Rifle Brigade posted his sentries and pickets; they were about forty yards in advance of the sap and occupied a small stone screen on the ridge, originally built by the Russians. Had Captain Balfour waited until the position he was to occupy had been pointed out to him by a Field Officer, which did not occur until some time after eight o'clock, I do not believe that we should have succeeded in performing any work.'

Lieutenant Cary died at Malta, from the effects of his wounds, on the 9th November.

With the death of Lord Raglan and the failure to capture the Redan and Malakoff, plans were once again being made by the Allies for a second assault on the same positions. General Simpson had been appointed to the command in his place, although the army would have preferred General Sir Colin Campbell, the only general officer left of any note, Generals Sir George Brown and Pennefather having returned to England and General Escourt having died of cholera.

On the 16th August the Russians made a determined and desperate attack on the French position across the Tchernaya, but the French repulsed them in an equally determined manner, causing terrible loss.

The Final attack on the Redan

AUGUST had seen the Russians build a bridge of boats to connect the north harbour by which most of the contents of Sebastopol were being removed. It was becoming quite obvious that the Russians intended to abandon the city, which would have given the Allies a very hollow victory after a siege of eleven months and the date of 8th September was now fixed for an assault. The French were determined it would succeed this time and planned to employ a much larger attacking force. The British, though using more men than on the failed assault of the 18th June were only a fraction of the size of the French. With the death of Raglan and the appointment of the reluctant and pessimistic Simpson the British were reduced to bit-part players in the campaign, which was now being run by the French.

The troops for the British attack were to be once again drawn from the Light and 2nd Divisions. A fact which seems to have escaped those in charge is that these two Divisions had already received severe casualties on the 18th. Besides being on constant duty in the trenches, they also had a large number of young troops in their ranks fresh from England. A far better plan would have been to use the Highland Brigade and 3rd Division.

From the night of the 5th September, a steady musketry fire was maintained along the whole of the enemy position. This was to prevent the Russians from repairing any of the damage inflicted by a severe bombardment started that day by the Allies, which continued for the next three days. The Allied artillery used 13,000 shells and 90,000 round shot, fired from 800 artillery pieces. Two Russian warships were hit during this bombardment which set them on fire and completely destroyed them. One of the main targets this time was to be the abattis, the main obstacle and cause of the British failure in the last attack, and large gaps were blown in its construction.

On the 7th September those men chosen for the assault were moved forward far too early to be ready for the attack, which gave them too much time in the trenches, pondering their fate while waiting for the advance. Orders were sent to the surgeons to clear out the hospitals and prepare for more wounded. The Foot Guards were directed to man the trenches on the right until relieved by the Highlanders on the morning of the 8th. The troops had also been issued with two days' rations with orders to cook them and fill their bottles with water; they also received an extra ten rounds of ammunition.

The British plan of attack was for a covering party of 200 men, a ladder party of 320, a storming party of 1,000 and a further 1,500 support troops, all to be supplied in equal numbers from the Light and 2nd Divisions. Those men left over from these two Divisions, not needed in the initial attack, formed a reserve, based in the third parallel.

The manner in which these troops were to attack was to be altered from the previous assault. This time the ladder men and covering party from both Divisions were to advance abreast of each other, while the storming parties were to go one ahead of the other. Colonel Unett commanded the stormers of the Light Division with Colonel Windham in command of the 2nd Division.

The 2nd Battalion Rifle Brigade provided a large number of men for this action. Captain Fyers with one hundred Riflemen formed a covering party on the left, their task being to protect the ladder men and keep down the fire from the Russians on the parapet. Captain Balfour commanded another party of one hundred men and they occupied the broken ground and a rifle pit in front of and to the right of the British most advanced works and were also directed to keep down the fire from the parapet. A further two parties of Riflemen, consisting of fifty men each, were under the command of Lieutenants Baillie and Playne. They were stationed, one in the fifth parallel and the other in the Woronzoff Road, while the remainder of the Battalion, about two hundred and thirty strong, under the command of Lieutenant Colonel MacDonell, formed part of the general attack.

The morning of the 8th September was very dull and depressing. A bitter wind blew towards the Allied position, bringing swirling clouds of dust and smoke from the burning ships in the harbour, and the houses in Sebastopol, straight into the eyes of the men waiting in the trenches, but at the same time it would help to conceal them from the enemy. The batteries on the slopes opened up once again, receiving only a token reply from the Russian guns. Crowds had started to gather on the hills behind the British guns, made up of those men not on duty, the wives and tourists who had succeeded in avoiding the military cordon placed around the area.

The Band of the 2nd Battalion Rifle Brigade were once again ordered to play on the heights overlooking the action, for the pleasure of those spectators who found the waiting rather irksome. What the men waiting in the trenches thought of this goes unrecorded!

The French began the attack in one concerted rush on a number of different positions, having synchronized their watches so as to avoid the mistakes made in June. Their timing for the attack, the swiftness and the large numbers involved, resulted in the successful capture of the Malakoff with little or no loss. The Russians had been caught with their night's defenders having returned to barracks with the replacements still not in place. The French tricolour was soon flying over the captured fort, but it was now time for them to do some stout defending against the Russians who sent large numbers of men to regain the position.

The British signal for their attack was to be four rockets fired from the position of General Simpson's Headquarters, once it was known that the French attack had been successful. However, the men of the Light and 2nd Divisions, on seeing the French flag already flying above the Malakoff, did not wait for the signal and charged out from the cover of the trenches and headed for the Redan. The unscheduled advance by the Light and 2nd Divisions meant the ladder parties were not yet ready. With eight men to each twenty four-foot ladder, the surge of men caused some of the ladders to be left behind. Those groups that did get out with their ladders, instead of being in advance and abreast of the covering parties, were now in their rear.

Unlike the defenders of the Malakoff, the Russians in the Redan were waiting for the attack and had a number of guns fully loaded for instant use. Once the British troops were out in the open they were cut down in swathes by canister, grape, round shot and musketry. Though the casualties were severe, a number of men did reach the abattis; of the Light Division's twenty ladders, only about six reached the ditch. This however was not a problem as the men were still able to cross it as a large part of the ditch had deteriorated from the bombardment and weather. Both storming parties had reached the Redan although greatly reduced in strength. They started to climb the outer defences. A number of the young soldiers, having survived this far, were reluctant to advance any further and took shelter wherever it was possible to find any. Those who reached the parapet tended to fire into the Redan, rather than enter it, because of the large numbers of Russians opposed to them inside. Every now and again a sergeant or officer would try to rally the men into an attack, but only a handful would venture from their shelter and most of the group would end up killed or wounded.

With the men on the Redan making no progress, the assault was in immediate danger of being a failure and more troops were needed to go to their aid. Colonel MacDonell was still in the third parallel with his main party of Riflemen, which also included a number of officers who had just arrived from England. Because of their lack of knowledge of the trenches, Colonel MacDonell had kept them with the reserve. Word was now passed for the Rifles to advance quickly to the front. They then made their way to the fifth parallel under a heavy fire from all sides as they moved through the maze of trenches and approaches. Once collected, the bugler sounded the advance and the men were quickly over the parapet and out of the trenches into the open ground. They were immediately greeted by a storm of shot and shell, which brought death and destruction on all sides but the race was on and they were soon at the ditch and climbing the sides of the Redan. All formation was lost in the rush and at the Redan they were soon mixed up with the original storming parties. Captain Hammond with Lieutenant Ryder, continued with his company up to where Colonel Windham was positioned. The Colonel had been trying to persuade the men out from behind their shelters to make a concerted effort against the Russians, but each time the young soldiers would fall back to safer ground. Only one man of the 88th Regiment and two Riflemen followed him into the Redan and with such a small party it was impossible to achieve anything. A Sergeant of the Rifles came up and coolly encouraged the men to move which so impressed Windham that he went to seek his assistance. He had just reached him and placed a hand on his arm to attract his attention, when the Sergeant was hit by a bullet in his black belt which killed him.

The attack on the Redan

Captain Hammond and Lieutenant Ryder tried to restore some order. They had started the men moving, when Hammond was wounded in the hand and Lieutenant Baillie, on coming to his aid, told him to go to the rear. Captain Hammond replied that there was no time for that and ordered Lieutenant Baillie to collect some men and try the other flank of the Redan, while he advanced into the heart of the work with a Colour-Sergeant and some men of the Rifles. Lieutenant Ryder, meanwhile, had been shot in the throat and fell wounded. He was carried back to the rear but the Surgeon was too busy to treat him straightaway. Lieutenant Ryder, a youth of eighteen, got up, tied a handkerchief round his throat and made his way back to the Redan and was once again seen climbing the ladders in the ditch. The Riflemen on the right attack were now almost out of ammunition. Rifleman George Evernden and Sergeant Wiltshire left their position at the front and ran back through a storm of lead and returned with a barrel of ammunition.

Lieutenant Ryder rejoined Captain Hammond and a small group of Riflemen as they tried to cut a way through one of the embrasures. Hammond's sword could be seen flashing through the air as it cut down a number of Russians. Lieutenant Ryder fell dead, a bayonet having transfixed his forehead. The men with Hammond gradually fell, either dead or wounded, and Hammond received a bayonet wound just above his heart. He turned at the same time and started to run back out of the Redan, his arms outstretched. As he reached the ditch he dropped his sword and was caught by an officer of the 41st Regiment just as he fell, but was already dead.

With further support needed, the numbers attacking the Redan were greatly reduced. Colonel Windham, having sent back for support on a number of occasions, ended up returning to beg for more men himself. The Russians were clearing the attackers from the Redan at the point of the bayonet and the men were pushed back to the parapet. The wooden gabions in the parapet gave way and rolled down the reverse slope taking those men who had been standing there with them. The men started to drift back to the trenches, leaving their dead comrades lying over each other, in some places four deep.

However, during the night following the attack, Major Woodford (though slightly wounded) and Captain Balfour, with about 150 Riflemen, occupied the stone screen and rifle pit and the cave mentioned earlier. Major Woodford had obtained a promise from Sir Colin Campbell that if his Highlanders assaulted the Redan on the next morning, Woodford and his men would again form a covering party. The dawn of the 9th September revealed that the Russians were abandoning the flaming town of Sebastopol and the services of the exhausted Riflemen would not be needed. Meanwhile, just before dawn, Major Woodford took a party of men to the Redan and recovered the bodies of Captain Hammond and Lieutenant Ryder from the ditch.

The trench in front of the Redan the morning after the attack, 9th September 1855

When the casualty returns were brought in and the total cost of the attack was known, it was found that the action, lasting about two hours, had produced nearly as many casualties as the whole eight hours of fighting at the Battle of Inkerman. The number killed was 385, with 1,886 wounded and 176 missing, giving a total of 2,447, of these 156 were officers. To these figures should be added 24 for the Naval Brigade. The total casualties for Inkerman were 2,573.

Casualties for the 2nd Battalion Rifle Brigade on the 8th September were: Captain Hammond and Lieutenant Ryder, four Sergeants and nineteen Rank and File killed; Major Woodford, Captain the Hon. B. R. Pellew, Lieutenants Eyre, Riley, Eccles, Moore, Borough and Playne, eight Sergeants, one Bugler and one hundred and twenty eight Rank and file wounded.

During the month of September the return gives 25 men killed with 7 Officers and 181 men listed as wounded in action, of these fifteen died of wounds.

On the 20th September, the anniversary of the Battle of the Alma, parades were held to commemorate this and distribute as many of the medals and clasps that had been issued to commanding officers of the various Regiments. On average there were about ten medals to each Company which was bound to cause some resentment amongst the men.

In the Light Division a parade was held and the men were given their medals by Lord W. Paulet *en masse* with some show of ceremony. William Russell of *The Times* gives us a fair description of how some of the medals were given out: 'A Regiment was drawn up with the commanding officer in front, beside him stood a Sergeant with a big bag. 'John Smith' was called. 'Here.' 'Step forward,' and up came John Smith to the Colonel who dipped his hand into the bag, took out a small parcel and said, 'John Smith, you were at Alma, Balaclava and Inkerman.'

'Yes.' The Colonel handed him his parcel, and John Smith retired to his place in the ranks, carrying the said packet in his hand, which he opened at the dismiss.'

With the Russians retiring from Sebastopol and setting fire to all that could not be taken and the blowing up of ships' magazines and defences the war was just about over for the Allies.

The British troops now took possession of the Redan and Karabelnaia district. The Rifles took their share of duty in Sebastopol during the destruction of the dockyard and other works. A detachment of the 2nd Battalion Rifle Brigade consisting of eight officers, twelve Sergeants and 200 men, under the command of Captain Fyers, proceeded to headquarters where they acted as escort or bodyguard to the Commander-in-Chief. On October 14th Colonel Hill arrived from England and took command of the Battalion.

With telegraphic information having been received from England that a great attack was expected on the Inkerman section of the British Line, the 2nd Battalion Rifles were put under arms at an early hour on the 16th October. This was repeated on the following mornings for some time.

On the 15th November 1855, at about 2 o'clock in the afternoon, a tremendous explosion took place in the French siege train, situated at the head of a ravine which ran down towards Careenage Bay. Lieutenant Eccles and several men of the 2nd Battalion were wounded, two of whom died from their injuries. The legs, arms and trunks of men were blown into the camps of the Rifle Brigade and 34th Regiment, being on the extreme right of the Light Division. Amongst the heap of ruins, a man's arm was found scorched and burnt black, on which the tattered pieces of clothing retained the traces of a Sergeant's gold stripes.

Men of the 2nd Battalion injured in the explosion:—

4466 Rifleman	William Powell	Killed	
Lieutenant	W. H. Eccles	Wounded slightly	
Asst.-Surgeon	J. B. C. Reade	"	"
3941 Corporal	John Edwards	"	severely
2257 Rifleman	William Edmonds	"	"
4169 "	John Payne	"	slightly
3615 "	William Smith	"	"

On the 17th, Lieutenant Borough died of fever. With the winter setting in the Rifles were kept employed in road making, fetching up huts, in furnishing pickets, or providing guards in the town.

In February, the Peace Conference was held in Paris. Four days later an armistice was proclaimed and a month later the Peace Treaty signed. Meanwhile on the 24th February 1856, the Rifles, along with the rest of the Army, paraded on Telegraph Hill above Balaclava for the inspection by the Commander-in-Chief, now General Codrington. Marshal Pelissier was also present.

Although the cold was very severe and much snow fell in the early part of this year, the Riflemen, having the protection of the huts and sufficient rations, fuel and clothing, were in far greater comfort than during the preceding winter. A theatre was erected with wood brought up from Sebastopol and other amusements were introduced to while away the time when not required for duties. In a foot race of the whole army on March 19th 1856 Lieutenant Palliser of the 1st Battalion Rifle Brigade won the Officer's hurdle race, with Lieutenant Thomas, 2nd Battalion Rifle Brigade coming in second.

The whole of the British and Allied Armies paraded on the afternoon of April 17 for a Grand Review and inspection by the Russian General, Luders. The General having gone down the line, the troops then marched past and returned to their camps.

On the 24th May both Battalions of Rifles were marched to Balaclava plains to celebrate with the rest of the troops the Queen's Birthday. On this occasion the medals granted by the Emperor of the French were distributed.

On the 8th June the 2nd Battalion Rifle Brigade embarked at Balaclava on the sailing transport *King Philip* bound for England. They arrived at Portsmouth on July 11th to the sound of 'Home, Sweet Home' played by the Regimental Band which had returned to England earlier in the year. They then proceeded by rail to Aldershot. On the 16th July the 2nd Battalion Rifle Brigade, along with the 1st Battalion, were reviewed by her Majesty Queen Victoria. The appearance of the Riflemen, most of whom wore the Crimea Medal, many also the Kaffir Medal, some the Sardinian and other

Balaclava harbour

decorations, especially attracted attention. Both Battalions were again reviewed by her Majesty on July 30th.

The 2nd Battalion Rifle Brigade remained at Aldershot until June 1857 when on the 26th of the same month they proceeded to London, where they were present at the first distribution of the Victoria Cross. After taking part in the review which followed this ceremony, the 2nd Battalion Rifle Brigade proceeded that same evening to Liverpool, where they embarked the following day for Dublin. On their arrival at Dublin, Headquarters, with five Companies proceeded to and occupied Beggar's Bush Barracks, while the remaining Companies occupied Linenhall Barracks.

PART TWO

1st Battalion Rifle Brigade in the Crimea

The Voyage East

THE SERVICE companies of the 1st Battalion Rifle Brigade, having served in the Eighth Kaffir War during 1852–53 arrived back in England on the 7th January 1854. They rejoined the Depot companies in Dover at the Western Heights Barracks and in March the Battalion moved by rail to Portsmouth where they occupied Clarence Barracks. A little before this, however, an order was received for one hundred men to volunteer into the 2nd Battalion Rifle Brigade who were at that time preparing for active service.

Orders were then received for the 1st Battalion Rifle Brigade to hold itself in readiness for active service and transfers were taken from several regiments to bring the battalion up to war strength. This increase consisted of one Staff Sergeant, ten Sergeants, ten Corporals, one Bugler, and two hundred and forty rank and file. One hundred of these volunteers came from the 60th Rifles, but many of these reinforcements were young soldiers, some of whom had not yet been dismissed drill.

In June 1854, the battalion received final confirmation to make ready and join the Army in the East under Lord Raglan. The Battalion had been augmented to a strength of twelve companies, eight service and four depot, the latter to remain in England.

The Battalion's campaigning in South Africa the year before made them the only one of the original 32 battalions in Raglan's army with recent active service experience.

On the 13th July 1854, the Rifles, now under the command of Lieutenant Colonel Beckwith (Colonel Buller C.B. having previously proceeded to the East in command of a Brigade) embarked at 3 p.m. from the dockyard at Portsmouth on board the R.M.C. S.S. *Orinoco* commanded by Captain Wilson. The *Orinoco* was a Royal Mail Company steam ship aided by sail and was not really suitable as a troop ship and the men were rather cramped because of the lack of space. Meals had to be taken sat upon the decks as there were neither tables nor forms for them to use. To add to this discomfort they were almost blinded by coal dust and complained constantly of always being dirty; no matter how much they cleaned themselves they never looked any better for it. The officers, however, seemed to have fared rather better especially when it came to feeding arrangements, an illustration of this being given by the menu for 20th July:—

'Vegetable Soup, Giblet Soup, Roast Beef, Corned Beef, Roast Leg Mutton, Stewed Shoulder Mutton, Stewed Breast Mutton, Roast Leg Pork, Roast Goose, Boiled Ham, Boiled Fowls, Stewed Ducks, Roast Fowls, Curry and Rice, Stewed Potatoes, Apple Tart, Gooseberry Tart, Plum Tart, Cranberry Tart, Plum Puddings, Macaroni and Cheese, Cabinet Puddings and Custards.'

In all fairness to the Officers of the Rifles this fare was provided at the expense of the ship's Captain, who no doubt wanted to impress his illustrious passengers. By the end of the year many of these officers would be looking back with longing to the fine provisions served on board the *Orinoco*.

At 1 p.m. on the 14th July, the *Orinoco* steamed out of Portsmouth harbour and anchored at Spithead, having the following officers and men of the 1st Battalion Rifle Brigade on board:—

Lieutenant Colonels S. Beckwith and A. H. Horsford, Captains E. Rooper, E. A. Somerset, H. Hardinge, J. R. Glyn and A. A. Cartwright, 1st Lieutenants A. W. Clifton, A. W. Godfrey, H. Tryon, C. Buller, C. S. Flower, H. G. Lindsay, T. H. Bramston, C. T. Bourchier, Hon. G. B. Legge and E. W. Blackett, 2nd Lieutenants W. Deedes, T. S. Morgan and W. J. M. Cuninghame, Staff Surgeon W. Bowen, Asst. Surgeon J. E. Scott, Pay Master J. E. Large, Quarter Master H. Peacock, 54 Staff-Sergeants, Colour-Sergeants and Sergeants, 21 Buglers, 50 Corporals and 850 Riflemen, a total of 975. A detachment of the 68th Light Infantry Regiment consisting of 131 of all ranks was also on board, giving a combined total of 1,106 officers and men.

On the 15th July the *Orinoco*, having got under way going out by St. Helens, stood on course and, with fine weather by the 20th, was soon passing through the Straits of Gibraltar, arriving in Malta harbour at 10 a.m. on the 24th July, 220 hours after leaving Spithead. Here the detachment of the 68th was landed.

The authorities now ordered the ship to be coaled and at midday on the 25th the *Orinoco* left Malta for Constantinople, entering the

Encampment of the 1st Bn. at Constantinople, 1854

Dardanelles on the 29th July to a rousing three cheers from the Riflemen lining her decks. The Bay was full of French ships at anchor, some with troops still on board. These had yellow quarantine flags flying at the masthead but they returned the cheer in a most friendly manner, showing no outward signs of sickness. At the entrance to the Dardanelles the *Orinoco* had to pass two powerful batteries which commanded the entrance, one each side, which meant that no ship could pass without being in their range. Having had fine weather most of the way, the *Orinoco* continued to Constantinople, arriving on the 30th. It was here that orders were received to proceed immediately to Beicos Bay, and there await further orders, which they did, anchoring at 6.30 p.m. that same day.

During this part of the journey the officers being short of entertainment decided to have a little wager amongst themselves. The outcome was that Lieutenant Augustus Clifton swam from the *Orinoco* to the furthest French ship, towing a dozen bottles of champagne, thus completing and winning the wager.

On the 1st August the *Simla* passed with the 4th Light Dragoons on board, and on the 2nd August the *Agamemnon* arrived with orders for the *Orinoco* to proceed to Varna and they set off that same afternoon. However, after passing through the Bosphorus they were signalled by the *Simoon*, who had been following them, to return to their former anchorage which was opposite a stone erected in commemoration of the treaty of 1853 between Turkey and Austria. The men were kept on board ship but some of the officers did manage to get ashore. On the 4th August a group of the battalion's junior officers were relaxing in a jocular mood outside a hotel which was close to the quay. General Sir George Brown came ashore and knowing of his strict sense of dress and discipline, the officers scattered in panic and confusion, rather than receive the rough edge of Sir George's tongue or worse!

Sickness and cholera had now broken out on board the *Orinoco*. On the 6th August this caused the death of Rifleman James Rowland of 'K' company, followed three days later by the death of Rifleman John Read. It was now thought prudent to land four companies on the Asiatic side of the Bosphorus, with the remaining four companies of the battalion disembarking on the 10th. They made camp on a ridge of hills above the town of Bekos which overlooked the entrance to the Bosphorus. Although there was everything to recommend the position with a clear sky and a healthy breeze from the Black Sea, the cholera kept a firm hold of the Regiment.

During the months of August and September the following men died of cholera:—

11th August	Riflemen Charles Sumler and John Dawkins.
12th August	Riflemen Stephen Tickner, John East, Robert Railler and Charles Cannon.
13th August	Riflemen William Dillon, and John Hodge
16th August	Riflemen Joseph Wingate and John McAnerny
17th August	Riflemen William Cook.
18th–19th August	Colour Sergeant John Brown, Sergeant James Wilcox, Bugler James Cork, Riflemen Samuel Adams, James Hawes, John Barker, Samuel Jones and John Taylor.

22nd August to the beginning of September:—
Riflemen Charles Green, William Hudson, Richard Whitaker, James Teasey, William Allen, Charles Cross, William Unwin, George Stephen, Holford Pavitt and Michael Murphy.

Cholera was prevalent throughout southern Europe during the summer of 1854 and it soon spread through the French then the British armies, then to the ships' crews on the Black Sea. Camps were moved to new sites where the air was thought to be healthier but the epidemic raged on.

William Russell of *The Times* described a visit he made to the French General Hospital at Varna in his letter of the 9th August 1854:—

'I rode up there at twelve o'clock the other night for medicine for an officer, a friend of mine, who was taken ill in the evening. Along two sides of the hospital was drawn up a long train of araba carts, and by the moonlight I could see that some of them were filled with sick soldiers. I counted thirty-five carts, with three or four men in each. These were sick French soldiers sent in from the camps, and waiting till room could be found for them in the hospital. A number of soldiers were sitting down by the roadside, and here and there the moonbeams flashed brightly off their piled arms. The men were silent; not a song, nor a laugh! A gloom, which never had I seen before among French troops, reigned amid these groups of grey-coated men, and the quiet that prevailed was only broken now and then by the moans and cries of pain of the poor sufferers in the carts. Observing that about fifteen arabas were drawn up without any occupants, I asked a sous-officer for what purpose they were required. His answer, sullen and short, was, — 'Pour les morts-poules Français décèdes, Monsieur.'

The band of the 1st Battalion Rifle Brigade was asked to play at the British Embassy on the 15th August under the baton of its renowned bandmaster Mr. William Miller. This was probably due to the arrival of some high ranking dignitaries from England. A few days later Mr Miller and the regimental band was asked to play down in the valley below the camp. A number of the battalion's officers went down to listen including Lieutenant Godfrey, who caused a bit of a stir amongst the red soldiers camped close by. He turned up dressed in his patrol jacket uniform wearing a Fez! It is little wonder that Sir George Brown caused such panic amongst the Rifles' officers on the 4th August if they were making up their own dress regulations!

On the 24th August H.R.H. The Duke of Cambridge, Commander of the 1st Division, who had arrived at the British Embassy for a short time, inspected the camp and expressed his approval of the soldier-like presence of the battalion.

Before leaving England the Battalion had handed in the old Brunswick Rifle and received on board, still in cases, the new Minié Rifle. At some time earlier in the year they had already received a consignment of the Minié Rifles, about enough to furnish and train a company, which gave a number of men experience in handling the new arm. When the battalion landed in Asia they constantly practised using the new rifle. On the 30th August the camp was struck at rouse, and by 11.30 every man and all the baggage was again on board the *Orinoco*, which then moved on down to Kulalie leaving buried on the hill as a memorial to their former camp site, one Colour Sergeant, two Sergeants, one Bugler and twenty four Rank and File.

The next day a number of invalids had to be landed at Scutari. Lieutenant General Sir George Cathcart, the designated commander of the 4th Division, which the 1st Battalion was to join, came on board on the 1st September and he was heartily cheered by the men, being a great favourite of theirs from his days as their commander in South Africa. He had brought with him a present for each man of the Battalion in the shape of a water-proof ground sheet, previously unknown in the Army. This was to prove invaluable to them later in the campaign, so much so, that no other regiment was as well off as the 1st Battalion Rifle Brigade.

On the 2nd of September, having the *Pedestrian* and *Rodesley* in tow with a battery of artillery on board, the *Orinoco* left her anchorage, and proceeded out of the Bosphorus. On rounding the point into the Black Sea, the tow ropes broke owing to the heavy swell and a strong wind, which caused her to put back to Buyukdere Bay, the transports narrowly escaping shipwreck. A day later the *Orinoco* started out again having only the *Pedestrian* in tow, and arrived off Varna on the 6th, only to find that the Army had left the day before with the fleet for the Crimea. Here she was ordered to join the army in Baldjick Bay where it was now assembled, and they started off that same day.

It was while anchored here that a number of Rifles officers of the 2nd Battalion and others on the Staff came aboard for a hearty reunion with entertainment provided by Mr. William Miller and the regimental band. The next day the whole fleet got under way and proceeded on the course indicated in five lines.

On the 8th September the *Orinoco* was fortunate to escape being blown up. Around three o'clock a fire alarm was raised, it having been discovered that some patent fuel mixed with the coal had become heated and caught fire. There were about 90 tons of ball cartridges stowed in the coal as the ship had no protection of a regular magazine. Dense smoke issued from the coal, so all hands set to work with the soldiers at the pumps and the stokers cutting passages through the coal which extended to the stern, in order to get to the source of the fire. Bags of biscuit and all the other stores above the ammunition had to be brought up and put on deck. This gave them a clear access, should the powder be required to be brought up on deck and thrown overboard. The men worked all night in removing the coal and trimming the vessel. A trench was actually cut in the coal around the burning fuel which was then extinguished by the hoses. The coal was found to be reduced to cinders, and a beam of the ship had shared the same fate. Though the situation was one of extreme danger all the men employed worked very calmly and quietly; the crew of the vessel being towed by the *Orinoco* had no idea as to the danger they were all in.

Landing in the Crimea

THE EXPEDITION anchored in Kalamita Bay on the 13th and the disembarkation commenced at 9 a.m. on the following day, the first troops being on shore by 9.45. The landing continued all day. The 1st Battalion Rifle Brigade, now forming part of the 4th Division, were ordered off about 3 p.m. in large punt-like boats which had been specially prepared for the landings. The Rifles once ashore remained on the beach between Lake Kamishli and the sea.

The general order for the whole force required each man to wrap up 1 pair of boots, 1 pair of socks, a cotton shirt and the forage cap in the blanket, which was then folded in the greatcoat

The Riflemen had been issued with three days rations, a full water bottle and 60 rounds of ammunition. They carried the greatcoat and its kit wrapped in the water-proof sheet, which Sir George had provided; this kept the contents completely dry and concealed. This pack was then carried in the knapsack straps, the large heavy box-shaped knapsack less the light marching kit having been left on board the *Orinoco*, as the Staff believed that, after all the sickness, the men were not strong enough to carry them.

With the Rifles in the 4th Division were the 20th Regiment, 21st Royal North British Fusiliers, 68th Light Infantry and the 63rd Regiment with two companies 46th Regiment, all under the command of Sir George Cathcart.

The night of the 14th September was very wet and the men lay down to sleep in the open where they had been standing in column. Close by on the beach lay Sir George who endured the hardships of the night with his men. It must be said, however, that some Rifles' Officers did manage to obtain some degree of comfort by scraping large circular holes out of the sand and building fires in the centre. This kept them sheltered from the biting wind and reasonably warm. A number of large boats which had been beached during the night were used to stoke-up the fires, so by dawn very little of them remained. The rest of the army on landing had moved forward to some higher ground and also spent a miserable night out in the open.

The following day the Cavalry, Artillery and Commissariat stores, which included the tents, were landed, but the latter were re-embarked before the army marched on the 19th. On the 16th Captain Rooper took out a patrol of four companies of Rifles from the 1st Battalion to get transport for the army. He came back with 120 carts and a great number of turkeys and other items of use to the army, all paid for by the Rifles to the delight of the local inhabitants.

On the 17th whilst the landing was still taking place, a light force under the command of the Earl of Cardigan was sent to seize all the transport which could be found. This force consisted of some cavalry, horse artillery and the four companies of the Rifle Brigade who had not been on patrol the previous day. The Riflemen went off at a cracking pace glad to be on the move. A few miles from the beach they marched through some salt marshy ground, which looked more like snow or slush. This brine however got into the men's boots, particularly in the case of those who had turned up their trousers and after some hours of marching their feet became absolutely raw. They had marched out a distance of at least twelve miles and found it hard going to keep up with the cavalry, who were off again as soon as the riflemen came up, giving them no time to rest. The force visited two or three villages, from which they collected a large number of country carts and other vehicles; they also seized, along with their drivers, all the bullocks and camels they could find.

The force did not leave the last village for the return march until after dark and as the Cossacks had been sighted, they marched back prepared for action expecting to be attacked. A number of men who had become quite lame from the salt in their boots were conveyed in the captured waggons, arriving back at camp in the early hours of the following day.

At daybreak the tents were struck and sent on board the transports. The 1st Battalion Rifle Brigade spent that night fully equipped for the march, formed in a circle round a number of captured horses. About midnight the men had permission to sit down, front and rear rank alternately. This harassing duty continued until the general advance.

On the morning of the 19th, a man from another regiment was flogged as an example for stealing a sheep, one of a number that were running loose about the camp at this time.

The Advance to the Alma

THE WHOLE army now started on its march to Sebastopol with the 4th Division in reserve, their task being that of rearguard. The Division was told off into two brigades, the 1st Brigade under Brigadier General Torrens, and the 2nd, when he finally joined, under Brigadier General Goldie of the 57th. General Torrens was left on the beach with the 63rd Regiment and the two companies of the 46th Regiment with the 4th Light Dragoons whose duty it was to look after the remaining stores and see them re-shipped.

The army now in order marched at daylight on the 19th, but the 1st Battalion Rifle Brigade (strength now 23 Officers, 49 Sergeants, 19 Buglers, 783 Rank and File) did not leave their ground until 9 a.m. and proceeded over the plain in extended order, to the rear and left of the army. The march, although not more than twelve miles, was very fatiguing owing to the heat and want of water, and a vast number of men fell out, some never to rise again. Of those that fell out in the 1st Battalion, most had re-joined by nightfall except 2404 Rifleman George Aldridge and 3538 Rifleman William Fisher who both died on this march. Besides the equipment mentioned, the men also carried a number of picks, shovels and camp-kettles for each company. How many of these items actually reached Sebastopol is unrecorded but many never got past the Alma!

Kinglake mentions in his history of the Crimea that the bands played on this trying day's march, but under such conditions it would be highly unlikely that much music was played after the initial advance. The Rifles make no mention of the bands playing in the 4th Division and their own regimental band could not play even if they were able, as all the band instruments had been packed on board ship with Bandmaster Miller returning to England. The band now ceased to function as a musical unit with the bandsmen taking on their secondary role of stretcher bearers. They were attached in small groups of two or three to each company, their music-playing days over until they returned to England after the war. This also was the case with a number of other regimental bands in the Crimea.

The 1st Battalion arrived at its bivouac close to the River Bulganak about six in the evening, one company, Major Rooper's, being detached to protect the left flank. About midnight Lieutenant Colonel Beckwith went down with the cholera and died soon afterwards. Lieutenant Colonel Horsford now succeeded to the command of the Battalion. On the 20th the Battalion was ready to move off just after daylight, having been issued with three day's rations. It did not actually leave its ground until 7.45 a.m. when the 4th Division took ground to the left by a flank movement in order to place itself in a proper position relative to the rest of the army. The order being given for the army to advance in direct echelon of divisions from the right, each brigade formed in contiguous columns of battalions at quarter distance. The 1st Battalion Rifle Brigade had been divided between the two brigades of the 4th Division with a wing of four companies attached to each brigade.

With the 4th Division in reserve, the 1st Battalion Rifle Brigade marched the whole day in skirmishing order and in this formation the army approached the banks of the river Alma. The 4th Division was held in reserve, its duty to protect the rear, in case the Russians tried to outflank them as they neared the Alma. The enemy on several occasions extended his cavalry to their right, which Sir George Cathcart answered by a corresponding movement on the part of the 1st Battalion Rifle Brigade. Although the enemy's force in cavalry on the British left was seen to be very great, they did not press their numerical advantage, so well did Sir George manage his small force.

Though the 4th Division played no active part in the Battle of the Alma, their holding in check a large body of Russian Cavalry aided in the success of the allied victory. The army approached within long range of the enemy's guns at 1.35 p.m. The Light and 2nd Divisions was deployed into line. The enemy opened with their batteries which were in position on the three ridges of hills on the south side of the Alma. The order was then given for these divisions to cross the river, with the Light Division supported by the 1st Division and the 3rd Division in support of the 2nd, with the 4th Division in reserve.

The Battle of the Alma

As soon as the heights were carried the 4th Division and cavalry crossed the river, the latter moving by the road while the Rifles and other regiments cut straight through the gardens and vineyards. As the infantry passed through the vineyards they pulled bunches of grapes from the vines and as the cavalry passed they threw some to them. The Rifles continued up the hillside, passing numerous dead and wounded Highlanders, when a cannon ball came bounding down towards them. Lieutenant Godfrey shouted to warn the men who were in its immediate path, who then opened out to let it pass. On reaching the top of the hill there was a sudden descent into another valley which was strewn with dead and dying Russians. Once inside the Russian entrenchment the Rifles were halted and bivouacked for the night. A large part of the Russian army was still in sight, retiring in great disorder. Lord Raglan and his staff came riding along the line and the whole army cheered him. Rifleman Richard Rose of the 1st Battalion Rifle Brigade was wounded when nearing one of the turf walls of the vineyards. He was the only member of this battalion wounded at the Alma.

The Battalion was ordered to bivouac on the south side of the Alma, just above its banks, and for that purpose had to retire down the hill again. That night the men lay down on the battlefield, surrounded by the dead and wounded, whose cries could be heard all night but nothing could be done for them until the following day.

The French had commenced the Allied attack on the right of the Alma position and their extreme right managed to turn the Russian left but being un-supported the whole French attack stalled. It was at this point that Lord Raglan ordered the British advance which aided in the success of the French attack and they also took possession of Prince Menschikoff's carriage, his servants, and the papers in which he described the position as impossible to be taken in three weeks.

The British Army's loss was as follows:—

112 Officers killed and wounded. 96 Non-commissioned Officers killed and wounded. 1,800 Rank and File killed and wounded. Total casualties 2,008.

After the Battle

SEPTEMBER 21st, the 4th Division moved at daylight and proceeded to the summit of the Russian position, where they were desired to halt. After a short time here they were ordered to form their camp, with the 1st Battalion Rifle Brigade occupying the ground which had been held by the Russian right, thus forming the left of the British Army.

The whole of this and the following day the Battalion was employed in burying the dead and conveying the wounded to the field hospitals. An example of how ill-prepared the British Army's medical staff was for the war was the fact that the 1st Battalion Rifles only had two Surgeons and one hospital Sergeant with any medical knowledge to serve the whole battalion and only the bandsmen to act as stretcher-bearers! While the battalion remained here the cholera continued to thin its ranks, and it is little wonder because what with no proper sanitation and the increasing stench of the position it was becoming most offensive. The lack of attention to the wounded was heart-breaking, and many who died from their wounds could have been saved if they had been treated sooner.

Lieutenant Bramston of the Rifles, on going over the battlefield the next day, found about twenty men of one regiment who had been carried down and all laid together. Sadly not a soul had come near them to dress their wounds or even look at them.

Lieutenant Godfrey also viewed the field that day and especially the Great Redoubt where most of the main fighting took place. It was still covered with dead and many wounded. He went down to the river to bathe and came upon the Rifles' young Assistant Surgeon Shorrocks lying almost senseless from cholera near a ruined building where the sick of the battalion had been placed. He had him carried inside, but he died later that day. Rifleman John Pine of the 1st Battalion was also searching the battlefield, but for a different reason. He was trying to find the body of his brother who had fallen in action with the Second Battalion. John, with the aid of some comrades of his brother, found Thomas close to the Great Redoubt, being one of the most advanced of the battalion when cut down practically under the muzzle of one of the guns. They buried him as best they could but with great regret that no parson was at hand to say a final prayer. The British dead seemed to be buried mostly in individual graves by their comrades and friends while the Russians were buried in mass graves. The collection of the Russian wounded was also a dangerous exercise, as a number of men found out to their cost. The Russians, not always being grateful for the efforts made on their behalf, actually fired their muskets at the very man who minutes before was offering them water or medical aid. This action so incensed a number of the men that in some cases the wounded Russian received a severe boxing for his lack of gratitude. From this lesson the British soldier learned that, on approaching a disabled Russian, it was prudent to remove any weapons from the immediate vicinity first.

After the battle Lieutenant Godfrey also visited the Second Battalion hospital near the river and found they only had one tent to serve the whole of the battalion casualties. A number of the wounded were still lying about without any form of shelter. One man was shot through the head, body and legs, his face was also swollen and covered in blood. Godfrey, thinking the man was dead, asked the orderly how he had been wounded. He replied that, 'From the number of wounds the man had, thought it was done by a shell.' But to Godfrey's astonishment the wounded man said 'That's all you know about it, I was shot!' Asked if he was in much pain he answered 'No.'

On the 22nd, Lieutenant Godfrey, who was in charge of the 1st Battalion casualties, managed with the help of his men to carry the sick down to the General Hospital. These men had to be carried down in their blankets as, owing to an oversight on landing, the stretchers had been left on board ship. The General Hospital turned out to be a ruined house on the other side of the river Alma and it was already full of sick and wounded from the other regiments of the army. In addition to the British casualties a couple of hundred Russians were lying wounded in its yard, all in desperate need of medical help and attention.

While on the Alma position the 1st Battalion Rifles lost through cholera Assistant Surgeon Shorrocks, one Sergeant and thirteen Riflemen.

Advance to Sebastopol

ON the 23rd the army left the heights of the Alma and moved to the Katchka Valley. The 4th Division again formed the rear-guard. It marched in order of battle in two parallel lines formed by the regiments of the brigades, with a wing of the Rifles in front and the other in rear, all in skirmishing order, so that in the event of an attack a large square two deep could be formed with the cavalry and artillery in the centre. After a march of about seven miles they reached the Katchka valley which, being unopposed, they crossed, halting for the night on the other side.

The Rifles paraded at seven o'clock on the morning of the 24th, but did not march off until ten o'clock having some sick men to carry down into the village. The Scots Greys and the 57th Regiment joined the army this day with the latter joining the 4th Division. The march to the top of the Belbec was only four or five miles, but the ground they had to cover on the left flank was very rough and hilly. This caused the advance to be very slow. The 4th Division had to halt on the hill over-looking the valley for some time, while the whole of the army descended into the valley and crossed by the same bridge. These valleys of the Katchka and Belbec were most picturesque and covered in acres of vineyards. After a further long halt in the valley close to the river the Rifles marched up the hill and bivouacked with the rest of the division close to the main army. Cholera was still evident in the battalion's ranks and, as the Rifles reached their allotted camping ground, Sergeant-Major Tucker called out to the 'coverers' to take up their position and then gave the word 'Steady.' He then dropped his stick, fell to the ground and later that night he died. Colour-Sergeant Richard Cornelius was promoted to Regimental Sergeant Major, which position he held throughout the rest of the campaign. During the night of the 24th/25th there were a couple of alarms. The men being woken by the rattle of small arms fire, the order was given to the men to stand to their arms. This proving to be a false alarm the men stood down and went back to sleep, only to be woken again a couple of hours before daylight, when a great clatter of cavalry caused the soldiers to shout that the Cossacks were amongst them. This turned out to be some of their own cavalry going down to water!

On the following day (the 25th) the army made a further advance, but the 4th Division was left on its ground to protect the sick and baggage and to allow the supplies to come up.

Early the next day at 5.30 a.m. the Rifles moved out and, throwing out skirmishers, marched along the high road to Sebastopol for about 3 miles, then turned to the left, through a forest to Khutor Mackenzie. Here they were halted for quite a considerable time to allow the baggage and supplies of the army to precede them. After passing through the forest they came upon some Turkish soldiers and a little further on a part of the French army. The Rifles now halted on the plain for breakfast, near to a ruined farm which had belonged to a Scotsman, this was Khutor Mackenzia or MacKenzie's Farm, as the Scottish soldiers called it. The French had set fire to the house and outbuildings, and filled up the wells much to the annoyance of the Rifles as they had left that morning without filling their water bottles! The hill was covered with broken Russian baggage waggons, and on the top of the hill close to where they were having breakfast

Balaclava harbour, one or two days after its capture

was an abandoned Russian tumbril full of ammunition, which was later blown up with grand effect.

Here it became known that the advance guard of the army under Lord Raglan had surprised part of the Russian army retiring on Bakcheserai, and had plundered and taken a vast amount of stores and baggage. The Russians had intended to cut off the supplies of the British Army which the 4th Division had already brought up. From Mackenzie's farm the Battalion descended to the plains of Tchernaya. The whole road was covered with the remains of the enemy's baggage train. They arrived at the banks of that river at 6.30 p.m. having been thirteen hours under arms.

The Battalion however was cheered by the news that the fort overlooking Balaclava had surrendered, and that the fleet was to assemble in the harbour. Crossing the valley the Rifles passed through a garden and orchard, and close by to the house was a stream where the men now filled their water-bottles. They bivouacked for the night on the top of the slope facing Sebastopol, overlooking the south harbour thus becoming the most advanced battalion at the front. This was of great satisfaction to the Rifles, having been for so long in the rear of the army they greeted this change of position with hearty cheers. One company was put out as an out-lying picket, while the rest tried to get something to eat, as no rations had been issued since the previous day. A couple of shells were fired at their position from the town which fell short apart from one which landed near the bivouac area and some rifles piled by the men were knocked down by the bursting of a shell. After dark some freshly killed beef was brought to the hungry Riflemen; this was eaten after having been boiled into a semi-cooked state.

On the 27th September, the Battalion was under arms at 6.30 a.m. but did not move until 10 a.m., allowing the whole of the supplies and all the impedimenta of the army to pass over the Traktir Bridge. The Battalion then followed and advanced almost to Balaclava, when it came up to the rest of the army, and passing it, ascended the hill to the right and approached Sebastopol over the plateau known as the Chersonese. Here it passed through the valley and the quarries, afterwards to be occupied by the 3rd Division.

Siege of Sebastopol begins

THE BATTALION paraded at 4 a.m. on the 28th September which became standard practice but once the danger of a surprise attack had passed they were allowed to fall out. At 8 o'clock Lieutenant Godfrey had to attend a court martial, which resulted in a flogging for the offender. The bugles sounded for the battalion to parade again but without greatcoats, blankets or haversacks. A Russian column having left Sebastopol, the 1st Battalion Rifles were ordered to advance to meet it until the rest of the division was assembled to come to their aid. The enemy however, immediately retired having set fire to some houses close to the town. Their intention was to draw the 4th Division in pursuit and within range of their guns. The division returned to their camp which was situated on a flattened limestone ridge extending in the direction of Sebastopol, a ravine separating it from the Inkerman Heights and another ridge on which was placed the battery of artillery of the English right attack. The Russian gunners now having got the exact range of the battalion position, the Rifles were moved about 100 yards to the rear into an area with rather more shelter.

From the time the Battalion left the position of the Alma to its arrival before Sebastopol, it lost by cholera, 1 Sergeant Major, 1 Colour Sergeant, 1 Corporal, and 7 Riflemen.

On the 29th September a picket of the Rifles shot at some Cossacks at a range of 900 yards and took one Russian prisoner. On the 1st of October, the strength of the Battalion was as follows:— 1 Field Officer, 5 Captains, 11 Subalterns, 1 Staff, 43 Sergeants, 19 Buglers, 691 Rank and File, showing a decrease of 1 Field Officer, 1 Subaltern, 1 Staff, 6 Sergeants, and 118 Rank and File since the Battalion landed on the beach at Kalamita Bay.

Although the battalion moved camp they were still exposed to the Russian fire and on the 2nd October a number of shells fell into the camp. Luckily enough none of the men were injured, but Corporal Davison of Godfrey's company had his pouch cut open by part of a shell and another man had his coat and blanket on his back damaged. The battalion moved again to the rear and east of the stone quarries and took up a position which it occupied for the remainder of the siege. Not long after moving out of their old position it was shelled with great precision! The high ground on which the battalion was now camped was later known as Cathcart's Hill. On its summit was an old Tartar Fort, which was used by officers from all parts of the army as a lookout post as it commanded the best view of Sebastopol. Even in this position the Russians were still able to reach the Rifles with their shot and shell. This fort was afterwards converted into a cemetery for officers.

Towards the beginning of October the men brought tents up from Balaclava harbour, five to accommodate two companies and three for the officers. Previous to this the men had made little bowers of the branches and leaves from the small oak-trees which grew in abundance in the area. A shell landed on a tent of the 68th Regiment, one man was killed, another mortally wounded in the head, while a third had a bayonet knocked into his side causing a terrible wound. On the 5th October Lieutenants Bramston and Legge, with fifty Riflemen, were sent out at 3 a.m. to escort an Engineer Officer on a reconnaissance close to the town of Sebastopol. Their mission was a success, with the engineer also managing to trace out the line for a British battery and approaches which were due to be started that very same night. They all returned just after daylight. Lieutenant Godfrey mentions seeing the tools for this work laid out in order, 'and a miserable-looking lot they were; many already broken.'

At the end of the first week of October some of the battalion's invalids returned from Scutari and related the terrible treatment of the sick and wounded after the Battle of the Alma. It was reported that in one ship, the *Caduceus*, 140 men died on the first day before they had even sailed. The bodies were thrown overboard without being sewn up in their blankets. The Captain refused to sail until some medical staff were sent. Two came and by the next day another forty men had died, these too were thrown into the sea!

On the 9th October a picket of two companies was furnished by the 1st Battalion Rifles to escort the engineers marking out the ground at the Greenhill Battery. The Riflemen descended about a mile into the ravine then laid down while the engineers marked out

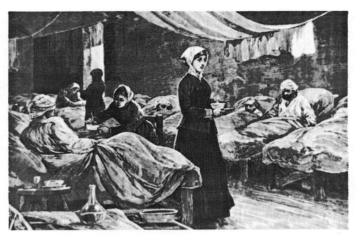

Scutari hospital: in the wards

the ground. Once completed they retired from the area, only just ahead of the Russians who were out looking at the same ground

The Engineers commenced to trace out the first parallel on the 10th October, and the right wing of the Battalion went down for the first time to those memorable trenches to cover the working parties, where they remained on duty for 24 hours.

The left wing of the Rifles paraded at daylight on the following day, joining up with some soldiers from other regiments. They all proceeded under the command of Brigadier Torrens to relieve the right wing of the Rifles in the trenches. The Brigadier took his force on a roundabout route on to the Simpheropol road which took them up a steep hill to the left, where they received a heavy fire. One man was killed and two wounded from the other regiments. On reaching the long parallel that the working party had thrown up during the night, Lieutenant Godfrey's Company was left about 30 yards to the rear where they lay down, the other companies going to the flanks. The men were under a heavy fire all day. Lieutenant Godfrey recalls how a part of a shell came so close to him that he felt as if he had been struck across the neck! In spite of this continuous shelling throughout the whole day only one man was hit, Rifleman George Newbury, from a shell splinter in the head. He had the wound dressed and continued to do his duty but the moving about caused the piece of shell to pierce his brain and kill him.

Just before sundown small parties of working men came to join them ready for the night's work. However, to do this they had to cross a section of open ground. These parties were treated to a most accurate shelling by the Russians but amazingly no one was injured. One man was seen to be knocked down and lay as if dead, but he was only stunned and not hurt. At night, with strong working parties coming from the camps, the parallel was extended to the Simpheropol road. Lieutenant Godfrey was sent down to cover the right with his company when an alarm was given of a sortie by the Russians on the left. The working party there, who were all unarmed, made a run for it. Godfrey kept the right in position by shouting for everybody to lie still and not to move as it was only a fake attack. He then took a dozen men and went to the front. The Russians brought some small field guns and rockets to bear on the works. These fell pretty thickly upon the covering and working parties but with little or no damage. The burning fuses could be seen in the dark and the men had time to get out of the way. This little affair did not last long and the men were able to resume their work, with the left wing of the Rifles finally being relieved by the right wing. This trench duty was from then on completed by alternate wings with help from the other regiments of the Division.

On the 12th October, whilst on duty in the trenches, a group of Riflemen of the right wing had a lucky escape when a live shell landed on the parapet above their heads. Rifleman Francis Wheatley jumped straight to their rescue and attempted to knock out the fuse with the butt of his rifle. This being unsuccessful he picked up the shell and threw it over the parapet where it instantly exploded. This act of valour was later rewarded by the award of the Victoria Cross and the cross of the Legion of Honour.

Around this time Lieutenant Godfrey found the situation of having three tents to house the battalion's officers unbearable, so he constructed for himself a small house of stone, half of which was underground and banked up with earth to make it warm and splinter-proof. For added comfort it also housed a small fireplace. Unfortunately, there was only enough room for him to sleep by placing his bed side-ways in the construction. However, this still made him the admiration of his comrades and brother officers.

On the 13th, with the left wing on trench duty, a heavy fire continued nearly all day and Rifleman John Mead was killed and a second man had his thigh broken by a splinter of a shell. Some troops of the 3rd Division on the left were not relieved till dark and so had to spend thirty-six hours in the trenches instead of the usual twenty-four. Some Guards and Highlanders from the 1st Division came and took their places. It was a small party of the Guards which brought some light relief, and afforded the Rifles some amusement, by their awkward attempts to dive for cover when a shot came near them. One gigantic fellow, as he came marching past, tumbled head first into a trench were he landed on top of a poor unfortunate Rifleman.

At daybreak on the 14th, the relief being a little late, the Riflemen expected to spend another twelve hours in the trenches, but the order was received to return to camp. This time the Riflemen made their own way back to camp instead of falling in and marching back by company. The Simpheropol road, by which they returned to their camp, was full of spent shot, the road being in such a deep ravine that troops moving along it were not visible from the Russian forts. A heavy fire was frequently kept up on the area whenever they suspected that troops were moving along it and the shot would fall or roll down its steep banks into the road.

Sometime after 2 o'clock in the afternoon an explosion took place in the British lines on the right attack, caused by some ammunition that was lying loose and exposed. Fortunately not a single man was hurt, only a horse and a tumbril were blown up into the air and fell

Bird's-eye view of Sebastopol, showing Allied siege lines

close to where the reserve were lying behind a mound of stones and rocks.

A party of sixty Riflemen commanded by Captain Cartwright were sent into the trenches at 3 a.m. as a specially selected section of 'Sharpshooters.' From here, under cover of darkness, they were placed into the best concealed positions that could be found, some four hundred yards from the Redan, whose fire they were to keep down. They succeeded in silencing the fire of a mortar battery first, then devoted their attention to the Redan. Some soldiers from the other regiments of the brigade had been employed on a similar duty but when the Russians opened fire they returned to the trenches in great haste. The Rifles remained in this position until nightfall, spending the whole day in no-man's-land between the artillery duel of both armies. The Russians plied this open ground with shrapnel but miraculously only two Riflemen were wounded.

At 10 a.m. on the 16th, while the left wing of the Battalion was in the trenches, the enemy opened a murderous fire on the whole length of the English trench, and continued for half an hour apparently determined to drive them from their position. The Rifles' only casualty was Colour Sergeant James Powell, who was disabled when hit in the back by gravel and stones thrown up by a shell.

The allies opened their fire at 5. 40 a.m. on the 17th and the first bombardment of Sebastopol commenced. The British were the first to open, followed soon after by the French. Unfortunately the latter's fire did not last long as their principal magazine exploded and rendered their chief battery useless. However, the fire continued on both sides till dark, but slackened very much on the part of the enemy by the afternoon; the round tower, the Malakoff and many of their guns in the Redan being silenced.

In the town the main magazine was exploded by the fire from the English batteries. Meanwhile, at noon, the fleet commenced their attack on the forts at the entrance of the harbour and continued until dark but with little success.

Lieutenant Godfrey had to go into the trenches on the 18th October to relieve Captain Ned Somerset who was ill. It was a quiet night for the Rifles but Brigadier 'Rounds' Torrens, so called from the stiff shirt collars he wore, made the men ill at ease because of his restless nature, thus preventing them getting to sleep. The Brigadier had two narrow escapes during the day. The first occurred while sitting on a form with two soldiers and a sailor when a round shot came and knocked over all three, killing one soldier, wounding another, and stunning the sailor, whilst the Brigadier escaped unhurt. Later a round shot knocked away a gabion he was standing against.

The following day before daybreak another party of Riflemen went out in advance of the batteries as on the 17th. This time each man was provided with a pick and shovel so as to make as much cover as possible before dawn. These men were all volunteers, Sergeant Fisher was also amongst this party, whose job it was to pick off the Russian artillery gunners. The reward for such a dangerous duty was that it only lasted for twelve hours, whereas trench duty lasted twenty four hours. A Rifleman on this duty was seen to pick off eight men from a Russian battery and the party returned after dark with very little loss.

Colonel Horsford of the Rifles with Smith and Maitland went out at 1.30 a.m. on the 20th October to reconnoitre the Redan; they could make out nothing more than the hill on which it stood. They also observed that it would be too steep for infantry to get up in line. Captain Cartwright was also sent out this day with his company, to join a force made up of two battalions of infantry and some cavalry. They travelled beyond Balaclava, but did not come across the enemy. Three Russian Artillery men deserted this day and a Russian lady was taken prisoner while sketching in the camp.

On October 22nd at 3 o'clock in the morning Colonel Windham of the 4th Division Staff marched the covering party to the trenches and then took Sergeant Rutland and six men of the Rifles with him. They followed a company of the 21st Regiment to a house in the left ravine. Once they reached it they found that the artillery had been erecting a battery on a hill to its left. About two hundred yards in front of this battery Windham found a French picket and a working party of the latter making a battery within five hundred yards of the salient angle. This at least was a move in the right direction and Windham continued forward edging off to the right with his escort of Riflemen. They got a good view of the town and harbour, but could discover little of the ground on which the Redan stood, despite getting within three hundred yards of the town.

The Battle of Balaclava

ON the morning of October 25th the 1st Battalion Rifles fell in as usual an hour before dawn, which they did every day throughout the campaign, and as nothing was seen to cause any alarm they were ordered to stand down and returned to their tents. Hardly had they fallen out when an order came for them to fall in again. They were immediately marched off at the double towards Balaclava. The whole of the 4th Division, with the Rifles advanced, took the longer route instead of taking the shorter telegraph road through the French lines. This march was about seven miles. However, after doubling and marching alternately, the Rifles soon moved across the heights and descended into the valley of Balaclava. News now reached them of the attack on Balaclava by the Russians, the gallant repulse by the 93rd Highlanders and charge of the Heavy Brigade of cavalry. The Russians had attacked the redoubts on the ridge of hills known as the Causeway Heights in front of Balaclava in great force, which were held by the Turks, armed with some English guns. The Turks in the main abandoned these redoubts though some N.C.O's and men did try to put up a fight, but the position was soon overrun. The Rifles arrived at the Heights just as the Light Cavalry Brigade was about to make its famous charge, and a number of Riflemen were able to witness this glorious blunder! This has often as not been attributed to Captain Nolan but in all fairness was more the product of a series of errors and misunderstandings on the part of all the principal players.

Lord Raglan's initial plan at the outset was for the 4th Division to support the cavalry's recapture of the redoubts by advancing east along the Causeway Heights towards No 3 Redoubt, while the 1st Division advanced, in support of the 4th Division, along the South Valley. Raglan's plan failed because the Cavalry misunderstood their orders and General Cathcart took his time getting into position and was too late to assist the Light Brigade in any way.

The Rifles advanced in wings. Colonel Horsford with his right wing took up a position with its left resting on the road from Sebastopol to the Traktir Bridge. The 68th Regiment were deployed in line on his right, with Major Rooper and his left wing on the right of the 68th in support of Captain Barker's battery of artillery.

The enemy brought forward a field battery of six guns and opened fire on the line causing problems for the right flank. Lieutenant Godfrey and some Riflemen were sent out to try and silence these guns, which they did in a very short time. The task was made more difficult because only a slight undulation offered any kind of cover. The Riflemen who were by now lying down picked off the gunners whenever they made an attempt to man the guns, and after about twenty minutes the Russian guns were forced to retire. The Rifles occupied two of the forts which were recaptured after having advanced their right shoulder and lined the ridge. Some Russian riflemen were also very active at this time but the brow of the ridge protected the Rifles from them. Some skirmishers were posted on the right to annoy the enemy. Only one man was hit during the whole of the day by a round shot which struck him in the leg. The men were without rations all day having made such a hurried start in the morning. Sergeant John Fisher and his companion Sergeant Jack Round shared a piece of pork fat provided by the latter. This was the only food they received all day, which was more than most. The 4th Division remained on this ground and in the same position until dark. It was now decided that the forts should be abandoned for the winter, the position being too extended to maintain without the aid of a large force, and so the 4th Division was ordered to retire to camp.

On the 26th the Russians came out from Sebastopol and attacked the extreme right of the British position which was occupied by the 2nd Division. The pickets of this Division held their ground while the division got under arms. This gave time for the field batteries to be put into position and the pickets to be reinforced. The enemy having advanced in a mass of columns, the British guns and infantry caused such loss that they retired. As they re-entered the town, the Lancaster guns opened up on them and their loss was estimated at five hundred killed. On this occasion the 1st Battalion Rifle Brigade, though the most distant from the right was on the scene of action in a very short time, but not until the enemy had retired. This action was later known as 'Little Inkerman.'

The weather had now turned very cold and stormy. Lieutenants Clifton and Legge reported sick, the former with dysentery and Captain Ned Somerset had already gone to Headquarters to recuperate from his illness. Lieutenant Godfrey had to attend a number of courts martial on the 30th October even though he was feeling quite ill. With so much sickness amongst the officers and men the duties they had to provide were made all the more difficult. The officers, however, were pleased to see Lieutenant Flower report back fit for duty.

A sale took place on the 31st of October of the effects of the cavalry officers killed at Balaclava. Colonel George Evelyn who was serving on the Staff of the Turkish Army under the command of General Cannon and formerly in the 1st Battalion Rifle Brigade attended this sale and tells us that 'A pair of warm gloves sold for thirty shillings while horses went cheap!'

On the 1st November, the morning state for the 1st Battalion Rifles was as follows:—

2 Field Officer, 5 Captains 11 Subalterns, 6 Staff, 38 Sergeants, 18 Buglers, and 550 Rank and File, shewing a decrease of 6 Sergeants, 1 Bugler and 141 Rank and File, since the arrival of the Battalion before Sebastopol.

Battle of Inkerman

SUNDAY 5th November 1854, an hour before daybreak, the Rifles fell in as usual dressed in their greatcoats as the weather had turned very cold. Musketry was heard to the right of the position, and so Lieutenant General Sir George Cathcart ordered the whole of the 4th Division under arms. At the same time about one thousand men were just entering the camp having been relieved from the trenches and inlying pickets. These men were soaked to the skin, cold and hungry, and Sir George allowed them to remain in camp. He then moved off in the direction of the firing to where Colonel Horsford had halted with his Battalion of Rifles, as they had advanced earlier at the sound of the first alarm. He had ordered the other Regiments of the Division to follow him immediately to the position of the windmill, near the camp of the 2nd Division. The

Lord Raglan conferring with General Canrobert at the Battle of Inkerman

windmill was being used as the principal magazine, but before reaching it Sir George, because of the increasing fire, realised that the situation needed more than the numbers he had with him. He sent his A.D.C., Captain Greville, back to the 4th Division camp to order General Torrens to advance straightaway with every able man left there, which included about eighty men of the Rifles.

As Colonel Horsford and the Rifles neared the 2nd Division camp they were greeted by a number of cannon-balls which came bounding from all directions. Though it was now daylight not much was visible because of a thick fog and drizzling rain. Already there were a number of dead lying about, and the wounded were being carried passed the advancing Rifles to the rear. The Russians had brought guns up to the position where the advanced pickets would have been, while the British Artillery was on the ridge across the road above the 2nd Division camp. The Rifles at this point were still marching in columns of fours when Sergeant Fisher had a lucky escape. A cannon-ball passing through the column grazed his arm and just missed the nose of a staff officer's horse and continued until it hit a horse picketed close by. Colonel Horsford now gave the order for the battalion to advance in line on the left of the Inkerman road. On reaching the heights General Pennefather commanding the 2nd Division asked Sir George for assistance, who accordingly handed over the Rifles. General Pennefather, now rode up to Colonel Horsford and told him he was very hard pressed on the left of the centre ravine and wished reinforcements to be sent there. The first three companies were immediately detached to the left under the command of Major Rooper, who deployed them into line below the crest of the hill and passing over it advanced down the other side. This was Quarry Ravine and it was covered in waist-high stunted oak trees. Here some shapes could be seen moving about but at this distance it was still hard to make out whether they were the enemy or our own troops. They were soon in no doubt when these shapes poured a heavy rifle-fire into the advancing Rifle Wing. It was in fact a column of the Russian left wing under the command of Pauloff, part of Dannenberg's force. The advancing Riflemen now halted and opened fire. For a short time the Russians returned their fire then began to waver as the Riflemen dashed through the bushes towards them. This forced them to retire to their supporting forces which could now be seen in large numbers on top of the hill. Major Rooper halted his men and had them lie down under cover of the bushes to await the renewed attack by the enemy, who, having had their numbers swelled by further reinforcements, came again solidly towards them. Sergeant Fisher could not contain himself any longer and jumped up shouting,'Come on let's get at them,' Major Rooper, being close by, told him to lie down and wait until he got the order.

At last Sergeant Fisher got his wish and the Rifles advanced against the enemy masses who were preceded by skirmishers but it was only these latter troops who fired at the Rifles. The Russian columns just advanced behind their skirmishers, but all the time their artillery continued to fire, which caused most of the Rifles' casualties. Major Rooper's detachment advanced against this dense column and pushed them back but they in turn with their weight of numbers pushed the Riflemen back. This tussle was kept up for some time, each side pushing the other back as they gained the advantage. All the time the Russian Artillery ploughed into the British force and a number of Russians were hit by their own fire. As the battle continued the Rifles became detached as a solid unit and continued the fight in small groups which gradually became mixed up with men from different regiments. Sergeant Fisher was certainly wearing a lucky charm in this action because while taking aim at a Russian, a bullet hit his rifle between the stock and barrel which completely doubled it up causing the muzzle to point behind him! Lieutenant Tryon shouted to him to find another and he had to discard a number of rifles before coming upon one which was serviceable.

A little later in the action Sergeant Fisher was confronted by a large Russian Sergeant whom he attacked with the butt of his rifle. The Russian did not put up much of a fight and threw himself down on his knees at Fisher's feet saying he was a Pole and asked for mercy! Fisher removed the sergeant's sword and, as there was now a lull in the fighting, marched him to the rear, putting him with other prisoners. On the way the Russian pulled a medal off his breast and gave it to him. It was for the campaign of 1849, inscribed for the pacification of Hungary and Transylvania!

Rooper's wing of Riflemen and the detached units of the other regiments, now all mixed up, were on their last legs, tired from the fatigue of constant fighting with little rest and no food. They made a last token line to face the advancing Russians in what would be a final charge and would result in a fight to the last man. Corporal Sills fell badly mangled by a round shot, another Rifleman was hit in the side by a shell, which exploded on impact and he was blown to pieces. At this point the French came up and went straight into the action yelling 'Moscow.' Most Riflemen were out of ammunition and at one point had been reduced to throwing stones at the enemy! Attempts had been made to bring up fresh ammunition but all met with failure with the pack horses either being killed or running off terrified from the explosions of the enemy artillery. With the timely appearance of the French, Major Rooper advanced his wing of Riflemen as far as the low wall at the head of Quarry Ravine known as the 'Barrier' and were re-united with the rest of the battalion.

At the same time as Major Rooper's wing went off to the left, Colonel Horsford took the remaining three companies off to the right. He deployed them into line and, advancing to the Kitspur, then continued on to the head of the St. Clement's Gorge which they held for some time while to their right a fierce fight was taking place at the Sandbag Battery. From here they then fought their way to the Barrier. At times they had to open their files to allow stragglers and wounded to pass through, and at one point two companies of the Guards who were then retiring. Finding themselves without support and the ammunition starting to run short, Colonel Horsford halted his wing.

About 12.30, Captain Somerset, who had been obliged to go to headquarters because of ill health, had with much difficulty made his way to the front. He joined a party of the 1st Battalion Rifles that he found in rear of the two-gun battery under the command of Ensign Brett. It would seem that these men were those who had been on trench duty and originally left in camp. At the same time as Captain Somerset arrived Lieutenant Morgan came rushing down to their position with a message from Colonel Horsford stating that he was anxious to collect as many men of the battalion as possible in front at the Barrier. Captain Somerset and Ensign Brett with about one hundred men now advanced to Horsford's position.

During the action a number of Riflemen fought independently or in twos and threes and were often mixed up with men of other regiments. The fog and the fact that most of the troops were dressed in greatcoats made it almost impossible to distinguish their comrades. Lieutenant Tryon found himself with a handful of men fighting with the 57th Regiment in resisting an attack on the ridge. Tryon was using a discarded rifle which he always did when one became available, this made him a favourite with the men. The Riflemen took cover where ever they could among the scrub oak on the rocks and in time some ran short of detonating caps. After using up all those of their fallen comrades they turned to those of the dead Russians which, although larger than their own, worked equally well. Some Riflemen, taking cover in the brush wood on the left of the Barrier, picked off the gunners of the Russian battery on Shell Hill. Lieutenant Godfrey had also been lucky in the day's fighting; the peak of his cap was cut, a ball hit him in the ribs which took his breath away and another bullet broke the sheath of his sword burying itself in the iron.

With the advance of the French, Colour Sergeant Higgins collected some thirty men of No. 2 company, (his company commander Captain Cartwright had been killed earlier at the Barrier from bullet wounds in the eye and chest) forming up his men on the left of the French Division joining them, in driving the Russians down the ravine.

Towards the end of the day's fighting Colonel Horsford took those men of the battalion who were still with him and advanced from the Barrier and pushed up Shell Hill to where a Russian Battery had stood. They ascended the hill in almost constant hand to hand fighting. They fixed swords (bayonets) and charged the remaining Russians from the ridge, keeping up a telling fire on the retiring masses. Only four tumbrils of ammunition remained intact in their hands with two others smashed to pieces, the guns having already been withdrawn. Colonel Horsford had been slightly wounded a little earlier but did not report himself as such, a shell having

Russian attack at the Battle of Inkerman

exploded on the ground between his legs, the force of which lifted him off the ground.

During the action the band had been busy collecting the wounded and carrying them as best they could to the rear. Band Corporal David Peachey was ordered by the 4th Division Quarter-Master-General, Major Smith. to go and find General Cathcart's body and bring it off the field. Pointing to the direction in which the General had last been seen alive Peachey set off with a sergeant and six men of the 20th Regiment. They had to crawl carefully along under as much cover as was possible. After a little while they came upon a party of French soldiers firing across some hollows in the ground at the retreating Russians. Peachey advanced to the officer in charge of the party and with some difficulty, got him to understand their mission. The officer ordered his men to cease fire and pointed to some rough rocks, to which Corporal Peachey's party advanced. Here they discovered the General's horse, a little distance away lay the General's body, shot through the left breast. Almost lying over the General's body was Colonel Seymour, Assistant Adjutant General, who was bayonetted three times in the breast. Peachey's party brought Sir George's body back and were then told to return for Colonel Seymour.

Lieutenant Colonel George Evelyn on hearing the sounds of the advancing battle decided to join up with his old comrades of the Rifles. On nearing the action he was met by a party of Riflemen bearing Coote-Buller of the Rifles who had received a shot in the leg, which had broken it. Evelyn stopped the men to help bind up his leg, having put some medical items in his pack before setting out. They had stopped in an advanced position when a number of men began retiring past them before a rapidly approaching enemy, whose shouts were now quite close. Bullets started to strike the bushes around them when two of the men started to get a little nervous for their own safety, but Evelyn reminded them of their duty to their charge. Being without a stretcher or blanket to convey Buller, they had to carry him as best they could some couple of hundred yards out of the line of fire. This position proved to be even more hazardous, as the Russian gunners concentrated shot and shell on this area, ploughing up the ground, with shells bursting in all directions. Bandsman Shroeder of Evelyn's party was killed by a round shot. Having procured a blanket they again carried Coote-Buller out of the danger back to Surgeon Scott of the Rifles.

Battle of Inkerman. Engraving by J. J. Crow

Captain Henry Clifford of the 1st Battalion Rifle Brigade was A.D.C. to General Buller, his old Rifles' Commanding Officer. They were accompanying Colonel Egerton and two hundred and fifty nine men of his 77th Regiment when out of the fog, only fifteen yards away, appeared the Russians in great strength. It was a moment or two before Captain Clifford could convince Buller that they were the enemy. Clifford eventually got Buller to order the 77th and other troops to fix bayonets and charge. This small force were soon in hand to hand combat with the Russians who, because of their large numbers, were able to outflank the small British line. Captain Clifford gathered together about a dozen men and drawing his pistol, he and his little band dashed amongst the flanking Russians bayoneting them in every direction. One of the bullets in his revolver had partly come out, causing it to jam, which prevented him from firing. The Russians fired close to Clifford's head but caused no harm. Having now drawn his sword, he cut off the arm of a Russian who was in the act of bayoneting him. A second Russian seeing this turned to run when Cifford's sword caught him in the back of the neck, killing him on the spot. Just after this he saw another Russian taking aim at one of the men of the 77th. Clifford rode up to him and cut at the Russian's head, but his sword struck the extended arm of the man almost severing it from his body. For his gallant actions Clifford was later awarded the Victoria Cross.

Meanwhile Colonel Horsford was positioned on the top of Shell Hill with the bulk of his battalion of Rifles firing off the last of their ammunition into the retreating Russians who were heading back into Sebastopol. This is how the Battle of Inkerman ended. The ground they held was strewn with dead and wounded men and horses, fragments of guns, muskets, and all kinds of equipment. After a time stationed in this position, the Rifles' Quartermaster came up with a party of Pioneers carrying a barrel of rum which they served out to the men who made them most welcome having had nothing to eat throughout the whole day's fight.

As it became dark the battalion was ordered to return to camp having been relieved by the pickets of the 2nd Division. Band Corporal David Peachey obtained leave to look for the body of Bandsman Shroeder whom he then buried in the dark. Ensign Brett was also out on the battle field in search of his brother, a sergeant in the Rifles who had been killed earlier in the day. A number of the men were also out on similar errands in search of friends and comrades. The wounded had nearly all been collected and returned to camp to be attended by the Regimental Surgeons. No. 2 Company was brought out of the field under the command of Colour Sergeant Higgins who had commanded it since the death of Captain Cartwright. Sergeant Fisher also brought his company out of the field, because of the absence of Ensign Brett, his company commander. The company Colour Sergeant, Powell had been killed which left Fisher as senior Sergeant.

The casualties for the 1st Battalion Rifle Brigade at Inkerman were:—

Captain Aubrey Agar Cartwright killed

Major E. Rooper severely wounded, (died later on the 11th November while on passage to Malta in the S.S. *Golden Fleece.*)

Lieutenant Coote-Buller severely wounded in leg.

Five Sergeants and 22 Rank and File killed, with a further five Sergeants and 26 Rank and File wounded.

Colour Sergeant Noseley wounded dangerously who had been at first reported killed was taken prisoner.

The Adjutant General's return of the 22nd November however gives:—

One officer and 22 rank and file killed, with three officers and eighty men wounded and six missing.

The Officers of the 1st Battalion present at Inkerman:—

Lieutenant Colonel Horsford, Major Rooper, Captains Somerset and Cartwright,

Lieutenants Coote-Buller, Godfrey, Flower, Cuninghame, Tryon, Deedes, Adjutant Morgan, and Ensign Brett.

The day after Inkerman eight Sergeants of the Rifles were selected to carry the bodies of Sir George Cathcart and Colonel Seymour, his Assistant Adjutant General, to the grave at the old fort; this afterwards became known as Cathcart's Hill. Captain Cartwright was also buried on the same day in the old redoubt on top of the hill.

The 1st Battalion Rifle Brigade claimed a Russian Bass Drum as a trophy from the battlefield of Inkerman and for many years it was played in the Regimental Band. It gradually fell into disrepair until only a brass eagle which was originally on the shell of the drum remained (see illustration on Plate 23).

The lessons learned at Inkerman resulted in the men being engaged in throwing up works to prevent another attack by the Russians. The Rifles supplied their fair share of covering parties on the extreme right which was quite some distance from the camp. This was in addition to covering the works of the left attack which was their normal regular duty.

There were not more than 8,000 British troops engaged at Inkerman whilst the Russian forces were estimated at 50,000, plus a most powerful artillery; their field guns being 18 and 24 pounders, whilst the British were only 9 pounders. One consequence of the great loss which the British Army sustained in this severe engagement was that the guard on the trenches was supplied from this time on by roster according to the duty strength of each Battalion, instead of each regiment taking the guard by wings as was previously the case.

Lieutenants Tryon, Bourchier, Morgan and Godfrey and two hundred men of the Rifles were sent at 7 o'clock in the evening of the 9th November as a covering party, to Inkerman hill, where the battle had been fought. It was now being entrenched and a redoubt and field work was being made where the advanced picket had been posted. When they reached this position they found a strong working party of Turks and Colonel Smith of the 68th Regiment in command of the covering party. He ordered the Rifles to protect the front and guard against surprise by having a long line of extended sentries several hundred yards in advance, so as to command the different ravines and approaches.

Lieutenant Godfrey was on duty again with his men under Colonel Smith on the 10th November, the Turks providing the working party. Godfrey protected the front with a double chain of sentries far out in advance and sufficiently strong to check the advance of an enemy column. They were placed so as to command all the approaches and posted a reserve in rear of the centre. Lieutenants Tryon, Morgan and Bourchier were also out with their men on similar duty.

In November, the following general after order was issued.

Headquarters before Sebastopol.
9th November 1854.
General After Order.

The Commander of the Forces returns his thanks to the officers and troops in the battle of Inkerman on the 5th instant, in which, aided by their allies, they succeeded in completely repulsing and defeating the enemy by whom they were attacked in very superior numbers, with masses of artillery, both of field and position, as well as of ship's guns.

The army have thus taken advantage of another opportunity to distinguish themselves, and of showing that upon all occasions and in presence of every difficulty, their determination to devote their best energies to the service of their their country is still the same.

On this occasion the troops had the good fortune to be associated with and supported by a division of the French army, and they will join in the expression of gratitude and admiration for their spirited advance at a most critical moment.

The loss sustained both by the French and British armies on this trying day cannot be too strongly deplored, and while he deeply regrets to have been deprived of the service of so many valuable officers and men, it is particularly painful to Lord Raglan to announce that among those that fell nobly discharging their duty, were Lieutenant General the Hon. Sir George Cathcart, Brigadier-General Goldie, and Brigadier-General Strangways, all officers of distinction and Sir George Cathcart especially, being one whose conduct elsewhere had particularly attracted the gracious notice of Her Majesty, and the attention of the country.

By order.
(Signed) J. B. B. Estcourt, Adjt. General.

On the 14th November, the Allied camps and fleets were exposed to the memorable gale which lasted for twenty hours; several ships were lost, among them the 'Prince' with the greater part of the warm clothing for the army. The harbour was a seething mass of foam, the ships being buffetted against each other and the quay. Some broke loose and smashed others to pieces. In the camps tents were carried away by the force of the gale, buildings collapsed, trees uprooted and blown about like match sticks. Wagons sailed through the air, horses and cattle were blown about for miles and a flock of sheep vanished. The sick and wounded were left without shelter exposed to the rain, snow and icy sleet that followed, while the winds cut like a knife. The little forage which had been preserved and jealously guarded for the horses was never seen again.

The spray from the sea came dashing over the cliffs many hundreds of feet high and fell like a heavy rain into the harbour. Coote-Buller of the Rifles still lying wounded in his tent was spared the harshness of the elements by the unselfish aid of Colonel Evelyn who hung on to the centre pole of his tent while two riflemen were constantly employed outside driving in the pegs. It is without doubt that this action saved the life of Buller. Throughout the gale men were still on duty in the trenches exposed to the severe conditions with no chance of relief until the storm had ceased. Lieutenant Tryon was on this duty with his men and Sergeant Fisher. To add to the severe conditions of the storm was the fact that the men were up to their knees in mud and slush and the only way they could gain any form of shelter was to huddle together. Sergeant Fisher was in charge of his company's grog and was hardly able to stand as he tried to issue it out to as many men as possible, but he only found half of them. Some of the men suffered cramp so badly that Lieutenant Tryon sent out for relief parties to carry them back to camp, but no help could be given, as the men left in camp were in much the same condition as those in the trenches. The trench parties later struggled back to camp as best they could and, with no tents, just lay down where they could in the wet. No food could be cooked or hot drinks given and their plight was most miserable. The Army lost a large number of men in consequence of this severe twenty-four hours of hardship, Sergeant Douglas of the Rifles being one of them. This was the commencement of the British Army's winter sufferings which highlighted how ill equipped it was for a winter campaign. From this date the weather grew steadily worse, and rations were served out very irregularly.

The Capture of the Rifle-pits

NOTHING much happened in the few days directly after the storm until the 20th November. In the rocky ground between the army's first and second parallels and in the ravine that ran towards the left of the British attack, about three hundred Russian sharpshooters had established themselves in some caverns and old stone huts once used by shepherds. These pits, caverns or 'ovens' as the men called them, were formed by the decay of the softer soil and rock by the wind and rain, which now left caves in the harder sections of rock in the sides of the hill.

From this position the Russian marksmen were able to fire directly into the British siege batteries on Green Hill and to enfilade the French batteries on the British left. The Russians had also made some improvements to the natural cavities and from the British position were scarcely visible, being about two hundred yards in front of the second parallel which was the most advanced trench at this time.

General Canrobert was determined that this Russian position should be taken and requested the aid of the British. Three companies of the 1st Battalion Rifle Brigade under the command of Lieutenant Henry Tryon were selected for this dangerous task. They were also accompanied by Lieutenants Bourchier and Cuninghame; the force consisted of six Sergeants and two hundred Rank and File. Their mission had been kept secret, the Sergeants and men having no idea what they had been selected for. The companies fell in at about four o'clock on the afternoon of the 20th November and then marched off to the trenches, but on the way Lieutenant Tryon halted them in a ravine which sheltered them from stray shots. Tryon formed the men around him and then explained to them what their duty was to be. The Rifles then continued down to the trenches where they lay down until dark. At seven o'clock they made ready for the attack. Tryon had them formed into three groups, the first with fifty men, Sergeant Hicks and himself; the second fifty with Sergeant Fisher under the command of Lieutenant Bourchier; while the remaining hundred were put into a position of support under Lieutenant Cuninghame.

Lieutenant Cuninghame's men remained in the 2nd parallel and opened fire on the Russians, who were soon returning it. This enabled the other two units to pin-point the exact position of the rifle pits to be attacked. Lieutenant Tryon now advanced with his two attacking parties, who moved out over the parapet in file, the front file of each fifty men being the Officer and Sergeant.

Tryon's Riflemen advanced on a point just clear of the Russians left, with their rifles at the shoulder and bayonets fixed. When the leading file came near enough for a rush, Lieutenant Tryon shouted the signal which was taken up by the whole party. They turned towards the pits, brought the bayonets to the charge and dashed forward.

Cuninghame's men who all this time had been firing away at the Russians immediately ceased their fire. This movement had taken the Russians completely by surprise and in no time the Riflemen were amongst them and a fierce hand to hand fight now took place. Tryon having emptied the contents of his revolver picked up a discarded rifle which he soon put to good use. After a short struggle the surviving Russians made a run for it. Cuninghame, on hearing the shouts of Tryon's Riflemen, advanced his party over the parapet and joined their comrades in the rifle pits. The Russian sharpshooters who had been relieved of their position were immediately joined by Russian Infantry and a terrific fire was directed into the Rifles in an attempt to force the attackers out of their newly acquired position.

Grape and canister rained down on the Riflemen which but for the darkness, good cover, both natural and man-made, would have thinned their numbers to an extent that holding the pits unsupported would have been impossible. They were, however, still suffering severe losses.

The Russians formed into deep columns and with sheer numerical advantage tried three times during the night to retake the pits. In the process of holding the pits Lieutenants Tryon and Bourchier were crouched on their hands and knees in one of the excavations with Sergeant Fisher and Rifleman Fearn. They were the only other ones in this area still unwounded. Tryon was loading his rifle under cover when Bourchier saw his head drop. He caught his arm and called

Firing from the advanced trench at the Quarries and Rifle-pits

his name but no answer came. A bullet had struck him on the right side of his head and killed him on the spot.

Lieutenant Bourchier now took command. Although it was Tryon's plan which initially captured the 'ovens,' the brilliant defence and repulse of the Russian counter-attacks were solely down to Bourchier's distinguished efforts and energy. Bourchier kept Tryon's death from the men as he was such a great favourite with them. To make the Russians think they had more men than they actually had, they constantly shouted to one another. The men were encouraged to continue shouting, but with the ammunition beginning to get scarce Bourchier made it known that, if it ran out, they would continue to defend the 'ovens' by bayonet.

Sergeant Hicks was positioned behind some stones with twelve men, but by the morning nine of these had been hit. At daybreak Bourchier had the men better posted and in perfect order to receive the enemy who now attempted another attack which failed. An engineer with a working party had joined during the night but had hard work constructing a trench under the severe fire of the Russians.

Lieutenant Bourchier's gallant band of stormers hung on to the position until the morning when they were relieved by another party of the 1st Battalion. They returned to the relative safety of the British lines and counted the cost of the night's work; their only reward being that some of the men had gained Russian greatcoats or blankets which had been forgotten in their escape.

After the war Lieutenants Bourchier and Cuninghame both received the Victoria Cross for their highly distinguished parts in this action. Had he lived, Tryon too must have received it, but at that time there was no provision for posthumous awards.

The casualties received by the 1st Battalion Rifle Brigade at the capture of the Rifle pits on the 20th November 1854 were:—

Lieutenant		Henry Tryon	Killed
2102	Rifleman	Thomas Barge	Killed
2995	"	Robert Beale	Killed
3319	"	George Boxhall	Killed
3220	"	John Brayley	Killed
3283	"	James Carter	Killed
3325	"	John Dod	Killed
2961	"	James Fox	Killed
2978	"	James Henry	Killed
2712	Rifleman	Joseph Baxter	Wounded severely
3439	"	Frederick Campbell	Wounded slightly
2893	"	John Flynn	Wounded severely
3086	"	James Grffiths	Wounded slightly
2838	"	Michael Hanfry	Wounded severely
3662	"	Edward Hawkins	Wounded severely
3001	"	Arthur Howard	Wounded slightly
3170	"	William Hutton	Wounded severely
2865	"	Christopher Jesson	Wounded slightly
3313	"	Richard Johnson	Wounded severely
3441	"	John King	Wounded slightly
2124	"	Patrick McNalty	Wounded slightly
3018	"	Robert Russell	Wounded severely
3316	"	John Turner	Wounded severely
2545	"	Francis White	Wounded slightly
3295	"	Robert Whitlock	Wounded slightly

The British and French commanders were both highly delighted with the success of this sortie. Both had published in General Orders an account and their thanks.

English General Order 24th November 1854.

The Commander of the Forces, cannot pass unnoticed the attack on the night of the 20th instant, of a detachment of the 1st

PLATE 1

1st Batallion, The Rifle Brigade

Death of Lieutenant Tryon, attack on the Rifle-pits

PLATE 2 RIFLE GREEN IN THE CRIMEA

Lt-Colonel Alfred Horsford

Lt-Colonel Edward Somerset

Major Lord Alexander Russell

Captain Henry Clifford, V.C.

Captain John P. C. Glyn

Captain Frederick Morgan

Captain Hercules Walker

Lieutenant Hore Ruthven

PLATE 4   RIFLE GREEN IN THE CRIMEA

Lieutenant William J. M. Cuninghame, V.C.

Lieutenant Claude Thomas Bourchier, V.C.

Lieutenant H. Tryon

Lieutenant George R. Saunders

PLATE 5

Colour-Sergeant John Fisher

Rifleman James Hawksford

Bugle-Major David Peachey

Bugle-Major David Peachey
in later life

PLATE 6   RIFLE GREEN IN THE CRIMEA

*Rifleman Francis Wheatley,
V.C., D.C.M.*

Rifleman William Reith

*1st Bn. Rifle Brigade officers in various forms of dress on return
from the Crimea*

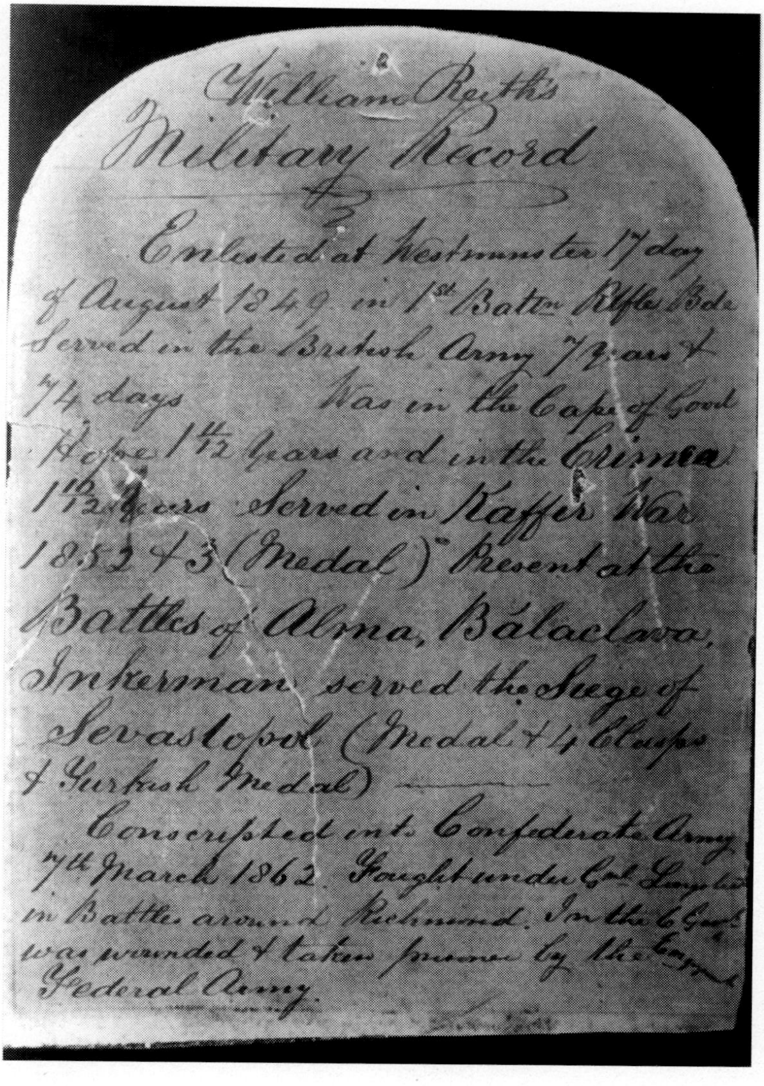

William Reith's
Military Record

Enlisted at Westminster 17 day of August 1849 in 1st Battn Rifle Bde Served in the British Army 7 years & 74 days Was in the Cape of Good Hope 1½ years and in the Crimea 1½ years Served in Kaffer War 1852 & 3 (Medal) Present at the Battles of Alma, Balaclava, Inkerman served the Siege of Sevastopol (Medal & 4 Clasps & Turkish Medal) —

Conscripted into Confederate Army 7th March 1862 Fought under Col. [illegible] in Battles around Richmond. In the 6 [illegible] was wounded & taken prisoner by the [illegible] Federal Army.

Record of Service of William Reith

PLATE 8   RIFLE GREEN IN THE CRIMEA

Officers and other ranks of 'K' Company, 1st Bn. Rifle Brigade

Colour-Sergeant, Sergeant and Rifleman

PLATE 9

2nd Batallion, The Rifle Brigade

*Riflemen Hannan and Ferguson,
the affair in the trenches*

PLATE 10   RIFLE GREEN IN THE CRIMEA

General Sir George Brown

Colonel A. J. Lawrence

Lieutenant Colonel A. MacDonell

Major William Norcott

PLATE 11

*Captain and Adjutant
John Ross*

*Assistant Surgeon
J. B. C. Reade*

Captain W. Colville

Captain F. R. Elrington

PLATE 12   RIFLE GREEN IN THE CRIMEA

Captain The Earl of Erroll

Captain W. A. Fyers

Captain E. Newdigate

Lieutenant John Knox, V.C.

Major J. R. Glyn

2nd Lieutenant C. R. Nicholl

Lieutenant F. E. Sotheby

Lieutenant Henry Newdigate

PLATE 14   RIFLE GREEN IN THE CRIMEA

Rifleman Joseph Bradshaw, V.C.

Rifleman Robert Humpston, V.C.

Rifleman Roderick MacGregor, V.C.

Colour-Sergeant James Winchcombe

RIFLE GREEN IN THE CRIMEA   PLATE 15

Colour-Sergeant Daniel Fisher

Provost Sergeant Mills

Rifleman George Evernden

Rifleman William Salter

PLATE 16 RIFLE GREEN IN THE CRIMEA

Corporal Edward Morley

Bugler Tobin, Rifleman Hill and Cpl Wiseman, D.C.M.

Crimean veterans of the 2nd Bn. Rifle Brigade

PLATE 17

Crimean War Medal 1854 with unofficial clasp for Balaclava

Turkish Crimean Medal with unofficial fixing suspension

PLATE 18   RIFLE GREEN IN THE CRIMEA

Medals of Rifleman Francis Wheatley, V.C., D.C.M. 1st Bn.

Medals of Captain the Earl of Erroll, 2nd Bn.

RIFLE GREEN IN THE CRIMEA — PLATE 19

Medals of Colour-Sergeant George Evernden, 2nd Bn.

Medals of Colour-Sergeant Daniel Fisher 2nd Bn.

PLATE 20   RIFLE GREEN IN THE CRIMEA

Other Ranks' shako badge for the Crimea period

Part of Bugle-Major's cloth rank badge, 1st Bn.

PLATE 21

Minié Rifle shooting badge

Short Enfield shooting badge

Colour-Sergeant Daniel
Fisher's cloth rank badge for
tunic

George Evernden's Colour-
Sergeant's rank badge for
greatcoat

Enfield Rifle. Detail of Lock

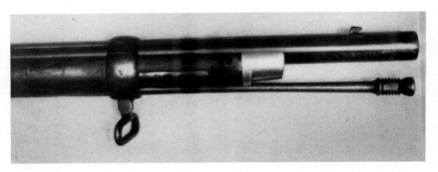

Enfield Rifle muzzle and ram rod, showing front band and sling fastener.

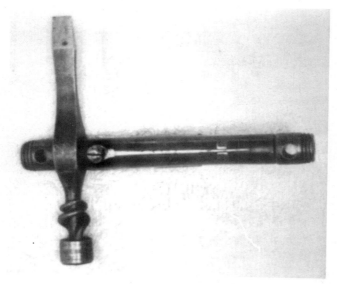

Combination tool for Enfield Rifle

Plaque from Russian Bass drum captured by 1st Bn. at Inkerman

PLATE 24   RIFLE GREEN IN THE CRIMEA

Albert Shako 1844–1855

Officers' shako badge of the Crimean period

The Marshal and a Rifleman, c.1857–1860

Battalion Rifle Brigade under Lieutenant Tryon, upon the advanced posts of the enemy which had been pushed forward so as to enfilade the English trenches and take in reverse those of the French troops.

The advance was made in the most spirited and determined manner and was completely successful, and though several vigorous attempts were afterwards made by the enemy to dislodge the gallant band, they utterly failed, and the ground remains in our possession.

Lieutenant Tryon, whose conduct was most conspicuous, was unfortunately killed and several valuable soldiers shared the same fate.

The General-in-Chief of the French army so highly prized the achievement, that he published a general order eulogizing the conduct of the detachment, and paying a just tribute to the memory of the officer who led it.

(Signed) *J. B. B. Estcourt, A.G.*

Translation of the French General Order:—
Camp before Sebastopol.
21st November, 1854.

On the night of the 20th or 21st, on a request made by me to Lord Raglan Commander-in-Chief of the English army, pointing out to him that the Russian riflemen had placed themselves under cover in front of the line from whence they could enfilade our workmen, one hundred riflemen under the command of Lieutenant Tryon left the trenches, and turning the flank of the enemy, charged and dispersed them.

The Russians formed in deep columns, attempted three times during the night to retake the place, after pouring in grape and canister on the English detachment, with that energy belonging to our allies they held firmly their ground, and we can now see them where the enemy once stood.

I wish before you all to render the homage due to so gallant an act, which unfortunately cost of the life of that brave officer Lieutenant Tryon; we will give him all the regrets so glorious an end deserves, it will be an additional link to the loyal fraternity of arms which unites us to our allies.

(Signed) *Canrobert, General.*

When the position was taken it was found to be one of considerable importance, as under cover of the stone work and broken ground the Rifles were able to approach within eighty yards of some of the Russian batteries. The Redoubts and Redan wall in particular were exposed to harassing fire from this spot, so naturally the Allies were determined to retain it. A covered way in due course was constructed from the British left attack, which enabled the men to approach and leave it unobserved; this ensured a strong picket was always maintained there. During the nights this strong and now sheltered position was well guarded against any sorties by the enemy, while during the day the Minié rifles kept up a constant fire upon anything that moved within the Russian batteries. So deadly was this fire that for four or five days neither the Redan nor Redoubt fired a shot!

The term 'ovens,' which the men gave to these excavations, was probably more apt than pits and they are not to be confused with the pits on the road from Balaclava to Inkerman from which the Tartars used to dig a kind of clay which is better known by the German name of Meerschaum.

On the 22nd November the Russians made another spirited attack on the captured rifle pits and advanced to within a hundred yards of the front of the position. Before being driven back they managed to inflict a number of casualties on the defenders, Captain Churchill and Lieutenant Morgan both receiving slight wounds to the face and Morgan had his cloak cut by musket balls in several places.

Casualties for the 1st Battalion Rifle Brigade on the 22nd November were:—

3083	Rifleman	Robert Allen	Killed
3427	"	Thomas Carr	Killed
	Captain	C. H. S. Churchill	Wounded slightly
	Lieutenant	F. C. Morgan	Wounded slightly
3002.	Rifleman	Charles Goad	Wounded severely
3477	"	W. D. Bailey	Wounded severely
3586	"	Peter Collins	Wounded slightly
2599	"	Charles Gibbons	Wounded severely
3273	"	James Hopkins	Wounded slightly
3208	"	Patrick Hughes	Wounded slightly
3482	"	Thomas Hutchinson	Wounded severely
3262	"	Charles Knapp	Wounded slightly
3258	"	John Matson	Wounded slightly

3628	"	John Robins	Wounded slightly
3555	"	Cornelius Simmons	Wounded severely
3677	"	James Simons	Wounded slightly
3099	"	George Sutton	Wounded slightly
3338	"	George Thorns	Wounded severely
3318	"	John Weston	Wounded slightly
3630	"	John Wilmot	Wounded severely.

Winter in the Crimea

ON the 28th November 1854 a draft of 1 Sergeant, 1 Corporal and 46 Riflemen landed in the Crimea; these men of all the drafts for the Rifles suffered more than any other. They came straight into the winter with no chance to harden to the conditions; twenty died, fourteen others either died or returned home sick, a total of thirty four from the forty eight.

Just as day was breaking on the morning of the 2nd December, a party of two hundred Riflemen under Captain Churchill, Lieutenant Blackett and Ensign Brett were approaching the advanced trench to relieve the two hundred men of the 50th Regiment and were surprised to find it in possession of the enemy. The men of the 50th were retreating having been taken by surprise, seven of their men being killed by bayonetting in the trench. Captain Churchill divided his force and ordered one hundred men to fix swords and charge the captured breastwork keeping the second one hundred in reserve. The Rifles in no time recaptured the position with the loss of only two men wounded. The Russians had about twenty men killed. The Colonel of the Rifles on questioning one of the wounded Riflemen as to what took place was told 'Why Sir, to tell the truth the Russians relieved the 50th Regiment and we came up in time to relieve the Russians' Captain Churchill's men remained in the captured position as the guard for the day.

On the 12th December on the Woronzoff road a party of the Rifles under Captain Churchill and Ensign Brett, being part of the guard of the trench, was violently attacked by the enemy during the night. By showing a determined front and delivering an efficient fire, the enemy were at once driven off and were prevented from penetrating at this important point which was the key to the British position.

The number of duty officers and men was now rapidly decreasing. On the 27th November, Lieutenant Godfrey had died in camp of fever. It was brought on by carrying out his duties long after being attacked by illness; he was greatly loved by all ranks.

Lieutenant Colonel Horsford who had commanded the Battalion since the 19th September, when Lieutenant Colonel Beckwith was attacked by his fatal illness, had to retire to Balaclava on sick leave, on the 27th December, and shortly afterwards sailed for England. Major Somerset returned from sick leave on the 20th and assumed the command of the 1st Battalion.

The 1st Battalion Rifle Brigade had now lost so many men by sickness and death that, notwithstanding a draft of 154 Non-commissioned Officers and men which had been received in January 1855, the duty state showed as present and fit for duty after their arrival, only thirty-one Sergeants, seven Buglers and two hundred and thirty seven Rank and File, while two Sergeants, and one hundred and five men were otherwise on duties connected with the service of the army.

The weather was now most severe and the men's sufferings and privations began in earnest. Although Balaclava was only six miles away from the Rifles camp, the roads were practically impassable seas of mud. The men who had spent all night on trench duty were then ordered to start off on fatigue to Balaclava to fetch up rations; some dropped on the road from sheer exhaustion and ended up going into hospital utterly unable to make the return journey and several died on the road. The Cavalry were also employed on this same fatigue of bringing up supplies to the Infantry on the Heights,

Transporting supplies from Balaclava

each man riding one horse and leading another with bags of biscuit or meat slung across them. The once proud Cavalry were now only a shadow of their former selves. When the meagre rations were eventually given out, there was no firewood and the men had to try and cook the best way they could. Many made no attempt at cooking and ate their salt meat raw, swallowed their biscuits and sugar and threw away their coffee beans. These were bound to be amongst the first to die or go into hospital. Those men whose strength and energy enabled them to stay out of hospital were nearly all afflicted with scurvy. Besides the lack of rations and the severe weather the men's clothing and boots were all worn out and any rags were eagerly seized as a garment; biscuit bags were used to wrap around the legs to keep out the wet. To add to this it was now snowing and the Riflemen did duty in the trenches up to their knees in it. Even in their tents they could not escape as it was blown inside in drifts which at times covered the sleeping occupants.

On the 4th January 1855, by the efforts of the men of the Battalion, assisted by two carts and six ponies from headquarters put at the disposal of the Battalion by Lord Raglan and his staff, the materials for the first wooden hut were brought up from Balaclava to the front. The task was made all the harder by the death of a pony and the constant breaking down of one of the carts. The Battalion, although numerically weaker than any Battalion at the front (except perhaps the 63rd), showed a noble example and proved the possibility, which some had doubted, of bringing a hut up at this season from Balaclava to the plateau on which the army was camped. Driving snow and severe weather conditions continued until the 19th of the month.

At the same time detachments of the Rifles were still doing duty in the rifle pits captured by Lieutenant Tryon. The Russians, however, continued to treat this position with special attention, having in some cases trebled their sharp-shooters and doubled the round shot and shells. Corporal Ishmeal Read, Riflemen Charles Baker, Thomas Bartley, Walter Eagle, John Jones and Josiah Wood were all severely wounded by the fire of their sharp-shooters on the 2nd January 1855, and Corporal Read died from his wounds on the 14th January.

On the 26th, a draft arrived from England under Captain Walker, with two Sergeants, two Corporals and eighty-four Riflemen, while on the 27th a second detachment under Lieutenant Boileau landed with one Sergeant, one Corporal and seventy-one Riflemen.

During all this month of severe weather, the camp was frequently visited by Lord Raglan. (There had been complaints previously that he was never seen by the troops.) He generally ended up at the hospital marquee, and on one occasion, finding there was no port wine, sent four bottles from his own supply.

Thirty four men of the Rifles died in camp during the month of January.

On the first day of February, Colonel Norcott joined from the 2nd Battalion Rifle Brigade and took over the command of the Battalion from Major Somerset; Colonel Horsford having returned to England sick. Colonel Norcott addressed the Battalion on his first parade by informing them that he was the son of Sir Amos Norcott who commanded a battalion of Rifles at Waterloo, and that he was proud now to be doing the same. He at once proved his worth by devoting himself to bettering their conditions. Fatigue parties were employed to build a cook-house for the battalion, the stones being obtained from an old quarry about a mile away. Regular cooks were appointed and struck off duties, so that the men were able to receive hot coffee before going to the trenches.

If the men had gone to the trenches before the rations were received Colonel Norcott used to march down with the Quarter Master and his party, to see that the bread was served out to everyone.

A draft of one-hundred and two men from England arrived in Balaclava under Lieutenant Musgrave on the 17th February.

On the 22nd February 1855 a draft of one Corporal and eighty-nine Riflemen arrived. On the 24th the whole of the battalion marched down to Balaclava and handed over their Minié Rifles to the 18th Regiment who were still armed with the old Brown Bess. The 1st Battalion Rifles now received the new pattern 1853 Enfield Rifle.

An armistice was called on the 27th for the purpose of burying the dead who had fallen in an affair between the French and the Russians on the morning of the 24th.

The trenches during this month had to be carefully and constantly guarded. The work on the men, owing to the smallness of their number and the great severity of the weather, was enormous and many sank under the fatigue and anxiety. Supplies of every sort now

Burying the dead, January 1855

began to arrive daily, and were issued from the public stores as well as from private sources.

The siege continued without any remarkable change until the 12th March, when it was found that the enemy had taken possession of a rocky hill eight-hundred yards in advance of the Malakoff Tower. The Russians built up a strong work, notwithstanding our guns from the twenty-one gun battery opening on their working parties. Our Allies had undertaken to occupy this rocky hill some days earlier but this they had failed to do, allowing the enemy to construct that work called 'The Mamelon,' which later cost them so many lives to take and hold.

About the 14th, the weather changed for the better. It became fine and warm and all things seemed to take their colouring from the same influences. When General Simpson arrived on that day he could have had no idea of what the army had gone through, and indeed those who had been through the whole of it could hardly recognise the ground they occupied.

From the 15th of March the British witnessed the start of the nightly fights between the French and the Russians for the possession of the rifle pits under 'The Mamelon,' and in front of the Victoria Redoubt.

From the 19th to the 23rd, the enemy hardly fired a shot, but on that last night there was a great attack along the whole length of the Allied lines; it was very severe on the right attack, where the Light

Division alone lost nine officers and forty-three men killed and wounded.

At the same time the French had a most obstinate and bloody fight under 'The Mamelon,' losing upwards of 300 men, but holding their position.

On March 24th an Armistice was called from twelve until two in the afternoon for the purpose of burying the French and Russians who had fallen the previous night in the attack upon the rifle pits under the 'Mamelon.' The Russian officers came down in great numbers, and conversed together with the French and British officers. From this day to the end of the month, although there was little firing, it was evident that both sides were preparing for a great attack; cots, stretchers etc, were being prepared for the wounded.

The enemy commenced firing shells into the camp occupied by the Battalion, but without causing any injury. During the month, three Sergeants and eighty-two men died, one Sergeant and ten men died in camp, the remainder at Scutari and Kulalie.

Fire was re-opened at 5. 20 a.m. on the 9th April, and continued until the 12th. On the 13th, volunteers were called to man the rifle pits in front of No 7 battery. Lieutenant Anson and eighteen men volunteered for this duty, occupying the pits from daylight until dark suffering heavy losses; Sergeant Devitt and four men were killed. These pits were afterwards connected and formed the 4th parallel. The firing continued on both sides and on the 16th April, the magazine in No. 8 battery exploded, one man being killed and two artillery-men were severely wounded.

The Rifles and their comrades continued to improve the British works and push them forward until the end of the month.

During the month of May the siege continued with great vigour, but the fighting was chiefly between the French and the enemy. The expedition to Kertch also took place and was completely successful. On the 6th June the artillery re-opened fire, this being the third bombardment. On the 7th June, at 7 p.m. the French attacked and captured the 'Mamelon,' and the 47th and 49th Regiments of the 2nd Division took the Quarries and rifle pits under the Redan. The loss in carrying these works of the enemy was heavy, amounting to six hundred and sixty killed and wounded of whom forty-five were officers.

On the 9th June, there was another armistice to bury the dead.

The 13th brought another draft of two Officers, one Sergeant and fifty men for the battalion, just in time to take part in the first assault on the Redan.

68-pounder gun in the 8-Gun Battery

The First Attack on the Redan

THE ALLIES re-opened fire on the 17th and commenced the fourth bombardment, for which great preparations had been made. Sergeant Fisher was on duty at this time in the advanced Rifle-pits of the left attack, this duty having commenced after dark on the evening of the 17th June. He had previously been Orderly Sergeant of his company, warning the men for the different duties required during the assault, and once he had left, some of the older Riflemen decided to play a trick on Rifleman Flannery, (one of the draft who had not long joined). They told him Sergeant Fisher had warned him for duty with the 'Covering Party' of 100 men that was being found by the battalion, thinking this would have some adverse effect upon him. Flannery, however, went straight to Sergeant Fisher and asked if this was true, who informed him it was not, but asked him if he would like to go. Flannery replied that he would, thus turning the tables on his comrades' jest. To add further to the character of the man, those old soldiers who had joked with the novice Rifleman the night before, recovered his body after the attack, furthest in advance of all those who fell on the 18th, some several yards ahead of the body of Sir John Campbell who had been killed leading the assault.

Orders were issued late on the 17th, to attack the Redan in three columns at daylight the next day. The Light Division was to attack the proper right face, the 2nd Division the salient angle and the 4th Division the left face. The 1st Brigade of the 4th Division formed the storming party, and the 2nd Brigade the reserve. The 3rd Division was to carry out a second offensive but this was only to be a diversion for the main attack. Eyre's Brigade was to move between the British and French Armies and attack the various works at the Dockyard Creek, while the other Brigade under the command of General Barnard was to assemble in the Woronzoff Ravine and take the Barrack Battery in reverse once the Redan had fallen.

The 1st Battalion Rifle Brigade found one-hundred men as a covering party to the 21st Royal North British Fusiliers, who were told off to carry the wool bags for throwing into the ditches to enable the stormers to climb in and out of the enemy trenches with as little harm to themselves as possible. The Rifles were commanded by Captain the Honourable J. Stuart, with Lieutenants Boileau and Saunders under him.

The remainder of the Battalion under Colonel Norcott left camp at 2.15 a.m. The covering party, having left an hour previously, occupied the trench round the Quarries. The reserve proceeded to the caves above the Woronzof Road.

The French were to commence the proceedings by attacking the Malakoff Tower and earthworks and, when successful, the British attack was to commence. The French attack unfortunately failed. However, the signal was given for the British attack to commence, but the covering parties and stormers were not supported and the enemy was fully prepared for the assault, as they had not been shelled by the Allies for any length of time. They opened fire from the crest of the parapet with such storms of grape from their guns, that the British storming parties were mown down like grass.

The Riflemen positioned in the rifle pits had the task of knocking out as many of the Russian gunners as showed themselves. These pits had in fact been connected to form a trench and were the most advanced position of the left attack. The ground immediately in its view was that over which the 3rd Division under General Eyre attacked the Russian batteries in rear of the cemetery. This cemetery was occupied at night by Russian sentries but was evacuated at daylight. The 3rd Division advanced across it and captured some rifle pits in the low ground to the front of the Riflemen. These pits captured by the 3rd Division were occupied for a few days, then abandoned. Owing to their low position, they were of little use and

Bullets brought back from the Crimea by Colour-Sergeant John Fisher (actual size)

Camp of the 4th Division, 15th July 1855

exposed the defenders to a heavy fire from the Russians. One example of this was a Riflemen who, when looking through the same embrasure as Sergeant Fisher had his head taken off by a round shot.

The stormers of the 4th Division, the 57th Regiment under Colonel Shadforth and one hundred Riflemen under Captain the Honourable J. Stuart, were gallantly led by Sir John Campbell, who was killed almost immediately, but not before he had nearly reached the abattis. Colonel Shadforth was also shot dead and the attack failed. The 2nd Division did not move, having understood their orders to be to await the success of the Light and 4th Divisions.

The Rifles under Captain Stuart had Lieutenant Boileau wounded, from which he later died, with Sergeant Jerrom, Corporal John McEwan and Riflemen, Michael Cain, John Flanery, George Lines, and Charles Spreadborough killed, with Riflemen, David Bright, William Browne, Timothy Collins, William Dean Finch, Thomas Harrison, Richard Jenkins, Peter Lafferty, George Oliver, George Parker, William Robinson, Henry Scott, Joseph Russell wounded and Rifleman Thomas Deller Couch listed as missing.

The French attack having failed and the British attack which had only been intended as a diversion in their favour also proving unsuccessful, the troops were recalled and returned to their respective camps.

That night the enemy made a general attack along the Allied line but were beaten off without any loss to the defenders.

Under a flag of truce at 4 p.m. on the 19th June parties were sent out to collect the dead. The body of Sir John Campbell was discovered inside the abattis and that of Rifleman Flannery of the 1st Battalion Rifle Brigade close to the ditch two hundred yards in advance of where Sir John lay.

The following day the siege resumed in much the same way as before the bombardment. General Estcourt, the Adjutant General died of cholera, on the 24th and on the 28th at 8.35 p.m. the Commander-in-Chief Lord Raglan died. General Simpson assumed command of the army.

Six days later the body of Lord Raglan was conveyed on a gun carriage to Kazatch Bay, put on board the *Caradoc*, and accompanied by his personal staff immediately sailed for England.

The weather had now become very hot and the Rifles were issued with some canvas clothing, a sort of tunic and trousers. The men nicknamed them 'Sand Bags' which gives an idea of the colour and material. Though conditions had become much more comfortable for the men, water was still in short supply. The Riflemen had to fetch their cooking and drinking water from a spring some distance from the camp and so washing was a very low priority. Sergeant Fisher tells us that the first wash he remembers during the campaign was after the fall of Sebastopol in the harbour.

With the Rifles on duty in the trenches Colonel Norcott would be met at the end of each shift by his servant with his horse. On the morning of the 29th July Rifleman William Ninds was in the rear of Green Hill Battery waiting for Colonel Norcott as usual when a round shot killed both him and the horse.

During the whole of this month the French were actively employed in pushing forward the attack and approaching nearer to the Malakoff, but in doing so suffered a very heavy loss.

The British attacks were also pushed forward and greatly strengthened, a great number of guns were mounted and fresh batteries erected. The same was continued during the month of August, and on the 16th the enemy made a furious and determined attack on the positions occupied by the French and Sardinians overlooking the Tchernaya, but were defeated with the loss of four thousand five hundred men killed and wounded, with three hundred taken prisoners.

The Russian sentries and the Rifles were posted well out in front of their respective Batteries so consequently were a very short distance apart. The custom in the Rifles was that every sentry was doubled and a Sergeant was in charge of the line of sentries. The duty of the Sergeant was to constantly visit each double sentry and see that all were alert and awake, as owing to fatigue, the heat and the fact that to keep out of sight sentries were ordered to sit or lie down, they often fell asleep.

On the 17th, the 4th bombardment commenced and lasted for two days, after which it slackened. This was done to assist the French in pushing forward some works on the left.

By official returns made to the French headquarters, the number of Russians ascertained to have been killed on the 16th was three thousand three hundred and three.

The British Army was kept continually on the alert frequently under arms at night for at least several hours. The Russians commenced and completed during the month the bridge of boats and pontoons across the harbour. On the 29th, the magazine in the Mamelon blew up with a tremendous explosion, occasioning some loss to the French, and about seventy casualties in the British right attack.

Attacks on the British and French working parties were now of nightly occurrence, but the sap was pushed forward with great determination.

On the 5th September, at 5 a.m. the French opened a determined fire on the enemy's works and tower opposite their left attack. This was speedily taken up by the British Batteries, but only partially so. It was sufficiently heavy to do great execution to the enemy.

The Second Attack on the Redan

BY the afternoon of the 7th, it was known that the assault was to take place. Accordingly on the 8th, one half of the Battalion went into the trenches under Colonel Norcott, and the remainder, about two-hundred men under Lieutenant Colonel Somerset, moved out of camp at 11 a.m. and took up their position in reserve on the Woronzoff Road.

The 2nd Battalion Rifle Brigade furnished one hundred men under Captain Fyers as a covering party, and three hundred men under Major Woodford. These were thrown forward in skirmishing order near the abattis to try and keep down the fire from the crest of the parapet and to fire at the enemy's embrasures. The 41st and 90th Regiments formed the storming party.

The attack commenced exactly at noon, the French carrying the Malakoff instantly and without any resistance. The British attack on

Storming of the Redan. Print after Dupray

the Redan followed immediately, but not with equal success; being an open work in the rear, the Redan was more easily defended. The men had to advance one hundred and fifty yards exposed to the most terrible fire in front and flank; this prevented the stormers when they gained the parapet from entering the work. There was also a great fear that the Redan was mined, and as soon as the British had gained possession it would be blown up. This attack directed the attention of the enemy from the Malakoff, which was held by the French with extreme difficulty and great loss. They were mainly enabled to do this by the heavy fire which was kept up by Captain Strange's Quarry battery on the Russian reserves in rear of the Malakoff, which prevented them from completing any formation. They maintained possession of the salient angle until dark when they were withdrawn.

At midnight the Russians having evacuated the town and works of Sebastopol. They started to blow up their magazines and forts. On September 9th, at 3 o'clock in the morning the barrack battery went up with an enormous explosion; everywhere the town was on fire, and explosions from the enemy works were frequently heard.

As daylight broke it was discovered that all the large Russian ships, fourteen in number, were sunk, At ten a.m. the bridge by which the Russians had retreated was disconnected and towed over to the north side.

The loss on the 8th was very heavy, the British casualties amounting to two thousand five hundred and fifty five of which one hundred and fifty four were officers, twenty seven being killed.

The British now took possession and charge of the Redan and Karabelnaia district, the French the Malakoff and all the works to the left of the South Harbour. The destruction of the town was complete.

The 1st Battalion Rifle Brigade received their first issue of the Crimea War Medal on the 19th September 1855. Only a small amount had been sent out to the army and the Rifles issued theirs to those who had been longest in the campaign

The Russians still held the north side of the harbour and occasionally amused themselves by firing shells into the town.

On October 1st, Colonel Norcott appeared in Orders as, 'Having leave to proceed to England,' the command of the Battalion being assumed by Lieutenant Colonel Somerset.

On the 2nd October, the 1st Brigade, 4th Division received orders to hold themselves in readiness to embark at a moment's notice, and on the 7th the expedition under Brigadier the Hon A. Spencer sailed for Kinburne. The force consisted of about one thousand two hundred men with vessels of all sorts. It is not clear if any of the Rifles took part.

Sir Henry Bentinck gave up the command of the 4th Division to Major General Windham on the 11th and a telegram was received from England to the effect that the Allies were to expect a great attack on the Inkerman side of their position. On the morning of the 16th, the whole army was under arms. This was continued every morning, with the time being profitably employed in drilling the Battalions and getting them into good order, but the attack never materialised.

On the 24th October Lieutenant Colonel Somerset, having obtained leave to proceed to England, left the front and handed over the command of the Battalion to Lord Alexander Russell.

Colour Sergeant Noseley who had been reported as killed at the Battle of Inkerman rejoined the Battalion on the 26th October, to the great surprise of the officers and men dressed in Russian uniform. He had been wounded and taken prisoner by the Russians and was the only man of the Battalion in the hands of the enemy during the Campaign. He told his comrades how he was taken before one of the Grand Dukes (at the time of his capture in Sebastopol) who addressed him in good English.'You are of the Rifle Brigade?' 'Yes Sir' 'Ah! I know your regiment well and take great interest in them. Does Lawrence command your battalion?' 'No Sir, Colonel Norcott:' 'Ah! I know Norcott, did he command you yesterday (Inkerman) or Lawrence?' 'Colonel Norcott did sir. I'm of the 1st Battalion.' 'And were you engaged,' In the trenches, Sir.' The Grand Duke then inquired after several officers by name and said to Sergeant Noseley, 'Well, I'll see you are well provided for. I like the Rifle Brigade and always take an interest in them.' Noseley was taken well care of and fared better than the other prisoners who were sent from Simpheropol to Kharkoff.

During October the Battalion was employed road making and on the 4th November, they prepared the ground and in three hours put up one of the panelled huts that was large enough to house fifty men.

On the 9th, General Codrington was appointed to the command of the Army, General Windham to Chief of the Staff; General Garrett to command 4th Division, *vice* Lord W. Paulett to Light Division; Colonel Staunton 31st Regiment to command the 2nd Brigade.

Explosion in the French Magazine

ON the 15th November about 2 p.m. a tremendous explosion took place in a French magazine near the Light Division camp. The fire communicated with the French artillery camp occasioning great loss of life to both British and French and much destruction to the huts and tents. Sergeant Pescott of the 1st Battalion who had gone down in charge of a fatigue party with stretchers, received injuries from a rocket the effects of which caused his death. The following amount of ammunition was destroyed:—100,000 lbs of powder, 3,700 Russian shells. 12,000,000 ball cartridges, and 1,300 other combustibles.

For the second time since the arrival of the battalion in the East on the 26th November, no one reported sick and the Battalion was once again employed road making during the month. On the 12th December, news was received that Kars had surrendered. Captain Maclean, Lieutenants, Lord Edward Clinton, Dashwood, Vandeleur and Scott joined from Malta on the 27th. The first of the docks was blown up by the Engineers on the 9th January 1856 and, on the 21st, news was received that the propositions which had been set out by the Allies for peace had been unconditionally accepted by Russia.

A week later, another of the docks was destroyed and on the 29th, the Battalion was inspected by Colonel Staunton; the Russians sent a heavy fire into the Allied positions that same evening. On the 31st, the last of the docks was destroyed. Fort Nicholas was destroyed by the French on the 4th February. General Garrett inspected the Battalion on the 9th, and the French destroyed Fort Alexander on the 11th. The 1st Battalion Rifle Brigade moved to headquarters on the 20th.

The Army paraded on Telegraph Hill on the 24th and some white buildings were blown up on the 28th. Captain Rankin, Royal Engineers was killed superintending the work.

From the 4th to the 7th March, a lot of snow fell, and a draft of two hundred men under Lieutenant Slade joined from Malta on the 19th.

On the 13th April, General Luders and his staff met the Allied commanders at the Tractir Bridge, the Peace of Paris having been signed on the 30th March 1856.

The French Army paraded for the inspection of General Luders on the 17th, along the ridge of hills running from the Col towards the monastery and Kamiesch. The infantry was formed in line of contiguous columns of grand divisions with large intervals between the battalions, brigades and divisions, the artillery was in rear of the infantry and their front extended nearly three miles.

The British Army paraded that same afternoon in front of headquarters in line of contiguous columns at quarter distance, artillery on the left and the front extended about 12 miles. The difference in appearance of the two Armies was very marked, the British well clothed and fed, the French the very reverse. Throughout the winter of 1855–56 the British Army had learned the lessons of the previous winter and the men were supplied with plenty of warm clothing, shelter and food. The French were suffering greatly from disease. The General went down the line, after which the troops marched past, and proceeded to their camps.

On the 24th, the Army proceeded to the Balaclava Plains for the purpose of manœuvring. The Battalion paraded for the inspection of General Vaulinsky on the 25th who was in command of the Russian troops on Mackenzie Heights.

Rifleman Conolly of the 1st Battalion Rifles died on the 9th May as a result of a wound received on the 26th April caused by the explosion of a shell thrown down by a man of the 13th Regiment who was on fatigue.

The 68th Regiment embarked for Corfu on the 17th followed by the the 46th Regiment on the 20th.

The Army paraded on the Balaclava Plains on the 24th May to celebrate Her Majesty's birthday; and the medals granted by the Emperor of the French to Non-Commissioned Officers of the British Army were distributed.

Return to England

ON June 1st, orders were received to hold the Battalion in readiness to embark on board H.M.S *Apollo* for England.

At 8 o'clock in the morning on the 4th June the 1st Battalion Rifles marched to Balaclava and embarked at 10 a.m., left harbour at 1.30. and at 4 p.m. the *Medusa* took the *Apollo* with the Rifles on board in tow. They anchored off Scutari on the 6th, left the Bosphorus on the 7th arriving at Malta on the 13th. Then they sailed on the 14th anchoring at Gibraltar at 5 a.m. on the 22nd, leaving the same day and anchored at Corunna on the 27th. A number of men went ashore, a party of these which included Sergeant Fisher visited the grave of Sir John Moore and the *Apollo* left on the 28th.

The *Apollo* arrived at Spithead at 7 a.m. on the 5th July and went into harbour at 2 p.m. the same day. The Rifles were landed on the 7th and proceeded by rail to Aldershot.

Before the Battalion left the Crimea for England the following order was published by Major General Garrett, K.H., commanding 4th Division.

Camp before Sevastopol,
Division after order. 3rd, June, 1856.

Maj-general Garrett regrets that the separation of the 1st Battalion Rifle Brigade from the 4th Division, by their embarkation to-morow for England, calls on him to take leave of them.

The Major General will look back with pride and pleasure on those eventful days when they were under his command, first as Brigadier and afterwards commanding the division for upwards of a year and a half. During that period the willingness and smartness which the officers and men invariably evinced, whether in duties in the camp or in the trenches, clearly showed that, that magnificent 'esprit de corps' which descended from their predecessors the old 95th, still animates the young soldiers who were brought to supply the heavy casualties of the late campaign, which they quickly caught up from the fine old soldiers whose education had been formed in the rough and arduous enterprises of two Kaffir Wars. That noble 'esprit de corps' may never fail them is the sincere wish of the Major General, who hopes soon to see them exhibiting that spirit amongst their comrades in England.

On the 8th July, the Battalion was reviewed by the Queen, with a number of other Regiments when the following officers who disembarked with the Battalion were present, *viz:*—

Major and Brevet-Lieutenant Colonel Lord A. Russell,

Captain and Brevet-Major W. Walker, Hon G. Elliott, C. V. Oxenden, Hon J. Stuart, Hon. H. Clifford,

Captains W. J. Cuninghame, W. Norris.

Lieutenants Lord E. Clinton, C. A. Talbot, G. B. Saunders, C. E. Musgrave, C. B. Dashwood, J. P. Glyn, A. L. Tottenham, W. T. Rooper, J. Ashton, R. E. Harrington, H. S. Vandeleur, C. T. Bunbury, C. G. Slade, S. A. Gordon, H. B. Blundell, C. T. Murdoch,

Ensigns H. L. Wickham, W. C. Pardon.

Surgeon R. Bowen*, Assistant Surgeons J. J. P. Williams,. F. de Chaumont, Adjutant J. Brett*, Paymaster J. E. Large*, Quarter-Master H. Peacock.

Those Officers marked with an asterisk embarked with the service companies for the East at the beginning of the Campaign.

At the same time the following non-commissioned officers and men were selected to be addressed personally by the Queen, *viz:*—

Colour Sergeants J. Round, J. McGrotty, J. Barrows, H. Fothergill, J. Judge,

Sergeants C. Roydhouse, M. Haycock, S. Shaw,

Corporals J. Kudling, E. Taylor, T. Tarrant, R. Tarrant, J. Randall, A. Clarke, J. Hawksford, W. Tack,

Buglers W. Jackson, B. McMahon, W. Ackerman, W. Hardinge, A. McWilliams, R. Stewart, W. Gardiner, W. Gains,

Riflemen P. McCann, R. Harper, H. Bailey, J. King, W. Simms, R. Whittaker, M. Barker, W. Hodges.

Her Majesty delivered the following address:—

'Officers, non-commissioned officers and soldiers, I wish personally to convey to you for the regiments assembled here this day, my hearty welcome to your return to England in health and full efficiency.'

'Say to them, I have watched anxiously over your different trials and hardships which you have so nobly borne, that I mourn with deep sorrow for the brave men who have fallen for their country, and that I have felt proud of that valour which, with their gallant allies, they have displayed in the field.'

'I thank God that your dangers are over, whilst the glory of your deeds remains, but I know that should your services be again required, you will be animated by the same devotion which in the Crimea has rendered you invincible.'

By a circular letter from the War Office, dated 11th August 1856, the Battalion was reduced from 109 Sergeants, 41 Buglers, 2,000 Rank and File to 57 Sergeants, 25 Buglers and 1,000 Rank and File.

The Battalion was inspected at Aldershot on the 15th August 1856 by Major-General A. Laurence, C.B., who had commanded the 2nd Battalion Rifle Brigade during the earlier part of the campaign.

Veterans of the 1st Bn. Rifle Brigade, Hamilton, Canada, 1911

(Front, L to R) W. Wright*, R. Lannaway*, Band Sergeant William Gardner*, R. Jacques*, J. Hyam
(Centre, R to L) C. Cooper*, W. Burrows*, J. Fletcher, W Nash, D. Farr, J. Clark, F. Weaver*, J. Johnson
(Back, L to R) C. Blackman, T. Rutter, C. Locke*, R. Fleming, H. Owens, W. Fricker, E. Hodson
Those marked * are Crimean War veterans

PART THREE

Rifle Brigade Crimean Uniform, Arms and Equipment in 1854

Uniform

THE UNIFORM colour of the Rifle Brigade had always been what is now termed as Rifle-Green, which in practice meant almost black, owing to the difficulty of obtaining a fast dye. At one stage they actually had the uniforms issued in black, the theory being that they would, over a period of time, turn lighter and resemble the hue of Rifle Green. After considerable wear however, the men's green issue clothing tended to fade to various shades of green or even blue. Up until the uniform changes of 1829–30, the buttons had been silver but thereafter were changed to black. The officers' uniform had always differed considerably from the men's, since it followed the fashions adopted by the Light Cavalry, except for the headdress.

The Rifle Brigade was distinguished from other Rifle Regiments by:—

- *a.* The facings (black).
- *b.* The devices on buttons and pouch belts.
- *c.* The coatees of the other ranks, being double-breasted, with long tails like those of the Foot Guards, with two rows of buttons.

The following details of the Rifle Brigade's clothing, accoutrements and weapons in 1854 are taken from the 1846 Officers' Dress Regulations and Michael Barthorp's *Crimean Uniforms—British Infantry* (Historical Research Unit, 1974). The extracts from the Officers' Dress Regulations of 1846 applied to all Rifle Regiments.

OFFICERS

Dress-Jacket:—RIfle-Green made in the Hussar style; single-breasted, with three rows of buttons; black braid loops, and ornamental trimming. Prussian collar and pointed cuffs of the regimental facing.

Pelisse:—Rifle-green, in the Hussar style; single-breasted with four rows of black silk olivets, black royal cord loops, and ornamental trimming; black fur Prussian collar, pointed cuffs and edging; black neck-lines and tassels.

Shell-Jacket:—Rifle-green, laced according to regimental pattern.

Cap:—Black beaver, six inches and three quarters deep and a quarter of an inch less in diameter at top than at bottom; patent leather top, turned over the edge to the breadth of five-eighths of an inch, and stitched round; a band of the same, double-stitched, encircles the bottom of the cap; a peak of patent leather, two inches and three-eighths deep in front, and another one inch and a quarter deep behind; a bronze bugle in front, surmounted by a black silk cord rosette; bronze chain, fastening at sides with rose-pattern ornament.

Tuft:—A black silk ball and slide.

Trousers:—Rifle-green cloth, with a braid of black mohair, two inches wide, down the outward seam, or, for summer wear, green gambroon, plain.

Sash:—Crimson silk patent net, with cords and tassels; the cords not to exceed a yard in length; the tassels to hang in front below the sash, being attached by a small loop to the bottom button of the jacket.

Stock:—Black silk.

Gloves:—Black leather.

Forage-Cap:—Rifle-green cloth, perfectly plain, black leather peak and chin-strap. A Cap-Cover of oil-skin is permitted to be worn in bad weather, both with the dress-cap (shako) and the forage cap.

Cloak:—Rifle-green, lined with black.

Spurs:—Field Officers and Adjutant only, steel.

Regimental Staff

The Adjutant is to wear the uniform of his rank. The Paymaster, Quartermaster, Surgeon, and Assistant-Surgeon are to wear a plain shako; with no tuft; sash not to be worn.

Other Ranks

Details of Other Ranks' Dress are drawn from photographs, contemporary illustrations and Clothing Regulations, compiled by Michael Barthorp.

SENIOR NON-COMMISSIONED OFFICERS

Coatee:—Rifle-green, double-breasted with two rows of regimental black buttons, set at equal distances; plain black Prussian collar, plain black round cuff, two inches and three quarters deep; rifle-green slashed flap on the sleeve, with three buttons, two buttons at the waist; black turnbacks; no skirt ornaments. Buttons black with a buglehorn, surmounted by a crown, with strings going into the base of crown; between strings, initials RB.

Epaulettes:—Black cloth strap, with black worsted crescent; a short black fringe for Staff Sergeants only.

Badges of Rank:—Distinguished by chevrons as for the Infantry of the Line but in black lace and worn on both sleeves; the number of bars denoting rank as for the Infantry of the Line, but with the following exceptions:—

Sergeant-Major: the N.C.O. holding this rank in 1st Battalion Rifle Brigade in 1851 is recorded as wearing a large gold crown on both sleeves above the elbow, but it is unclear whether this was in addition to a one-bar chevron in black lace. A print in the author's collection for around the same period shows a similar senior N.C.O. with the crown as stated but above crossed swords in silver.

Colour-Sergeant: on the right sleeve, in gold, a crown above crossed swords with a bugle-horn below, all within an oval wreath, the whole above a single-bar chevron of double gold lace; on the left sleeve, a three-bar chevron of double black lace. From photographs taken at the time of the Crimean War and just after, it would appear that the gold lace was replaced by silver (see illustration on Plate 21).

Cap:—As for officers, but in black felt instead of beaver; the chin strap, for company sergeants, of black leather.

Tuft:—Black worsted ball.

Trousers:—As for officers, but without the black braid down the outer seam for company sergeants.

Boots:—Ankle.

Sash:—
    Staff Sergeants: as for Officers.
    Company Sergeants: crimson girdle, two inches and a half wide, worn under the waist belt.

Stock:—Black leather.

Gloves:—Black.

Shell-jacket:—Rifle-green, black facings.

Forage-Cap:—
    Staff Sergeants: as for officers.
    Company Sergeants: rifle-green Kilmarnock bonnet with black tuft; no insignia.

Greatcoat:—Grey, with cape; for sergeants and above, collar and cuffs in the facing colour.

RANK AND FILE

Clothed entirely as Company sergeants, but without the sash and gloves.

Good Conduct Badges:—Chevrons of single black lace, worn points up above right cuff.

Buglers:—Clothed as Rank and File. No contemporary evidence has been found to indicate any distinctive markings on the buglers' clothing, although some would seem to have been likely. A lithograph published *circa* 1834 shows a bugler of the 1st Battalion with black wings, and white piping, or single white lace, all round the collar, down the open front of the coatee, on both sleeve seams, round the top of the cuffs and all around the sleeve flap: the bugler in the Hayes lithograph, 'The Rifles,' *circa* 1846, appears to have piping round the collar and cuffs. The photograph in which Bugler Tobin of the 1st Battalion Rifle Brigade appears taken about 1856 shows the wings with gold or silver lace around the edges and in equal stripes across the black from the shoulder seam to the outer edge of the wing. Whether this is a continuation of the former regulation wings worn with the coatee or a new regulation pattern is not known.

Bugle-Major.—Clothed as Staff Sergeants, rank badges four black lace stripes above the elbow on each arm, with a double entwined bugle-horn badge above.

Bandsmen.—Clothed as Rank and File with black cord aiguillettes from right shoulder with wings and sword as for buglers.

Bandmaster.—Clothed as Sergeant-Major with black aiguillettes as Bandsmen.

Band Sergeant.—Clothed as Company Sergeants, but with officers pattern sash.

Equipment

Officers' Accoutrements

Sword belts.—The 1846 Dress Regulations give the following information:—

Waist-belt.—Black leather, one inch and a half wide, with slings, silver snake-clasp and mountings.

Pouch belts and sabretaches:—

Pouch.—Black patent leather, with a silver bugle horn badge on the flap.

Pouch-belt.—Black Patent leather, three inches wide, with silver regimental plate badge, whistle and chain, the latter, suspended from a silver lions head mount. (The belt was worn over the left shoulder.)

Tache-Slings.—Three, of black patent leather, half an inch wide, attached to rings of waist-belt and fastening with loops and buckles to rings of tache.

Tache.—Plain black patent leather, pocket nine inches deep, seven inches and a half wide at top, nine at bottom; face twelve inches deep, eight inches wide at top, eleven at bottom, perfectly plain, with three rings at the top for tache-slings.

Other Ranks' Necessaries and Accoutrements

Knapsack:—This was made of black painted canvas, reinforced at the corners with leather, and stiffened with wooden boards at the sides. A specimen in the National Army Museum measures 15 inches in breadth, 13 inches in height and 3 inches in depth. Two buff leather straps, one and a quarter inches wide, passed vertically around the pack, buckling underneath; the shoulder slings were fastened to the straps near the upper inside edge of the pack, and, after passing over the shoulders, were secured to other buckles attached to the straps on the underside. A connecting strap joined the shoulder slings across the chest, its length being regulated by a buckle. On some patterns the strapping was detachable, on others it was fixed to the knapsack. On top of the knapsack were three narrower straps for securing the greatcoat or blanket. All buckles were of brass, and in the Rifle Brigade the strapping was of black leather.

There was another type of knapsack in use at this period known as the Rifle Brigade pattern although this nomenclature did not restrict its issue solely to Rifle regiments. In general appearance it resembled the other type, but although research has not disclosed its precise measurements there is evidence to suggest that it may have been more capacious and that only the mess-tin could be secured to the top, the greatcoat being folded flat against the outside under the straps.

Mess-Tin:—The mess-tin was roughly semi-circular in shape, being 4 inches deep at its widest point with the flat surface, which fitted against the knapsack, measuring 6 by 4 inches. A pan, $3\frac{7}{8}$ inches deep and with a flat surface $5\frac{7}{8} \times 1\frac{3}{4}$ inches, fitted inside the top to serve as a plate and to provide a second partition within the mess-tin; the top was closed by a cover, which had a small flange fitting inside the pan. When assembled, the whole mess-tin fitted inside a black canvas cover, to which was fastened a black strap for securing it to the knapsack.

Calling it a 'priceless pot', an officer described its use as follows; 'In the morning [it] served as basin and footpan; on the march it conveyed the meat; in the evening, it was the receptacle in which water was boiled for tea; its lid doing duty for a plate, whenever called on.'

Sword belts:—Swords were carried by Staff Sergeants, Buglers and Bandsmen.

Staff Sergeants:—Shoulder belts as for officers, black waist belts.
Bandsmen and Buglers:—Black leather waist belt with brass snake clasp and frog.

Pouch and belt:—The pouch was made of metal, covered in black leather, and contained 60 rounds; sergeants' pouches held only 40 rounds. The inside was divided into compartments and also contained a tin magazine holding up to 100 percussion caps. The pouch was box-shaped, having a cover hinged at the rear, and a flap, which came right over the cover and the front of the box to hang about an inch below the base of the box, and which was fastened by a strap, fixed inside the flap, to a stud on the underside of the box. (See illustration)

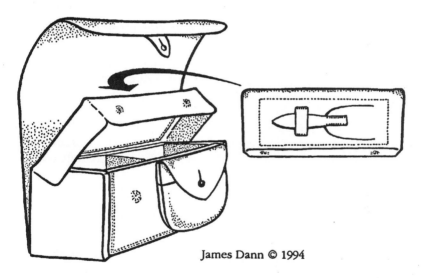

James Dann © 1994

The pouch was suspended over the left shoulder from a black leather belt, 2½ inches wide, the ends of which passed through two loops at the back of the pouch and fastened to buckles on the underside. Company Sergeants bore a badge, similar to the officers, and a whistle with chains, all in bronze. The belts of the Line and the Rifles were made in one piece. (Because of the length of the chain attached to the whistle it was common practice for it to be looped around the pouch belt behind the badge; later the chains were shortened by converting the chain into three separate lengths.)

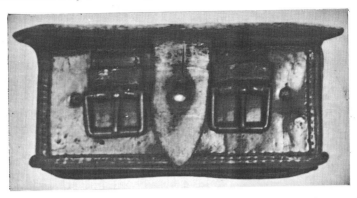

Other Ranks' ammunition pouch viewed from underneath, showing pouch belt fixing buckles, flap strap and stud

Bayonet belt:—In the Rifle Brigade, bayonets, which were always known as 'swords' whatever the pattern, were carried in a sliding frog suspended from a black leather waist belt, 2 inches wide, fastening with a brass snake clasp. On the right front of the belt was attached the ball bag, a small black leather pouch containing a zinc oil bottle, caps, and a few rounds for immediate use. Contemporary illustrations indicate that Riflemen wore the pouch belt over the waist belt.

Rifle sling:—Black leather 1 inch and a quarter wide with a brass buckle for regulating the length. The Rifle Brigade always had their slings loose.

Haversack:—These were made of coarse yellowish white linen, with the flap fastening with two buttons, and suspended from a shoulder strap of the same material. A painting by Thomas Baines of the 1st Rifle Brigade in the Eighth Kaffir War in 1852 shows the Riflemen with the black haversacks. Drawings made in the Crimea by the French officer, Vanson, indicate that they were about 14 inches deep and 8–9 inches wide.

Water Canteen:—The soldier's water container was the circular wooden keg, bound with metal hoops, which dated almost unchanged from the Napoleonic Wars, 7¼ inches in diameter and 4 inches deep. It held about half a gallon of water. It was unhygienic, heavy and compared unfavourably with the French and Russian patterns. It was suspended from a brown leather strap, 81 inches long and 1 inch wide, with a brass buckle at one end to regulate the length. It was normally painted dark blue and marked with the Board of Ordnance sign; a specimen issued to Private Coles, No. 8 Company, 3rd Bn. Grenadier Guards, bears this legend roughly scratched on it:—

B ↑ O
1854
D COLES
8 C 3B GG

In the painting of Colour-Sergeant Spence of the Light Company, 33rd Regiment, the canteen is marked, in white, 'LI 33R 1882', the last figure being the man's regimental number.

Blanket:—The issue blanket was buff in colour and bore a red band and the Board of Ordnance sign, also in red.

Cooking pot:—This pot, or camp kettle, was 7½ inches deep, 10 inches in diameter at the top, and 8½ inches at the bottom. It was provided with a bail handle and fitted with a flush cover, somewhat countersunk, to fit the knapsack closely.

Apart from the kit already mentioned, a proportion of the men carried bill hooks, picks and shovels; once ashore, each man was responsible for the collection and carriage of his own firewood; all of which had to be secured to the blanket pack. In the case of the 1st Battalion Rifle Brigade they also had the additional black groundsheets given to them by General Sir George Cathcart to adapt to their pack.

Arms and weapons

Sword:—Steel gilt half-basket hilt, with the Crown and Bugle inserted in the outward bars, and lined with black patent leather; the gripe of black fish-skin, bound with a spiral of three gilt wires; length of the blade thirty-two inches and a half, width at the shoulder one inch and an eighth, and at twelve inches from the shoulder one inch; thickness of back at shoulder three-eighths of an inch, and at eighteen inches from the hilt, a quarter of an inch; solid flat shoulder an inch and a half deep, and blade hollowed from the flat to within nine inches of the point, which is spear-shaped; weight not less than one pound fifteen ounces without the scabbard.

Scabbard:—Steel; for levees, drawing-rooms, and in the evening, black leather.

Knot:—Black leather.

One authority on swords states that the Rifle Brigade had the badge in the cartouche surrounded by a wreath. A sword carried in the Crimea by Lieutenant John Knox V.C., now in the Royal Green Jackets Museum, hes had the hilt and scabbard painted black, but whether this custom was adopted by all Rifle Brigade officers is unknown.

Staff Sergeants:—The swords and scabbards of Staff Sergeants of the Line and the Rifle Brigade followed the officers' pattern, except that Rifles' Staff Sergeants had black leather scabbards with steel mounting.

Buglers:—Short sword with lion's head pommel in brass.

Bandmaster:—Black waist sling belt; sword with half-basket steel hilt and steel scabbard.

Band Sergeant:—Accoutred as Bandmaster, but with black leather scabbard with steel mountings.

Bandsmen:—Black leather waist belt with frog; swords similar to buglers.

Pioneers:—A pioneer's sword or hanger was introduced in 1831, 26½ inches in length, it had a 22-inch long blade, which was 1¼

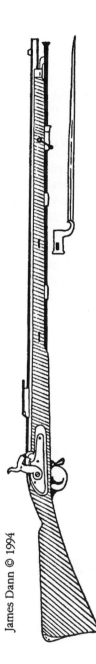

inches wide at the shoulder and had a saw back to within 7½ inches of the double spear point. Its stirrup hilt, grip and back piece, which was engraved with a lion's head, were all in brass. This sword apparently remained in use until 1856, but no contemporary illustrations showing pioneers actually carrying it have been discovered. It is not known if the Pioneers of the Rifle Brigade were issued with this sword at this time but the Pioneer Sergeant in the 3rd Battalion Rifle Brigade did have a similar weapon in 1857.

Revolvers:—The revolver first achieved wide popularity in 1851 and although no provision for them, as part of an officer's weaponry, was made in the Regulations until 1855, most officers in the Crimea seem to have purchased one. The most common types were the Colt Navy 1848 pattern, which had six chambers and was thumb-cocked, and the Adams 1851 pattern, which had five chambers and was self-cocking. Other details were:—

	Colt	*Adams*
Barrel length	7½ in	7 in
Total length	13¾ in	13½ in
Weight	2 lb 9½ oz	2 lb 15½ oz
Calibre	.358 in	.50 in

The Adams revolver was also made with four shorter barrel lengths, with correspondingly smaller calibres.

Rifles:—

Both Rifle Brigade battalions received the Minié rifle before landing in the Crimea to replace their old Brunswicks. Later in the campaign the Miniés were replaced by the Enfield Rifle 1853 pattern.

The Minié Rifle

The Minié Rifle:—

Lengths	Barrel	3ft 3in
	Arm	4ft 7in
	Arm with Bayonet	6ft 0½ in
Weight		9lb 8oz
Calibre		.702 ins
Sight	Graduated backsight to 1,000 yards	

The barrel had four grooves and the rate was much the same as the musket. The accuracy and range, however, showed a significant improvement. The effective range was considered to be 200–250 yards, but, at a white target 6 by 3 feet, at ranges between 500–800 yards, two out of five shots hit the target, and at 1,000 yards, one out of seven. At close range, a bullet could penetrate through at least two men, and at 1,000 yards into oak to a depth of 6–8 inches.

Bayonets:—

Detail of the Minié bayonets were:—
Weight	15½ oz
Blade length	17 ins

Blade construction equiangular, three fullers. Bayonets were secured to the weapon by a spring catch fixed under the muzzle which gripped the projecting collar of the bayonet. The weapons were carried in black leather scabbards of triangular sections with brass mountings.

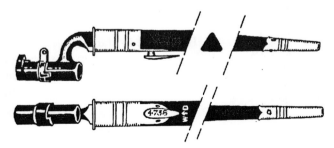

The Long Enfield Rifle and Bayonet

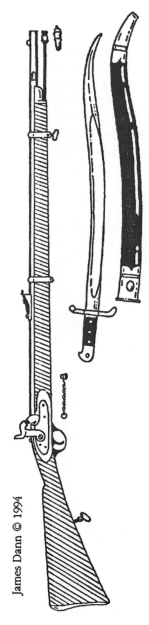

The Short Enfield Rifle

Enfield Rifle Pattern 1853:—

Model 1853, long with triangular bayonet. These will have been contracted rifles made in Birmingham or Liège, with either screwed or spring bands.

This arm represents one of the first examples of a weapon modified as a direct result of complaints from the battlefields. Numerous specific complaints from the Crimea resulted in the several modifications made to the basic design, which included the use of solid barrel bands secured by springs let into the fore-end ahead of each band on the right side, and a stronger hammer, the spur of which lost its curl. The sides of the backsight were flat and the ramrod channel slit was somewhat wider than the other two to assist in holding the ramrod in position. Subsequent to the basic changes made in this model, a new ramrod incorporating a cleaning jag on the head was introduced on which the form and position of the swell were changed, and the ramrod channel was widened beneath the upper band rather than forward of it.

Overall length 65 inches, barrel length 39 inches, calibre 0.577inches, rifled with three grooves of a uniform depth of 0.014 inch and making one turn in 78 inches.

Additional clothing, unofficial and official

During 1855, new pattern clothing had started to be issued to the British Army but there is no evidence as to when it started to arrive or be issued to the Crimean Army. The coatee was being replaced by a double breasted tunic for the men and a Light Dragoon tunic for the officers. A new pattern shako was also being issued which continued to have the front and rear peaks of the previous shako. The front was 5¼ inches high, 7⅛ inches behind and one inch less in diameter at the top than bottom. This gave it a tilted effect which resembled the French shako.

It is possible that it first arrived in the Crimea when worn by officers and men arriving as drafts from England to the various regiments. We have not been able to fix the exact date as to when the Rifle Brigade received the new issue clothing but Sir William Cope in his *History of the Rifle Brigade* states that, about April 1855, new pattern clothing was served out to both Battalions and that when the 1st Battalion received their new clothing it was partly coatee and partly the new tunic.

For further detail of this clothing, see *British Army on Campaign 1816–1902, Vol. 2, Crimea*, Osprey Men at Arms Series, by Michael Barthorp and P. Turner.

Apart from the official uniform and equipment already recorded in this chapter, a considerable amount of unofficial clothing was allowed or tolerated out of pure necessity. The harsh conditions and lack of official clothing dictated the need to keep dry and warm with the oddest of items being pressed into service. The clean-shaven army was allowed to grow beards, which all added to the most unbelievable appearance of a British Army on active service.

Many items were sent from England for the men at public expense, which included sheepskin coats, for officers and men. They were referred to as 'Bunnies,' whether this was a general term for all such clothing or just those worn by the officers which are reported to have been lined with rabbit fur.

In the National Army Museum's collection of Crimean photographs, we have seen some pictorial evidence of these sheepskin coats issued to the officers and men. A group photograph of the 68th Regiment shows the men wearing these coats with the wool or skin to the outside. They are also shown wearing a variety of caps and hats and thigh-length leather boots. Another photograph in the collection is of Officers of the 57th Regiment which again illustrates the various forms of the then popular 'pea jacket' worn over the shell jacket.

It is highly unlikely that this form of dress was limited to these two regiments, so one can assume that the men of the Rifle Brigade could also be seen wearing similar items.

The summer brought different problems and the men were re-issued with white covers for shakos and forage caps, and also a linen 'sandbag' suit, so called from its colour, the coat being cut like the new double breasted tunic. There is little pictorial evidence of this suit but Michael Barthorp, in his book *British Army on Campaign 1816–1902, Vol. 2, Crimea*, states that the sandbag suits were chiefly worn on working parties and when off duty. He also makes mention of an amateur watercolour of Riflemen parading for the trenches with the dress tunic worn over the sandbag trousers and an illustration of a Riflemen in this form of dress compiled from the author's description is also in the book. The *Journal of the Society for Army Historical Research*, Vol. XXXVI, page 95, 1958. has a photograph of a painting by P. A. Protais entitled 'British and French troops off duty in the Crimea.' The accompanying article suggests that the standing figure to the left is a Zouave but Michael Barthorp in his correspondence to us believes that the figure is of one of the 34th Regiment wearing a sandbag suit and a forage cap. We tend to agree with his findings, which gives an insight to this rarely illustrated uniform.

PART FOUR

Crimea Medals and Awards to the Rifle Brigade

Crimea Medals and Awards to the Rifle Brigade

WHATEVER the failures of the Crimean War, one plus for the campaign was the recognition of the common soldier's service and bravery in the field. The latter marked by the introduction of two gallantry awards, the Victoria Cross and the Distinguished Conduct Medal, with the Victoria Cross becoming Britain's highest honour. Besides these two bravery awards the British soldier was also allowed to wear the honours and awards granted by our Allies for the Crimea Campaign, such as the French Médaille Militaire, Legion of Honour and the Sardinian Medal.

For those not singled out for any special distinction during the campaign, the award of the Crimean War Medal was a lasting reminder of all the hardship and fighting they had been through. The medal was issued to all those who took part in the campaign from the 14th September 1854 through to the 8th September 1855, both dates inclusive. The next of kin of those men who were killed or died in the campaign also received the medal.

The Crimean War Medal was issued unnamed with five clasps or bars, but four was the maximum any one medal could have. The clasps were ALMA (20th Sept. 1854), INKERMANN (5th Nov. 1854), BALAKLAVA (25th Oct. 1854), SEBASTOPOL (1st October 1854 to 8th September 1855), and AZOFF (1855). The clasps read upwards, but can sometimes be found issued out of order. The last clasp AZOFF was awarded to the Royal Navy.

A number of medals were actually issued in the Crimea, mainly to the senior ranks and those who had been serving the longest in the campaign. This shortage of medals for all those who were entitled proved unpopular.

It is this immediate issue of medals which is responsible for many of the problems faced by collectors of these war medals. For that purpose we have noted our own observations on the Crimean War

Medals awarded to the Rifle Brigade. This might serve as a guide to those new to collecting medals and at the same time bring forward the experienced collectors' observations in their own particular field.

Some examples of how the clasps varied on the Rifle Brigade Medals and possible reasons for the different combinations are given below. These examples would just as easily fit in with the general pattern of naming in other regiments who served at the beginning of the campaign.

The first medal roll was made out so as to cover the award of the medal with no clasp, and the medal with clasps Alma and Inkermann. This covered all those Riflemen who landed in the Crimea on the 14th September 1854 as part of the original force

Rifleman [A] landed in the Crimea, but was sick and as a result returned to Scutari, where he recovered and returned to duty in the middle of October. He was present at Balaclava, but then became sick again and died in the camp hospital 1st November 1854. His name would appear on the roll as entitled to the medal only. However, by the General Order of 28 February 1855, his name would show him as entitled to the clasp Balaklava. By the General Order for 31 October 1855 a further clasp for Sebastopol was granted. In due course Rifleman [A]'s next-of-kin would have received his medal from the mint almost certainly with impressed naming and the two clasps Balaklava and Sebastopol.

SERGT FREDK ANSELL 2ND BN RIFLE BGDE.

CORPL I. READ 1ST BN RIFLE BDE.

J. FIELD. 1ST BATN RIFLE BDE.

S. SMITH. 2ND BATN RIFLES.

GEO. LOCKTON. 1ST BN RIFLE BDE.

G. LOCKTON. 1ST BATN. RIFLE BDE.

J. LITTLE. 2ND BTN RIFLE BDE.

M. MURPHY. 1ST BTN. RIFLE BDE.

Style of Royal Mint impressed naming

4086. PTE JAS HOLEM 2ND B.R.B.

2861. PTE WM VERNEY. 2ND BATT. RIFLE BRGDE

No 1878. WILLIAM WAKEHAM. R.B.

Styles of Depot naming.
The regimental number is the main addition

Riflemen [B] and [C] landed in the Crimea and both took part in the battle of the Alma. [B] was wounded and finally returned home. [C] survived, but died of cholera 29th September 1854. Both men would be on the roll for medal and one clasp Alma. The next-of-kin of [C] probably received the medal with the clasp Alma from the mint with impressed naming. [B], having returned to England, might have received his unnamed single clasp Alma medal in hospital, but had it engraved at his own expense or when posted back fit to the depot, where he had it done officially either by the punches used in the customary depot style of naming or engraved by somebody contracted by the depot. Both of these arrangements could include regimental numbers and battalion number if serving in a Regiment with more than one battalion, as with the Rifles. However, if Rifleman [B] had paid out of his own pocket to have the medal privately engraved, the medal might be engraved with a briefer inscription because of the cost involved.

Rifleman [D] was present at Alma, Balaklava and Inkermann, though the first roll would credit him with only the medal and two clasps, Alma and Inkermann. However, as he was still serving in the Crimea and by now a Sergeant, he received the medal before

PRIT JOHN COLEBORNE 2ND BN RIFLE BDE.

PTE WM. DAWSON 2ND BN R. BDE..

PRIV. THOS WATTS 2ND BATTN R. BRIGE.

PRIVE. JOSH. DYER 2ND BATTN B. RDE.

PVE JAS GRAY 2ND BATN. RF. BDE.

Privately engraved naming styles

Alexr Carey Band 2nd B R B.

Sergt John McNamara. 2nd Battn R.B.

Cr Serjt Fredk Piper. 2nd B R B

2nd Battalion engraved naming styles

returning home, probably unnamed with three clasps, Alma, Balaklava and Inkermann, subsequently receiving the Sebastopol clasp when back in England. His medal was now named either regimentally or at his own expense by a local jeweller. This seems to have been the case with the senior N.C.O.s of the 2nd Battalion Rifle Brigade, who either had the medal engraved in the Crimea or soon after landing in England in 1856. Their medals are engraved in a very attractive flowing style (see illustration), but not all Sergeants, it seems, conformed to this engraving as we have seen some senior N.C.O.'s medals with impressed naming.

Rifleman [E] was left at Varna in September 1854 and did not join his unit until 30th October 1854. He was wounded at Inkermann and six days later he was evacuated to the hospital at Scutari, where he remained for several months before being posted to the provisional battalion of the Rifles in Malta. He finally rejoined the battalion in the Crimea after the fall of Sebastopol and returned home to England in the May of 1856. The initial roll would list him as entitled to the medal and clasp Inkermann; however his service from the 30th October 1854 to 5th November 1854 before Sebastopol entitled him to this clasp, but as a very obscure Rifleman he did not receive his medal formally. When it finally arrived, it was probably nicely impressed by the Royal Mint and bore the clasps Inkermann and Sebastopol.

From these few examples it is easy to see how the different styles of naming evolved for the Crimean Medal. Once a man's details of service are known, the above examples can be used as a guide to what might be expected to be seen on his medal. Of course there

CORP George Laidler Rifle Brigade

Privately engraved

are always going to be exceptions to this and mistakes were made at the Mint. A good example of this can be given with the medals of Rifleman George Lockton of the 1st Battalion Rifle Brigade, who died while on service in the Crimea. He was first entitled to the medal and clasps for Alma and Inkermann and his next-of-kin in due course received his impressed medal with these clasps. The mint then issued a second impressed medal with the clasps for Alma, Inkermann and Sebastopol. Though the content of the naming is slightly different (see illustration), a possible reason for the issue of two medals can be given by the different type of die used for striking the medal, *i.e.* below the bust of Queen Victoria is the date 1854. On one medal this is quite small while on the second it is of a larger type.

Because of the quantity of medals required for the Crimean War, a large number also being sent to our Allies, the Royal Mint could not undertake to do all the work. They subsequently sub-contracted the striking of the medal to Heaton's of Birmingham, as a result of which, and the later authorisation of clasps, it is easy to see how two medals could be issued to the same man. Lockton was obviously first issued his two clasp medal from one mint; when it was made official that he was also entitled to the Sebastopol clasp his name probably came up on the list of the second mint, who on checking found he was also entitled to the other clasps and prepared a new medal for him with three clasps.

Besides the differences in strikings for the date of 1854, there are also some other noticeable variations to the medal which indicate possibly three or more die types. Much has been made of the varieties in the dies for the Crimean medal and also the differences found on the battle clasps. Fake and forged medals are at once associated with these styles. Though forged medals are around, and we should be aware of the fact, in the main they are linked to the expensive end of the market, such as the Light Brigade chargers, officers, or men entitled to bravery awards. The variation in the clasps would seem inevitable as the making of these clasps was seemingly entrusted solely to sub-contractors.

Some differences noted on the medals we have examined are:—

Wyon, the name of the engraver of the Crimean Medals, appears on both sides of the medal, but on the reverse (the side with the warrior and victory) his name has been noted in two styles, small and very small. We have seen three combinations of date and Wyon dies, these being large date small Wyon, large date large Wyon, and small date large Wyon. There is also a noticeable degree of variation in the line of the 1854 date on both large and small dates. Other points which show a marked difference are: the gap, where the dress of Victory shows behind the warrior's body and his right hand is larger than would normally be shown; the hand of Victory holding the wreath and the head of the warrior, the gap between these is sometimes more noticeable than normal; the rivet that allows the suspender to swivel has been seen in two styles: small head and a larger domed head.

The clasps to the medal have slight differences. The most striking is the variety with the line of the name struck much straighter than the normal curved accepted style. Fake clasps do sometimes come up on a medal along with genuine clasps and the easiest of these to detect are those with the back filled in, not indented as on the originals. Some men, however, had unofficial clasps made which they added to their medals, maybe aggrieved at not receiving a particular clasp. In a number of cases this unofficial clasp was for Balaklava, which at the time was receiving much attention from the public in respect of the men who charged with the Light Brigade. These clasps are easy to spot and cause no threat to the novice collector but should be kept with the medal, even if not entitled, as an added point of interest.

Of all the medal clasps awarded to the Rifle Brigade, the rarest is Balaklava for the 2nd Battalion, which was awarded to a detachment made up from the various companies to a strength of 2 Officers (Captain Inglis, Lieutenant Windham), 2 Sergeants,, 2 Corporals and 44 Riflemen. The next rarest clasp is also to this battalion for Inkermann, with a total of 351 clasps being issued to them.

The breakdown of Inkermann clasps for the 2nd Battalion is:—

1	Erroll's Company	9
2	Colville's Company	3
3	Fyers's Company	6
4	Markham's Company	3
5	Elrington's Company	95
6	Newdigate's Company	79
7	Inglis's Company	82
8	Forman's Company	73

For more details on different die combinations, see *Orders and Medals Research Society Journal,* Winter 1973, p. 178 and Summer 1974, p.55.

The first four companies were away at Balaclava and not entitled to the clasp, but a few men from these companies remained in camp on duty and in a number of cases were listed as being with Headquarters on the roll. When every available man left in camp was needed for the defence of the Heights at Inkermann, these men were called upon to help swell the numbers of the defenders. Captain Erroll's Company, the senior Company of the Battalion, had the headquarters staff on their strength and it is mainly these men that make up the nine entitled from his company. Forman's Company, as far as we know, took no active part in the battle, being stationed in the Lancaster Battery; they did however receive one casualty.

It was only men of the 1st Battalion who could have been issued with a medal bearing all four clasps. We do however know of two four-clasp medals to the 2nd Battalion but we have not been able to verify them on the medal roll. Of those men issued with the clasp for Balaklava, who were on detachment in the 2nd Battalion, none are shown as entitled to the clasp for Inkermann. So it would seem that the detachment at Balaklava on the 25th October were still on the same duty on the 5th November.

Besides the Crimean War Medal, all ranks received the Turkish Crimean War Medal, which had three different die types to cover the British, French and Sardinian troops, the flag of each respective country in question being to the fore. However the ship transporting the British medals sank in severe storms and, as a result, the shortage of medals in the British style was made up from those surplus to requirements from the dies used for Sardinia and France. Hence, British troops did not always have the British type of the Turkish Crimean medal issued to them.

The Turkish Crimea medal was only awarded to those men who survived the campaign. No medals were issued to the next of kin.

The differences in the three die types are as follows:—

British Medal:

A cannon with the British Flag second from right and Crimea 1855 below.

French Medal:

A cannon with the French Flag second from the right and La Crimée 1855 below.

Sardinian Medal:

A cannon with the Sardinian Flag second from the right and La Crimea 1855 below.

The reverse of all three medals have the Sultan's cipher within a wreath of Laurel, also the year of the Hegira 1271.

The Turkish medals were issued unnamed, but not until some time after the campaign was concluded. The 1st Battalion received theirs at Newcastle upon Tyne in 1858, while the 2nd Battalion had to wait until 1860 for theirs when serving in India. Many of these medals for the 2nd Battalion can be found with the ring suspension changed and replaced by the same suspension as on the Mutiny medals. Whether this was done as a battalion instruction or by individual choice is not clear, but a large group photograph of the 2nd Battalion taken in 1862 shows all the Crimean veterans with Mutiny suspension to their Turkish Medals. Some medals to the Rifles have also been seen with the ring removed and Crimea suspensions replacing them.

With this interchange of medals, Britain sent 15,000 British Crimean War medals to the King of Sardinia, who responded by sending 400 Sardinian Al Valore Militare medals to London in 1857 to be awarded to officers and men who had served in the campaign with distinction.

A list was drawn up by Lord Hardinge and General Codrington and as the medals were issued unnamed a minor sub-contractor was chosen to engrave them. This was one Elizer Nash of Clerkenwell. The Rifles were awarded sixteen of these medals most of which went to officers.

Over the years, when describing the style of naming on a medal, the term 'official' has crept in, especially on some dealers' catalogues when describing medals on their sales lists. It seems to be a term added to the advantage of the seller rather than an official term. A medal is either impressed or it is not impressed; depot naming with the use of a punch is quite different in style and cannot be mistaken for the impressed naming of a Mint. The term officially impressed gives the idea that there are other impressed styles also to be seen on the Crimea medal. Some will argue that officially impressed means that it was done by the mint, as only the mint impressed the medals. This is already taken for granted. A wise and valued collector of some standing put it this way; official impressing can be likened to a grocer selling butter but advertising it as best butter to gain an edge over a competitor or an increase in the price. We hope this will help to clear up some of the confusion in naming terms for the new collector of Crimean Medals.

Distinguished Conduct Medal

1st Battalion Rifle Brigade

1. 2138 Rifleman Nathaniel Arthur. Recommended by C.O. 19 Jan. 1855
2. 2162 John Brown. Recommended by C.O. 19 Jan. 1855
3. 2602 Sergeant John Burrows. Recommended by C.O. 19 Jan. 1855
4. 1846 Corporal Thomas Clements. Recommended by C.O. 19 Jan. 1855
5. 3714 Rifleman Timothy Collins. Recommended by C.O. 19 Jan. 1855
6. 1315 Sergt.-Major Richard Cornelius Sub. Queen recommended for medal with Annuity 2nd Feb. 1855. Also had FMM.
7. 2296 Rifleman Walter Eagle. Recommended C.O. 14 April 1855. Also FMM.
8. 1790 George Haines. Recommended by C.O. 19 Jan. 1855
9. 3147 James Hawksford. Recommended by C.O. 19 Jan. 1855
10. 3590 Henry Ingram. Recommended by C.O. 19 Jan. 1855
11. 1994 Thomas Leighfield. Recommended by C.O. 19 Jan. 1855
12. 2667 Corporal Henry Prompby. Recommended by C.O. 19 Jan. 1855
13. 1174 Sergeant Timothy Murphy. Recommended by C.O. 14 Apr. 1855
14. 3363 Rifleman Charles Rains. Recommended by C.O. 19 Jan. 1855 19 Jan.
15. 1871 Corporal Samuel Shaw. Recommended by C.O. 19 Jan. 1855. Awarded VC in Mutiny.
16. 1701 Rifleman Francis Wheatley. Recommended by C.O. 14 Apr. 1855
17. 2679 Joseph Wood. Recommended by C.O. 19 Jan. 1855

2ND BATTALION RIFLE BRIGADE

1. 2562 Sergeant Edward Boughton. Recommended by C.O. 19 Feb. 1855. Gratuity £10
2. 3885 Rifleman Hugh Hannah. Recommended by C.O. 19 Feb. 1855
3. 1912 Q.M. Sergt. William Harrington*. Annuity
4. 1893 Paymr.-Sergt. Henry Harvey. Recommended by C.O. 19 Feb. 1855. Gratuity £10
5. 1944 Rifleman Samuel Hogger. Recommended by C.O. 19 Feb. 1855
6. 3697 Timothy Lewis. Recommended by C.O. 19 Feb. 1855
7. 3584 Edward Marratt. Recommended by C.O. 19 Feb. 1855
8. 2179 Sergeant James Nutt. Recommended by C.O. 19 Feb. 1855
9. 3991 Henry Struck. Recommended by C.O. 19 Feb. 1855
10. 3770 Corporal Robert Wiseman. Recommended by C.O. 19 Feb. 1855

Companion of the Order of the Bath

Colonel	W. S. R. Norcott.
Lieutenant Colonel	A. H. Horsford.
Lieutenant Colonel	E. A. Somerset.

Victoria Cross

Captain Henry H. Clifford	Staff
Rifleman Francis Wheatley	1/Rifle Brigade
Lieutenant John Knox	2/Rifle Brigade
Lieutenant William James Cuninghame	1/Rifle Brigade
Lieutenant Claude Thomas Bourchier	1/Rifle Brigade
Rifleman Roderick MacGregor	2/Rifle Brigade
Rifleman Robert Humpston	2/Rifle Brigade
Rifleman Joseph Bradshaw	2/Rifle Brigade

---

* Enlisted 31/12/1845. Died 30/8/1855

Legion of Honour

Sergeant J. Andrews
Major E. W. Blacket
Lieutenant C. T. Bourchier
Ensign J. Brett
Captain H. H. Clifford
Captain Hon. W. Colville
Major F. R. Elrington
Surgeon J. Frazer
Captain W. Fyers
Captain J. P. Glyn

Lieutenant John S. Knox
Colonel A. MacDonald
Colour Sergeant J. Murphy
Captain E. Newdigate
Major W. S. Norcott
Colonel Hon. Leicester Smythe
Colonel E. A. Somerset
Rifleman Francis Wheatley
Major C. J. Woodford

Turkish Crimea Medal

There are no medal rolls for this medal at the P.R.O. for the Rifle Brigade. However the following memorandum is of interest:—

War Office correspondence books at the P.R.O. under W.O. 3/329: memorandum for the Military Secretary:

'The Adjutant General has the honour (*sic*) to inform the Military Secretary with reference to his memo of the 4 July conveying information of the intention of the Sultan to bestow silver medals upon the Officers and soldiers of the British Army and calling for a return of the number of medals which will be required, that after deducting from the number of Crimean Medals issued. those which have been delivered to the representatives of deceased Officers and soldiers there remains a balance, in round numbers of 74.000 living of all ranks who are entitled to receive the Turkish Silver Medal.

Horse Guards   *G. A. Wetherall*
1st Nov. 1856   *A. G.*

The Sardinian War Medal

1st Battalion Rifle Brigade

Colonel William Sherbrook Ramsay Norcott, C.B.

Served in the Eastern Campaign of 1854 and 1855, including the Alma and the siege of Sebastopol.

Lieutenant-Colonel Alfred Hastings Horsford,. C.B., K.C.B.

Served in the Eastern Campaign of 1854, including the Alma and Inkermann, and first part of the siege of Sebastopol, until compelled to return to England on account of ill-health, after which he commanded the third battalion.

Lieutenant-Colonel Alexander MacDonell, C.B

Brevet-Lieutenant-Colonel Charles John Woodford

Served in the Eastern Campaign of 1854 and 1855, the battles of the Alma and Inkermann, and siege of Sebastopol.

Brevet-Lieutenant-Colonel Lord Alexander George Russell.

Served in the siege of Sebastopol in 1855.

Brevet Major the Honourable James Stuart

Was present with the army during the whole war, having embarked with the second battalion for Varna, and was afterwards promoted into the first battalion. He was present at the Alma as Aide-de-Camp to Colonel Norcott, in command of the left wing of the second battalion. Served during the siege in the first battalion, and commanded the storming party on the 18th of June for which he received his brevet rank.

Lieutenant George Robert Saunders

Joined the battalion in December 1854, before Sebastopol, and performed his duties without interruption to the end of the war; was present under Major Stuart with the covering party on the 18th June 1855.

Corporal J. Rudling

Was present at the Alma, Inkermann, Balaklava, sortie on the Woronzoff road, the storming party on the 18th of June, and when the advanced party in the graveyard was attacked; also accompanied Major-General Windham on a reconnoitring party at the commencement of the siege. Was present at the front with the battalion from the landing in the Crimea until the withdrawal of the army.

Corporal Thomas Tarrant

Volunteered on the 17th of October to lie out in the front of the works to keep down the enemy's fire. He was present at the sortie on the 13th of August, 1855, and served through the whole of the campaign without leaving the front.

2ND BATTALION RIFLE BRIGADE

Lieutenant FitzRoy William Fremantle

Joined in the Crimea on the 1st of December, 1854 and did duty in the trenches from that date until the 18th of June, 1855. Was present at the last sortie made on the quarries on the 8th of June. Commanded the woolsack party of the right column of assault on the 18th of June 1855, on which occasion he was severely wounded.

Lieutenant John Croft Moore

Joined in the Crimea on the 10th of June 1855, and served in the trenches until the fall of Sebastopol. On the attack of the 8th of September he commanded an advanced party of about thirty men, which was pushed forward for the purpose of keeping down the fire of some embrasures on the proper right of the Redan, which enfiladed the attack. He was mentioned in General Simpson's despatch.

Sergeant J. Cherry

Two men employed as sharpshooters having ventured down to the gardens near the Woronzoff road, in July, 1855, one of them was wounded and disabled. Sergeant Cherry went to his assistance under a heavy fire, and returned to report that it was impossible to remove him during daylight. When it was sufficiently dark he headed a party, and brought in the wounded man. Volunteered for secret service on the 6th of September 1855, and was employed in covering a working party throwing up the new sap. Was wounded in four places. Served during the whole campaign.

Rifleman E. Tarvish

Served with great gallantry during the whole campaign in the Crimea, especially in the assault of the 8th of September, 1855, on which occasion he entered the Redan and was taken prisoner.

The Reserve Force for the Crimea

From The Malta Times 13 March 1855.

THE following according to the *Daily News* are the arrangements regarding the reserve force for the British army in the Crimea. The provisional depot will consist of drafts of the three battalions of the Guards and 40 battalions of the line, now in the Crimea, to constitute the first reserve force; and the proportion of officers to each draft of the depot is to be (ultimately) 1 Major, 6 Captains, 12 Subalterns. Distribution of companies, 8 in the Crimea, 4 at Malta, 4 at home, so as to have 2 supernumerary Captains, and 4 ditto Lieutenants at Malta, and 4 ditto Lieutenants with head quarters in the Crimea. The immediate strength of each draft at Malta will be— 2 Captains, 4 Subalterns, 6 Sergeants, 122 rank and file, and the whole force at Malta will number 5,160 rank and file. The 43 drafts will be formed into as many provisional battalions as there are divisions in the Crimea. The battalion for each to be commanded by a major, and the entire force to comprise two commands under Brigadier-Generals Williams and Rumley respectively. Lieut. General Fergusson on the staff at Malta, to have the chief command. The reserve at Malta will be detailed off into five provisional battalions, corresponding with the number of divisions in the Crimea, and they will be drilled and exercised in all camp duties, rifle practice, for which 10,000 smooth-bore percussion muskets are in requisition, pitching and striking tents, cooking, and the officers and men are to be placed under canvas and huts alternately. No soldier under 18 years of age is to be drafted to the army in the Crimea.

The number of Officers and Riflemen at Malta is unknown for either battalion of the Rifle Brigade. The numbers sent to the Crimea from this reserve is not recorded either. However, it is known that some men posted to this reserve never saw active service, remaining the whole time at Malta.

Distribution of the Victoria Cross, Hyde Park, 1857

ON the 26th June the 2nd Battalion Rifle Brigade left Aldershot for London to take part in the parade held at Hyde Park for the distribution of the Victoria Cross, by Her Majesty the Queen.

Practically the whole of London turned out to witness this historic ceremony, under the command of Sir Colin Campbell, G.C.B. The troops for the parade consisted of:—

The Life Guards, 6th Inniskilling Dragoons, 11th Hussars, two field batteries of the Horse Artillery, a company of Royal Engineers, a detachment of the Royal Navy, 1st Battalion Grenadier Guards, 2nd Battalion Coldstream Guards, 1st Battalion Scots Fusilier Guards, Royal Marines, 79th Cameron Highlanders, 2nd Battalion Rifle Brigade and detachment of the Military Train.

The crowd was swelled with the ranks of Chelsea pensioners, many of them veterans of Waterloo and the Peninsula, and the boys from the Duke of York's School, all soldiers' sons.

Just before ten o'clock a 21-gun salute was fired and a detachment of the Blues arrived at Hyde Park corner under the command of Captain Sayer as escort to Her Majesty who was riding behind them between Prince Albert and Frederick William of Prussia. Her Majesty was dressed in a round hat, with a gold band and a red and white feather on the right side, a scarlet bodice, open at the throat, crossed by a gold embroidered scarf, worn officer-fashion over the shoulder, and a dark-blue skirt. A daïs had been prepared :or the Queen but she remained on horseback next to a small table covered with a scarlet cloth, on which lay the Crosses, designed and executed by Messrs. Hancock, of Bruton Street, who had been supplied with metal from the captured Russian artillery pieces held at Woolwich Arsenal.

Colonel Lord Henry Percy, Grenadier Guards, was in command of the men who were to receive the Cross, and Lieutenant Knox,

Rifle Brigade and late Sergeant in the Scots Fusilier Guards, acted as his Adjutant. However, shortly before the parade it was decided that Her Majesty could not pin on the crosses through the thick cloth of the recipients' tunics. Lieutenant Knox was therefore told to get some ribbon, which was to be cut into little pieces and fastened on to each man's tunic. 'Who's going to pay for it?' asked Knox. He was promptly informed that he was to pay and that the money would be refunded, but it never was.

The men to be decorated were marshalled under the command of Lieutenant Knox who a little earlier had marched them down to the Park. They formed up opposite Grosvenor Gate, amid a storm of cheering. Sixty-two men were lined up and, as Lord Panmure, Secretary of State for War, read out their names they approached one by one, each recipient stepping forward and saluting, the sailors taking off their hats.

Her Majesty received a Cross from Lord Panmure, and bending from the saddle pinned it to the loop of ribbon with her own hand. The men of the Rifle Brigade were the last to receive their Crosses, and were lined up in the following order:—

    Brevet Major Hon. H. H. Clifford
    Rifleman Francis Wheatley
    Captain W. J. Cuninghame
    Lieutenant John S. Knox
    Rifleman Roderick MacGregor
    Rifleman Robert Humpston
    Rifleman Joseph Bradshaw
    Brevet-Major C. T. Bourchier

When all the Crosses had been distributed. the recipients were drawn up about fifty yards from the Royal Party, and a review took place, the troops marching in slow time between the heroes and their Sovereign to the admiration of all beholders. The Guards' band played 'See the Conquering Hero Comes,' the 79th Highlanders 'Auld Lang Syne,' the Marines 'Rule Britannia,' and the band of the 2nd Battalion Rifle Brigade struck up with their celebrated regimental quick march, 'I'm 95.'

The cavalry and guns then went by at the gallop—the 11th Hussars recalling vividly the Charge of the Light Brigade as they tore past with Cardigan at their head, and many a Balaclava man still among them.

After that, the whole force was drawn up in line; the infantry presented arms, the Life Guards, Hussars, and Dragoons their flashing sabres. Three hearty cheers were given for Queen Victoria, and the Royal cortege left the ground.

Then came a rush to shake hands with the heroes. It was impossible for every one of the hundred thousand spectators present to do so, but such a surging crowd surrounded the gallant sixty-two that they were in more danger than when gaining the award, which led them to cry out in desperation, 'Preserve us from our friends.'

The troops returned to barracks; the bands died away in the distance, the dust settled down once more, and all was over.

Medal Rolls, Remarks Columns.

THE medal rolls for the Rifle Brigade have been compiled from those held in the Public Records Office in London. All entries in the remarks columns are transcribed as they appear on the originals, which give no explanations as to what they mean though some are easy to work out. The condition of the rolls in places is very poor, some pages having pieces missing; the end of the 1st Battalion roll, for example, just gradually disintegrates. In other places the roll has faded so badly that it is not possible to make out the full details. In the transcribed rolls we have put [...] to indicate that a name or further names are missing, or in some cases just the man's number or rank is visible. From the position in the gap on the roll it is sometimes obvious what letter the missing name begins with.

The 1st Battalion roll is listed in alphabetical order, but the 2nd Battalion comes in company order; we have listed both rolls as they are shown. The advantage of this for the 2nd Battalion is that when reading that battalion's history a man can be followed through the campaign more easily as this battalion is broken down by wing or company more than the 1st Battalion.

Having compiled and preserved the rolls in this book we have at least ensured that no further information will be lost from the originals.

Besides the official medal roll remarks we have added the known casualties and further medal entitlements. The abbreviations used on the roll have been transcribed onto the roll as shown in the original and some of their meanings are quite vague. We have given our own interpretation of these, but in some cases they might not be the true meaning and will have to be treated as a guide.

H+R.	Home to Regiment (as opposed to home to discharge etc.)
WO.	War Office.
SO.	Special Order.
D.	Depot.
B.	Balaclava.
C.	Clasp.
Bal.	Balaclava.
Sent Away.	Could mean a casualty sent to Scutari or Malta.
KIA.	Killed in action.
DOW.	Died of wounds.
W.	Wounded.
Sl/W or Sly/W.	Slightly wounded.
Sev/W.	Severely wounded.
W/Dead.	Wounded dead (died of wounds or died later from disease)
Regt 18/7/57.	Medal sent to the Regiment on the date shown. In some instances the date might be shown as much later, indicating he had left the service and the medal was sent direct to him or, if he had died, it was sent to his next-of-kin.
1st.	1st, after a man's name indicates more than one man of the same name and he is listed as first second or third etc. on the roll.
2nd.	As above.
SA53.	This shows those men known to be entitled to the South Africa 1853 medal for the Seventh and Eighth Kaffir Wars.
Mutiny	These men entitled to the Indian Mutiny medal with or without clasp.
DCM.	Distinguished Conduct Medal.
VC.	Victoria Cross.
FMM.	French Médaille Militiare.
Turk.Med.	Turkish Crimea War Medal.
Sard.	Sardinian War Medal.
Leg.of Hon.	Legion of Honour.

Sometimes a man has a date next to his name showing when he died. Where no place is shown the muster rolls state 'Died in the Crimea.' The spellings of names was also a problem, as a man's name might be listed with more than one spelling. In some cases he could even have a change of Christian name, but in most cases we have been able to follow him through the rolls because his regimental number confirms the right man. However, some men are shown with two or three different regimental numbers, which we have listed.

The entitlement of clasps especially on the 2nd Battalion rolls is also a problem. The clerks who worked on the rolls often put ticks on the originals when making calculations for various reasons which only add to the confusion. Some get carried away with their ditto marks, however we have done our best to transcribe these as accurately as possible. When a man has a clasp for an action in which his company was not present, it does not necessarily mean he was not entitled to it. The men were transferred from company to company for promotion reasons, or in a number of cases because one particular company might have lost the greater part of its experienced men. Other problems we have come upon are that a man might only be shown on the roll as entitled to one clasp but his medal might have been issued with a number of clasps. An example of this is James Howshaw, the servant to Brigadier Buller. On the Rifle Brigade roll he is only entitled to Sebastopol, but on a staff return was entitled to the other clasps, having qualified for the Sebastopol clasp with the Rifles when posted back to the battalion on Brigadier Buller's return to England.

Balaclava is the spelling we have kept to in this book, though on the medal the clasp is shown as Balaklava. Sevastopol, the Russian spelling, is also given as Sebastopol on the medal, while Inkerman is shown as Inkermann on the medal.

PART FIVE

1st Battalion Rifle Brigade Medal Roll for the Crimea

Lieutenant Colonels

Sidney Beckwith	A—S	Died 25/9/54 of cholera
Alfred H. Horsford	AIBS	To the 3rd Battalion
Ramsey Norcott	A—S	On Leave
Edward A. Somerset	AIBS	On Leave

Majors

Henry Hardinge	AIBS	
Edward Rooper	AIBS	Wounded Inkerman DOW 10/11/54 on Voyage to England
Lord Alexander/ G. Rusell	—S	Landed in Crimea 13/7/55

Captains

Edward W. Blackett	AIBS	To 2nd Battalion
Claude T. Bourchier V.C.	AIBS	To 3rd Battalion
Thomas H. Bramston	AIBS	Transfered Grenadier Guards
Coote Buller	AIBS	W/Dgly. 5/11/54 to Depot 12/12/54
Aubrey A. Cartwright	AIBS	KIA Inkerman 5/11/54
Charles H. S. Churchill	AIBS	Sly/W 22/11/54 on Leave
Augustus W. Clifton	A–BS	SA'53
William J. M. Cuninghame	AIBS	On Leave
William H. Deedes	AIBS	To 3rd Battalion
Cook S. Flower	AI–S	Sly/W Inkerman 5/11/54. Retired
John P. C. Glyn	—S	
Arthur W. Godfrey	AIBS	Sebastopol Died 27/11/54
Hon. George B. Legge	AIBS	Promoted to 2nd Battalion
Henry G. Lindsay	A–BS	Promoted to 3rd Battalion
Frederick C. Morgan	AIBS	Sly/W 22/11/54 on Leave
Charles V. Oxenden	—S	Landed in Crimea 12/6/55
Hon. James Stuart	—S	
Henry Tryon	AIBS	KIA Sebastopol 20/11/54
George H. Walker	—S	Landed in Crimea 1/1/55

Lieutenants

Hon. Augustus Anson	—S	Landed in Crimea 27/1/55. To 3rd Battalion
Joseph Ashton	—S	Promoted to Lieut. in Rifle Brigade from Sgt-Major Coldstream Guards 28 Feb 1855 antedated to 8 Nov 1854. Entitled to a 4-clasp Crimean Medal but would only be entitled to Sebastopol on Rifle Brigade roll. Retired 26 Sep 1856
Charles A. P. Boileau	—S	Landed in Crimea 27/1/55 Sly/W 18/6/55. Mortally wounded 1/8/55. Died Malta
John Clark	—S	Landed in Crimea 17/6/55
J. P. Green	—S	Landed in Crimea 17/6/55
Christopher Musgrove	—S	Landed in Crimea 22/2/55
William Norris	—S	
Hore Ruthven	—S	Landed in Crimea 13/5/55
William T. Rooper	—S	Landed in Crimea 13/7/55
George R. Saunders	—S	Landed in Crimea 11/1/55
Charles. A. C. Talbot	—S	Landed in Crimea 17/11/54. On Leave
Arthur L. Tottenham	—S	Landed in Crimea 12/6/55

Adjutant / Ensign

John Brett	AIBS	On Leave

Surgeon

Robert Bowen	AI–S	On Leave

Assistant Surgeons

Francis De Chaumont	—S	
*James E. Scott	AIBS	Transferred 41st Regt
James A. Shorrocks	A—S	Died Sebastopol 21/9/54 cholera
John P. Williams	AI–S	

Paymaster

John E. Large	AI–S

Quarter Master

Henry Peacock	AIBS

Sergeant Majors

1315	Richard Cornelius	AIBS	SA'53 England
1397	Henry Tucker	A—S	Died Kalchsoi cholera 24/25/9/54

Quarter Master Sergeants

1883	Charles Ward	AIBS	
777	William Young	AI–S	Discharged

Paymaster Sergeant

2598	Charles J. Ablott/Ablitt	AIBS	Scutari

Armourer Sergeant

3218	James Gilles	AIBS

Hospital Sergeant

1425	Robert Hills	AIBS

Orderly Room Clerk

2683	David Milne	AIBS

Bugle Major / Bandmaster

1101	Alexander Miller	AIBS	Depot (Band)

Colour Sergeants

2607	John Burrows	AIBS	
1336	William Cornelius	AIBS	SA'53
2651	Henry Fothergill	AIBS	
1450	George Garner/Camer	AIBS	
2575			Killed at Inkerman 5/11/54
2595	John Green	AIBS	W. Inkerman 5/11/54. to England
1978	John Hicks	AIBS	Malta
1708	William Higgins	AIBS	
2135	John Judge	AI–S	
1791	William Knight	AIBS	
2058	John McGrotty/McGrotly	AIBS	Wounded 5/11/54 Inkerman
1174	Timothy Murphy	AIBS	Malta
2643	George R. Nosley	AIBS	KIA Inkerman 5/11/54
1563	David Osborne	AIBS	Malta
2664	James Powell	AI–S	Wounded 13–17/10/54. KIA Inkerman 5/11/54

2879	John Round	A–BS	
1494	Charles Tapp	A—	Died 25/9/54

Sergeants

3052	George Abery	AIBS	SA'53
3149	Thomas Arnold	—S	Landed in Crimea 12/6/55, Died 11/7/55 Crimea WO
2820	George Bateman	AIBS	KIA Inkerman 5/11/54. SA'53
3389	William Brett	AI–S	KIA Inkerman 5/11/54
2757	George Cain	—S	
2170	Thomas Cain	AIBS	
2079	Patrick Carroll	—S	Landed in Crimea 26/1/55
1768	Benjamin Chawner	—S	Landed in Crimea 28/11/54. England
	J. Clark	—S	
3307	J. William Curtis	AI–S	
2933/57/ 2937	Michael Devitt	AIBS	KIA 12/4/55 WO
2764	Charles Douglas	—S	Died Scutari 17/3/55 WO
2924	John Fisher	AIBS	
3098	John Forsyth	AIBS	Wounded Inkerman 5/11/54. 1/12/54 Scutari
3587	Charles Garfield	AIBS	DOW Inkerman 5/11/54 (england)?
2414	William Gibson	—S	Sly/Wounded 9/8/55.
4045	John Givens	—S	Landed in the Crimea 13/7/55
2278	George Hall	AIBS	
2612	William Hall	—S	
2472	William Hamilton	AIBS	Died Scutari 3/3/55
3077	John Harrington	A—S	Died Scutari 17/2/55
	R. E. Harrington	—S	
2449	Moses Haycock	AIBS	SA'53 Medal
2957	William Hill	AIBS	Deceased
1382	Amos Hobion	—S	Landed in the Crimea 27/1/55. England
2874	George Jenkins	—S	
2490/2690	Philip Jenkins	AIBS	WO Deceased
2086	George Jerrom	AI–S	WO KIA Redan 18/6/55
1346	William Jerrom	AIBS	Wounded Inkerman 5/11/54 (Band). Died Scutari.
3208/3298	George Jones	AIBS	L.T.C.
2024	John King	AIBS	
3229/3239	Richard Knapp	AIBS	
2461	C. Lambert	A—	
1946	Thomas McCullen	AI–S	KIA 5/11/54 Inkerman

1736	Charles McNally/McNalty	AIBS	27/11/56 Edinburgh
2779	James Mason	A—S	Died Scutari
3610	William Matthews	—S	
3876/3853	Robert Morgan	—S	Landed in the Crimea 17/6/55
2466	Henry Nightingale	AI–S	Wounded 5/11/54 Inkerman. Died Kulali 10/4/55
3304	Thomas Palmer	A—S	
1934	William Palstone/Patstone	AI–S	
1483/1683	David Peachey	AIBS	(Band)
1705	James Pearce	—S	
3204	Charles Peskett	A–BS	Sev/Wounded 15/11/55 French Siege Train. Died 18/11/55
3120	Joseph Pickford	AI–S	
3038	Edwin Pritchard	A——	Died Crimea 21/9/54
2667	Henry Prompby	AIBS	
2185	John Richards	A—S	
2862	James Rudling	AI–S	
3125	J. Sharpe	A——	
1871	Samuel Shaw	AIBS	Wounded 5/11/54 Inkerman
2009/2909	William Sills	AIBS	KIA Inkerman 5/11/54
3049	Frederick Smith	—S	Landed in the Crimea 15/3/55
2934	William Smith	A–BS	Sly/Wounded /15/11/55. Alma crossed out?
3055	W. V. Smith	AIBS	
2911	Charles Stroutger	A—S	(Treoulger?)
1951	George Taylor	AIBS	Wounded Inkerman 5/11/54
2858	John Vaughan	AIBS	Wounded Inkerman 5/11/54
2942	James Wain	AIBS	
1738	William Ward	AIBS	
5585/3853	James Watt	—S	Landed in the Crimea 17/6/55. Scutari
3336	Edwin Wallington	—S	Landed in the Crimea 13/7/55
2910/2916	James Wild	AIBS	
2605	Alfred Wilson	AIBS	Deceased

Corporals

3362	John Allen	AIBS	Wounded 5/11/54
3233	John Archer	AIBS	
2723	Samuel Barwell	AIBS	Sl/Wounded 11/12/54 England
2678	Thomas Bradbury	AIBS	
3288	David Brooks	A–BS	Died Date Unknown
3248	Richard Brooks	—S	Sev/Wounded 21/11/54. 1/1/55 Deceased

2986	William Brown	AIBS	19/1/1855
3035	James Budden	AI–S	England
1794	John Burton	AIBS	
2839	William Carroll	—S	
3019	Joseph Cawcutt	AI–S	
2929	John Chapman	AI–S	
1846	Thomas Clement	—S	
2786	John Connelly	—S	Landed in the Crimea 28/11/54. Corfu, Sick
3423	James Davison	AIBS	17/3/55 Scutari. England
3193	John Downs	AIBS	Deceased
3306	Henry Elliott	AIBS	Deceased
2171	Richard Fitzgerald	A—S	
3107	William Friend	—S	Landed in Crimea 26/1/55. England
3002	Charles Goad	AIBS	Sev/Wounded 22/11/54
1571	Charles Goddard	AIBS	Killed Inkerman 5/11/54
3116	John Gullett	AIBS	
3289	R. Harmer	AI—	
2049	W. Harpur	AIB–	
3309	John Hayes	AI–S	Died Scutari 28/2/55. WO 16/3/57
2229	Edward Higgins	AIBS	SA'53
2119	John Higgins	AIBS	SA'53
3537	Thomas Hollingsworth	AIBS	6/1/55 Scutari. Deceased WO 16/3/57
3104	George Hook	A—S	England
3226	John Hornsey/Harvey	AIBS	
3320	William Hunt	AIBS	England
2762	Richard Jenkins	A—S	Sl/Wounded 18/6/55 Redan
3625	Louis Phillip Kerr	AI–S	Deceased WO 16/3/57
3084	Thomas King	AI–S	SA'53
2218	George Laidler	AIBS	England
3081	George Lales	—S	Landed in Crimea 27/1/55
3159	John Lee	AIBS	KIA Inkerman 5/11/54
3037/3136	Jacob Lucas	A—S	
3272/3772	John McEwan	AI–S	18/6/55 KIA Redan
2124	Patrick McNulty	–IBS	SA'53 Sl/W 20/11/54
3792	William Mansell	—S	
3065/3165	Henry Mathew	A—S	Died 16/10/54
3610	William Matthews	—S	Landed in Crimea 26/1/55
3887	William Mont	—S	
3884	Gilbert More	—S	

3299	George Robert Perry	AI–S	14. 2/55 Scutari Deceased WO 16/3/56
3374	Thomas Pike	—S	
3267	Ishmeal Read	AI–S	Sev/Wounded 2/1/55 DOW 13/1/55 Scutari
3529	John Riorden	AIBS	
3264	George Rock/ Rook	AI–S	14/1/55 Scutari Deceased
3343	Charles Roydhouse	AI–S	
3037	Lucas Saunders	–IBS	SA'53 Died 6/12/54
3447	William Sayer(s)	AIBS	Deceased 16/1/55
3685	John Shirley	—S	
4085/4083	George Shorto	—S	Landed in the Crimea 13/7/55
3040/3046	Thomas Simpson	AIBS	Died 20/11/54
3183	William Smith	AIBS	Deceased WO 2/3/55
2847/9/ 2849	Martin Spencley	A—S	22/12/54 Scutari Deceased
4286	Alfred Stagg	—S	Landed in the Crimea 13/7/55
3484	J. Stivens	–I—	
2847/9	George Swaines	AIBS	Deceased 1/3/55
3087	William Tomkins	AI–S	England
3133	Thomas Tooley	AI–S	England
2808	James Traylen	AIBS	
3321	Alfred Traylen (Trayler)	A—S	
3485	John Tuck	AIBS	
2007	William Turner	AIBS	SA'53 Medal
3041	Joseph Wallace	AIBS	SA'53 Medal
3736	Thomas Ward	—S	Landed in Crimea 17/6/55. Sly/Wounded 10/7/55
2325	William Webb	AI–S	SA'53 Medal. England
3155	Thomas Wilson	AIBS	Deceased
3628	John Wilkinson	A–BS	
3576	George Wright	A–BS	England
3249/3449	Joseph Woods	—S	Landed in the Crimea 22/2/55

Buglers

3269	George Ackerman	AIBS	SA'53 Sl/Wounded 8/9/55 Redan
2770	William Ackerman	AIBS	SA'53 Medal
1846	T. Clements	AIBS	SA'53 Medal Promoted B/major
3250/8	William Cockerton	AIBS	Died 9/1/55 Scutari Aged 17 Years
2767	Richard Cummings	AIBS	Died Scutari 31/12/54 WO 24/9/56
2325/35	James Gains	AIBS	

2207	William Gardiner	AIBS	Canada Medal, SA'53 Medal, L.S.&G.C. Medal, Mer. Ser. Medal, Served in Regimental Band. Photo in 1911 R.B.C.
2333/53	Michael Harding	AIBS	
2771	William Harding	AIBS	
2122	Elizah Huston	AIBS	Wounded 5/1/54 Inkerman
4360	John Jackson	—S	Landed in the Crimea 13/7/55
2360	Alfred Johnson	AIBS	
2639	James Kearns	AIBS	
2024/2126	Arthur McWilliams	AIBS	
2793	John Matthews	—S	Landed in the Crimea 17/6/55
3042	James Nabbs	AI–S	England
2634	George Richards	AIBS	
2375	Charles Stewart	AIBS	SA'53, Turk Medal, LSGC, Served in Band
2719	Robert Stewart	AIBS	
3056	William Wylie	AIB–	2/1/55 Scutari

Riflemen

3432	Henry Abbott	AIBS	17/2/1855 Crimea. Deceased WO 16/3/57
4198	William Abbott	—S	Landed in the Crimea 13/7/55
2746	Edward Abery	AIBS	SA'53 Medal
2812	Richard Ackerman	AI–S	Wounded. 5/1/54 Inkerman. England. DOW 14/11/54
4146	George Adams	—S	Landed in the Crimea 22/2/55. England
2950	Richard Adams	AIBS	SA'53
3855	Robert Adams	—S	Landed in Crimea 28/11/54. England H+R 13/10
4530/4536	Henry Aery	—S	Landed in the Crimea 12/6/55. Scutari
4069	James Alderton	—S	Landed in Crimea 26/1/55
2748/2404	George Aldrige	A—	Died 20/9/54 Crimea
2854	David Allock	A–BS	SA'53 Medal
3205	John/Thomas Allen	AI–S	30/1/1855 Deceased WO 1/57
3362	J. Allen	AIB–	
3082	J. Allen	A—	
3408	Richard Allen	AIB–	
3083	Robert Allen	—S	KIA 22/11/1854
4058	Robert Allum	—S	Landed in the Crimea 13/7/55
1341	Thomas Allum	—S	
1491	T. Allum	AI—	SA'53 Medal
2535/55	Michael Ambrose	AI–S	SA'53 England H+R 14/11/56

4641	Charles Andrews/ Anderson	—S	Landed in Crimea 22/2/55
3999/3909	John Andrews	—S	Landed in Crimea 27/1/55
4212	John Applebee	—S	Landed in Crimea 13/7/55
3379	Frederick Archer	A—S	
4112/4712	James Archer	—S	Landed in Crimea 22/2/55
2747	Thomas Archer	—S	Landed in Crimea 28/11/54. Deceased
4839	Robert Armstrong	—S	Landed in Crimea 13/7/55
3538/58	William Armstrong	AIBS	
4047	William Arter/ Arther	—S	Landed in Crimea 28/11/54. Scutari. England
2138	N. Arthur	AIB—	SA'53 Medal
4887	Thomas Ash	—S	Landed in Crimea 17/6/55
3481	Samuel Ashbolt	AIBS	England
3795	Samuel Ashton	—S	Landed in Crimea 28/11/54. England
4096	William Ashton	—S	Landed in Crimea 13/7/55
4300	William Atkin/ Atkins	—S	Landed in Crimea 13/7/55
3671/3675	Fredrick Atkinson	A——	25/4/1855 Scutari
4559	George Atslow/ Alston	—S	Landed in Crimea 13/7/55
2397/2393	Robert Austin	—S	Landed in Crimea 22/2/55
4669	Edward Ayling	—S	Landed in Crimea 13/7/55
3089	Charles Bailey	AIBS	Sev/Wounded 21/12/54,. Died 5/1/1855 Crimea. Died of Wounds. WO 16/3/57
4640	William Bailey	—S	Landed in Crimea 13/7/55
2558	George Bailey	AIBS	SA'53 Medal
4386	George Bailey	—S	Landed in Crimea 22/2/55
2909	Henry Bailey	AIBS	SA'53 Medal, French M.M.
3477	William Bailey	AIBS	Sev/W 22/11/54 DOW 27/11/54
4585	William Bailey	—S	Died Scutari. 24/6/1857. Landed in Crimea 17/6/55
3896	William Baines	—S	
3068/3488	Charles Baker	AIBS	Sev/Wounded 2/1/55. Died WO 16/3/57
2721/2727	John/ Wm. Baker	AIBS	13/2/1855 Died Scutari
3619	Joseph Baker	AIBS	Died 20/11/. Scutari 14/1/55
3817	Thomas Bakewell	—S	Landed in Crimea 28/11/54. Died WO 16/3/57
4577	Edward Ball	—S	Landed in Crimea 12/6/55
2832/2834	Samuel Ball	A——	Died Date Unkown

3709	Jonathan Ballard	AIBS	Died 5/12	
4160	Alfred Ban/ Bap	—S	Landed in Crimea 22/2/55	
2407	Henry Bapett	—S	Transfered to 3rd Bn	
5190	William Barker	—S	Landed in Crimea 13/7/55	
4610	Thomas Barnett	—S	Landed in Crimea 13/7/55	
3762	John Barber	AIBS		
2752	Fredrick Bard/ Beard	AIBS	Dead Wounded 5/11/54 Inkerman	
2102	Thomas Barge	AI–S	Killed 20/11/54	
3466	John Barker	AI—	Sev/Wounded 4/12/54. ?? 19/8/54 Beikos, Asiatic side of the Bosphoros	
3896	William Baynes	—S	Landed in Crimea 26/1/55	
4551	William Baldock	—S	Landed in Crimea 22/2/55	
3031	Mark Barker	AIBS	Scutari	
3444	William Barker	—S		
2971	T. Barkley/ Bartley	AI—	Sev/Wounded 2/1/55	
1210	Henry Barley	AIBS	England D. 24/6/57	
3874	John Orcourt Barlow		—S Landed in Crimea 27/1/55	
3462	George Barnard	AI–S		
3574	Charles Barrow/ Barron	AIBS	Sev/Wounded 10/12/54. W 5/11/54 Inkerman	
3415/3450	William Barrowdave	AI–S+	Killed 5/1/55 Crimea	
2799	John Barry	AIBS		
4628	James Bartholomew	—S	Landed in Crimea 17/6/55	
3296	John Barton	AIBS	England	
3386	William Barwell	AIBS	Sly/Wounded 27/11/54	
2407	H. Bassett	AI—		
3708	Caleb Bateman	AI–S		
3583	John Bates	AIBS	England 20/11/54	
2620	Stephen Bates	AIBS	Died L4/2/1855 Scutari	
2888	Horace Batkin	AI–S		
2712	Joseph Baxter	AIBS	Sev/W. SA'53 Died 30/1/55 Scutari	
3942/4521	Robert Baxter	—S	Landed in Crimea 22/2/55. Scutari	
2988	Joseph Bayliss	AIBS	SA'53 Medal	
3921	Charles Betteridge	—S	Landed in Crimea 26/1/55	
4527	Thomas Beale	—S	Landed in Crimea 27/1/55 Died 9/9/55	
4075	Thomas Beaumont	—S	Landed in Crimea 27/1/55	
4425	George Bennet	—S	Landed in Crimea 17/6/55	

3017	Matthew Beader	AIBS	England Regt 18/7/57
3843	Walter Beadon	—S	Landed in Crimea 28/11/54. Scutari
3435	George Beak	AIBS	Died 8/3/55 Scutari. Regt 18/7/57
2995	Robert Beale	AIBS	Killed 17/11/54 (20/11)
3559	Joseph Bearer/ Beaser	AI–S	Died 25/1/1855 Crimea
5225	William Beathy	—S	Landed in Crimea 13/7/55
2837/73	William Beatly/ Beatty	AIBS	Wounded 5/11/54 Inkerman
3276	James Beatson	AIBS	
2736	Edwin Beaumont	AI–S	Died 23/12/54
4075	Thomas Beaumont	—S	Landed in Crimea 27/1/55 Scutari
3186	S. Beckett	A——	
2919	Henry Bedby	—S	
3933	David Beight	—S	
3445	Emanuel Bell	AI–S	England 20/2/1855 Scutari
3921	Charles Bellridge	—S	
1513	George Bennett	AI–S	Died 24/6/54
3137	George Bennett	AIBS	Died 17/1/54 Scutari
4425	George Bennett	—S	
3361	Samuel Bender/ Benden	—S	Landed in Crimea 27/1/55. 25/2/1855 Scutari H+R 14/10
1290	Richard Benskin	AI–S	Died
4539	John Benson	—S	Landed in Crimea 22/2/55 England
4243/5243	Robert Bep	—S	Landed in Crimea 13/7/55
3478	Edward Berry	AIBS	
3394	Henry Berry	AIBS	
4574	George Best	—S	Landed in Crimea 12/6/55
4431	Edward Bettridge	—S	Landed in Crimea 13/7/55
3868	William Bettridge	—S	England
2919	Henry Bibby	–IBS	Wounded 5/11/54 Inkerman
4210	William Bidwell	—S	Landed in Crimea 13/7/55 Scutari
3823/3828	Daniel Biggins	—S	Landed in Crimea 28/11/54. Dead 22/12/1854
3744	Henry Billen	—S	Died WO
4596	Henry Bingham	—S	Landed in Crimea 12/6/55 Died
3222	Thomas Bingley	AI–S	
3415	J. Binns	AIB–	
3402	John Birch	AIBS	DOW. 5/11/54 Inkerman

2291	George Birch	AIBS	Died WO
3851	George Bird	—S	Landed in Crimea 28/11/54. Died 17/2/55 Scutari
3403	George Bishop	AIBS	DOW 5/11/54 Inkerman
1661	Edward Blake	AIB—	28/1/55 Scutari.
3310	James Blanchard	AIBS	Killed 22/8/55 H+R 29/12/56
1615	John Blanks/ Blunks	AIBS	Died 6/2/55 Scutari
2947	Alfred Blucher	—S	Landed in Crimea 26/1/55
4144	Frederick Blunt	—S	Landed in Crimea 13/7/55 England
3759	James Blunt	—S	Landed in Crimea 26/1/55. Scutari
3809	John Boddy	AIBS	Scutari WO 24/9/56
3847	William Bodger	—S	Landed in Crimea 26/1/55. Scutari
4551	William Boldock	—S	
4340	Charles Bolting	—S	
3334/3434	Daniel Bone	AIBS	17/2/55 Scutari
3649	William Bonham	AIBS	DOW 7/11/54 Paylist Inkerman
4167	John Bond	—S	Landed in Crimea 27/1/55
3410/3416	Thomas Boon	–I-S	26/1/55 Scutari Wo8/12/56
3922	Richard Borgess	—S	
3235/3335	Joseph Bostock	–I-S	
4340	Charles Botting	—S	Landed in Crimea 13/7/55
4298	Thomas Bottom/ Bolton	—S	Landed in Crimea 13/7/55
2710	Henry Boulton	AIBS	Scutari WO
3119	William Boustead	A—S	

3937	Richard Braybrook	—S	Landed in Crimea 17/6/55. Scutari 24/6/57
3580	James Braybrook	AIBS	Died Scutari 16/3/55
3822	Thomas Braybrook	—S	Landed in Crimea 28/11/54. England (not shown in Muster Rolls). Died 11/2/55
3220	John Brayley	AIBS	Killed 20/11? Scutari 20/12/54. WO 24/9/56
4266	William Brown	—S	Landed in Crimea 17/6/55. Balaklava
3933	David Bright	—S	Landed in Crimea 26/1/55. Sev/Wounded 18/6/55 Redan
4368	James Bryant	—S	Landed in Crimea 27/1/55. Killed in Trenches 12/4/55
3377	William Bridger	AIBS	
3592	Richard Britt/ Butt	AIBS	24/1/55 Scutari
3009	John Broome	AIBS	12/1/1855 Crimea
4225	Charles Brown	—S	Landed in Crimea 17/6/55
3945/3954	Charles Brown	—S	Landed in Crimea 13/7/55
3369/3349	Ellis Brown	–IBS	Sly/Wounded 2/12/54 England
3160	George Brown	AIBS	Killed 12/4/55
3807	Henry Brown	—S	Landed in Crimea 27/1/55. Sly/Wounded 18/6/55 Redan
2162	John Brown	—S	Wounded 5/11/54 Inkerman England
4239	John Brown	—S	Landed in Crimea 17/6/55
4405	John Brown	—S	Landed in Crimea 22/2/55. Regt. 19/8/56
4848	Richard Brown	—S	Landed in Crimea 12/6/55
3194	Rody Brown	AIBS	SA'53 Medal
4558	Charles Brozier/ Brazier	—S	Landed in Crimea 22/2/55
1263/1363	Robert Bruce	AI–S	Malta Regt. 19/9/56
2889	Michael Bryan	AIBS	
3505/3509	George Bryant	A—S	
4409	Thomas Bryant	—S	Landed in Crimea 22/2/55
3063	Alfred Bryant	—S	Landed in Crimea 28/11/55
3198	James Buckley	A—	Died 22/9/54
3988	Stephen Bull	—S	Landed in Crimea 27/1/55
3803	William Bull	—S	Landed in Crimea 28/11/54
3922	Richard Burgs	—S	Landed in Crimea 12/6/55
4065	Thomas Burns	—S	Landed in Crimea 28/11/54
3819	John Burrell	—S	Landed in Crimea 28/11/54. Scutari

5211	John Buffham	—S	Landed in Crimea 13/7/55 Scutari
3938	Stephen Buld	—S	
4443	Benjamin Bule/ Bale		—S Landed in Crimea 17/6/55
1899	James Buller	AIBS	SA'53 1//2/55 Scutari. Died WO 4/6/56
2840	William Bullock	AIBS	England
4063	James Bullsman/ Bullman	—S	Landed in Crimea 12/6/55
4563	John Bunting	—S	Landed in Crimea 27/1/55. Sev/ Wounded 26/3/55
3203	Samuel Burchell	AIBS	
3382/3383	John Burgess	AIBS	Wounded 5/11/54 Inkerman
3872	John Buridge	—S	Landed in Crimea 28/11/54
1954	T. Burley	AIB–	
3616	F. Burman	AIB–	22/1/55 Scutari
4394	John Burmen	—S	Landed in Crimea 13/7/55. Deceased
3043	William Burnett	AIBS	22/1/55 Scutari
4043	William Burnnett	—S	Died
4610	Thomas Burrnett	—S	Regt. 18/7/57
4224	Alfred Burns	—S	Landed in Crimea 17/6/55
2907	Michael Burns	AI–S	
3415	Thomas Burns	—S	
1954	Thomas Burns	[...]	Has the same No. As T. Burley ?
3819	Charles/John Burrell	—S	Landed in Crimea 28/11/54. Died Scutari
4423	David Burridge	—S	Landed in Crimea 22/2/55
4394	James Burrin/ Burrier	—S	Killed 10/8/55. WO 8/12/56
3616	Frederick Burrman	—S	Died
3326	W. [Henry] Burrows	AIBS	Sly/Wounded 26/7/55. Photo R.B.C. 1911 gives initial as W
4087	Henry Burrows	—S	Landed in Crimea 13/7/55
2997	Benjamin Burton	AIBS	
1963/1973 3621/3624/	James Butcher	AIBS	Scutari Regt 20/7/57
644	Patrick Butler	AIBS	Wounded 5/11/57 Inkerman
3552	Samuel Butler	AIBS	Died 30/1/55 Crimea
4526	William Butterwick	—S	Landed in Crimea 17/6/55. Regt. 19/9/56
3137/3157	George Button	AIBS	Wounded 5/11/54 Inkerman. England H+R 23/10?

3712	Joseph Caddy	AIBS	Wounded 5/11/54 Inkerman. England So 18/8/56
2465	John Calderbank	AI–S	KIA Inkerman 5/11/54. SA'53
3734	Patrick Calvey	AIBS	KIA 18/6/55. H+R for WO L/5/56
3439	Fredrick Campbell	AIBS	Sly/Wounded 20/11/54. DOW 26/11/54
3920	Thomas Cane	—S	Landed in Crimea 28/11/54. Died 21/8/55 Crimea
2757	G. Cann/ Cain	AI—	Wounded/Died 24/6/55
2905	Peter Carney/ Cairney	—S	Landed in Crimea 26/1/55. Died 9–10/8/55
3656	James Carr	—S	
2839	William Carroll	—S	Landed in the Crimea 26/1/55
4002	Thomas Cartwright	—S	Landed in the Crimea 26/1/55
4320	Edward Clarke	—S	Landed in Crimea 13/7/55
4048	Henry Callier	—S	Landed in Crimea 13/7/55
3427	Thomas Carr	AIBS	KIA 22/11/54
1635	Eli Carson	AIBS	Died 28/12/54 Crimea. SA'53
3871	David Carter	—S	Died 1/11/55 Crimea
3323	George Carter	A–BS	Wounded 5/11/55 Inkerman. Died 29/11/54. H+R for WO 31/12/56
4142	Henry Carter	—S	Landed in Crimea 26/1/55
3283	James Carter	AIBS	DOW 20/11/54
3975	Charles Cartwright	AIBS	Wounded 11–12/8/55. Died WO 16/3/57
3648	Joseph Cartwright	AIBS	Died 1/3/55 Crimea WO 16/3/57
4002	Thomas Cartwright	—S	Sev Wounded 7/6/55 Quarries. Died 31/7/55
4517	John Catchbill/ Catchbite	—S	Landed in Crimea 22/2/55
2919	Charles Catchpole	AI–S	Wounded 5/11/54 Inkerman. DOW 10/12/54. Scutari
3557	John Catford	—S	Scutari
3446	George Cato	A—S	Died 8/12/54 Crimea
3539	J. Caycaed	AIB—	
4424	George Challis	—S	Landed in Crimea 22/2/55
3742	John Channing/ Charming	AIBS	
2733	George Chapman	AIBS	SA'53 Medal
2558/2587	Horatio Chapman	A—S	Died 4/10/54. SA'53 Medal
3392	Walter Chapman	–IBS	

3946	John Cherry	—S	Landed in Crimea 17/6/55. Wounded/Sev 21/8/55 Balaclava
3567/3587 3793	Charles Chilton William Chittleborough	AI–S —S	Landed in Crimea 17/6/55
3697	James Christie	AI—	25/11/54
2937	A. Clarke	—S	SA'53 Medal
4357/4557	Charles Clarke	—S	Landed in Crimea 22/2/55
3311	Daniel Clarke	AIBS	Sly/Wounded 10/7/55
4529	Emanuel Clarke	—S	Landed in Crimea 13/7/55, Sent to England. Mint
2669	George Clarke	AI–S	SA'53 Medal
4593	George Clarke	—S	Landed in Crimea 12/6/55. Wounded Dangerously. 5/7/55. Died 13/7/55
3328	John Clarke	AIBS	Scutari
4125	Robert Clarke	—S	Landed in Crimea 13/7/55. Died 1/8/55
3728/3738	John Clarkson	AIBS	
3464	Edwin Clayton	AIBS	
2853	James (T) Clayton	AI–S	
3431	John Cleary	AIBS	
3/2815	Cornelius Clews	AIBS	Wound Inkerman 5/11/54. Wound/Dead 6/8/55. SA'53 Medal.
3983	Robert Clifford	—S	Landed in Crimea 26/1/55
2958	John Coats	AI–S	25/1/55 Scutari. Died WO 16/3/57+sa'53.
3613	John Cockley/ Coakley	AIBS	W 5/11/54 Inkerman. Died 18/12/54.
3861	Thomas Cockburns	—S	Landed in Crimea 26/1/55
3150	Joseph Coe	AIBS	Died 3/3/55 Crimea
4048	Henry Collier	—S	
4126	William Cole	—S	Landed in Crimea 13/7/55. Scutari Mint 31/1/57
4166	Henry Coleman	—S	Landed in Crimea 17/6/55
4043	Henry Coalman/ Coleman	—S	
4088	James Collins	—S	Landed in Crimea 13/7/55
2760	John Collins	AI–S	6/2/55 Scutari Died WO 16/3/57
3586	Peter Collins	AIBS	Sly/Wounded 22/11/54. England. Mint 20/10?
2148	Samuel Collins	AIBS	
3714	Timothy Collins	AIBS	Sly/Wounded 18/6/55 Redan

3356	William Colnett	A—S	Died
2504	William Compton	AIBS	Died 1/3/55 Crimea
2786	John Connolly/ Conolly?		
2506	Patrick Connolly	AI–S	Died Scutari 13/1/55
2195	Michael Conron/ Couron	AI–S	Died Scutari 20/12/54 WO 28/4
2273	Charles Constable	AIBS	Died Scutari 2/1/55
4211	Joseph Cook	——S	Landed in Crimea 17/6/55. Regt. 19/8/56
4433	Thomas Cook	——S	Landed in Crimea 17/6/55. England Mint 31/11?
1632	Edward Coombs	AI–S	England
4293	Charles Cooper	——S	Landed in Crimea 13/7/55. Sly/Wounded 22/8/55 Regt 19/8/56. H+R 29/11/56
4325	Edward Cooper	——S	Landed in Crimea 17/6/55
4660	James Cooper	——S	
1500/1506	John Cooper	——S	Landed in Crimea 13/7/55. England D(epot) 24/6/57
3797	Charles Cooper	——S	Landed in Crimea 27/1/55
3053	Thomas Cooper	AIBS	Photo in R.B.C. with initial C
3764/3754	Edward Copmer/ Copner	AI–S	Died 13/12/54 Crimea
3558/3568	John Cordner	AIBS	
4221	David Costello	——S	Landed in Crimea 12/6/55. Sent to England
3300/3350	William Cotton/ Colton	A—S	
3989	Thomas Deller Couch	——S	Landed in Crimea 26/1/55. Missing Redan 18/6/55. Died 10/7/55
2688	Robert Coulter	AI–S	Scutari
3256	John Coulton	AIBS	Died 20/3/55 Crimea
3824	George Courson/ Collison	——S	
3472	J. Cousins	A——	
4441	Alfred Cox	——S	Landed in Crimea 17/6/55 Dead
3357	Alfred Cox	——S	
4486	Fredrick Cox	——S	Landed in Crimea 12/6/55 Scutari
3906	Thomas Cox	——S	Landed in Crimea 28/11/54. Scutari
3895	William Cox	——S	Landed in Crimea 27/1/55

3383/5	Joseph Cragg	AI–S	England S0 23/12/56
3659	Charles Crauston	AIBS	Died 1/11/55 Scutari
5223	James Crawford	—S	Landed in Crimea 17/6/55
2429	Caleb Croft	—S	Died 12/2/55 Scutari
3740	John Croonan/ Cronan	—S	Landed in Crimea 28/11/54. Died 26/6/55 Crimea
3700	T. Cropon	–I—	
4449	Samuel Crouch	—S	Landed in Crimea 13/7/55. Died 29/8/55
5228	Thomas/john Crow/ Crowe	—S	Landed in Crimea 17/6/55
3700	Thomas Croxton	—S	
3423	Richard Cruse	AI–S	Died 23/2/55 Crimea WO 18/11/56
2876	Thomas Cryer	AIBS	Scutari
4470	John/ William Cummings	—S	Landed in Crimea 13/7/55. Died 8/9/55 W0
4468	Edward Cunningham	—S	Landed in Crimea 13/7/55. Wound/Dangly 2/8/55 Scutari
3121	Edward Curle	A—S	Died 1/2/55 Scutari
4616/4416	John Curtis	—S	Landed in Crimea 22/2/55. Scutari
3703	Thomas Dafters	A—S	
4156	John Daley	—S	Landed in Crimea 13/7/55
3232	George Daines	AIBS	
4061	Francis Darcey	—S	Landed in Crimea 26/1/55. England
4178	David Davis	—S	Landed in Crimea 13/7/55
3735	Edward Davis/ Davies	—S	Landed in Crimea 17/1/55
3635	Jepic/ Jesse Davis	—S	Landed in Crimea 28/11/54
4097	Robert Davis	—S	Landed in Crimea 26/1/55. Died 22/2/55 Crimea
4562	Thomas Davis/ Davies	—S	Landed in Crimea 22/2/55
3230/3250	Daniel Davis/ Davies	AIBS	Wounded Inkerman 5/11/54 Died H+R 9/12/56
3400	Edwin/ Edward Davies	AI–S	Sly/Wounded 8/9/55 Redan. Medal H+R 26/?/56

3512/3572	Thomas Davis/ Davies	AIBS	
2573	William Davis/ Davies	AI–S	
2728	William Davis/ Davies	AI–S	KIA 5/11/54 Inkerman England
3779	William Davis/ Davies	AIBS	Sly/Wounded 28/6/55 And 3/8/55. Regt 19/8/58
3274	John Davison	AIBS	Died WO 10/1/55 Scutari
4960	Joseph/John Dawson	—S	Landed in Crimea 13/7/55 Scutari
3364/3702	Walter Dawson	—S	Died 23/1/53 Scutari
3302	James Day	AIB–	31/10/54 Balaklava
4426	James Day	—S	Landed in Crimea 22/2/55. Scutari
3387	William Day	AI–S	England D(epot) 24/6/57
4362	James Dayton	—S	Landed in Crimea 26/1/55. to Mint
4287	James Dean	—S	
4287/4237	James Dean	—S	Landed in Crimea 13/7/55
3664	William Dean	A——	Died 22/9/54 Crimea
2721/3731	George Dear/ Deal	AIBS	
3430	John Delaney	—S	Landed in Crimea 17/6/55. Killed 3–4/8/55 WO 24/9/56
3957/3959	John Deller	—S	Landed in Crimea 27/1/55. Died 3/4/55 Crimea
4594/4591	Henry Demaitt/ Demsnin	—S	Landed in Crimea 17/6/55
1531	John Demmett	AIBS	
3404	Francis Denn(e)y/ Debby	AIBS	Wounded 5/11/54 Inkerman. England H+R 13/2?
3653/4	James Denny	AIBS	H+R 19/1/57
4117	John Dewhurst	—S	Landed in Crimea 22/2/55. England
3530	Patrick Dewhurst	—S	Died 31/7/55
3849	John Dickenson	—S	Landed in Crimea 28/11/54. Died 18/3/55
4570	Thomas Digby	—S	Landed in Crimea 22/2/55
3905	Henry Dobbey	—S	Landed in Crimea 28/11/54. Died 20/2/55 Scutari
3300/3364	John Docker	A–BS	Died 19/4/55 Scutari
3325	John Dodd	AIBS	KIA 20/11/54

3772	Henry Doe	A—S	Died 29/10/54 England
4402	William Doe	—S	Landed in Crimea 26/1/55
2779	Michael Dohoney	AIBS	
4365	William Donahue	—S	Landed in Crimea 22/2/55
3429	Frederick Done	A—	Not recorded Scutari
2914	William Doran	AIBS	Wounded/5/11/54 Inkerman. England Mint 20/9/57
3530	Patrick Dougherty	AIB–	1/8/55 Same No. as Patrick Dewhurst?
3005	J. Dowling	AI—	
1985/6	James Dowell/ Dowsell	AI–S	
	William Drayton	—S	Landed in Crimea 13/7/55
2203	William Druse/ Druce	AIBS	England WO 16/3/57
3882	Edward Dryer/ Dyer	—S	Sly/Wounded 23/1/53
4467	James Dudney/ Dendney	—S	Landed in Crimea 13/7/55. So 16/4/57
2580	John Duggan	AIBS	
	Arthur Dunn	—S	Depot 20/1/?
1404	Patrick Dunn	AIBS	England
2831	Robert Dunn	AIBS	28/1/55 Scutari. Wo16/3/57
4376	George Durant	—S	Landed in Crimea 22/2/55
3414/3	Frederick Durham	AIBS	
3016	George Durrant	—S	Landed in Crimea 9/4/55. Scutari
3822	Edward Dyer	—S	Landed in Crimea 28/11/54
3420	John Dyson	A–BS	Died 9/3/55 Scutari
2296	John Eagle	AIBS	KIA 12/4/55. SA'53
2682	Walter Eagle	AIBS	Sev/Wounded 23/11/55. England H+R 1/3/? SA'53, FMM
3139/3199	John East	A—?	12/8/54 Died Beikos, Asiatic side of the Bosphorus
4448	James Ebbard	—S	Landed in Crimea 17/6/55. Died 1/7/55
4217	Hugh Eccles	—S	Landed in Crimea 12/6/55
3543	J. Edwards	A—	
4536	James Edwards	—S	Landed in Crimea 12/6/55
4373	William Edwards	—S	Landed in Crimea 13/7/55
3582	Thomas Elgar	AIBS	
3975	Henry Wells Elkin	—S	Landed in Crimea 26/1/55. England Scutari

4630	Edward Elliot	—S	Landed in Crimea 13/1/55 Scutari
3306	Henry Elliot	AI—	25/3/55/ Scutari
3970	Peter Elliott	—S	Landed in Crimea 26/1/55
4901	James Ellis	—S	Landed in Crimea 17/6/55. Sev/ Wounded 15/8/55
3652/3632	Thomas John Emmerson	AIBS	Died 5/12/54
4012	Robert English	—S	Landed in Crimea 26/1/55
2185/8	James [...]		
2188	Francis Evans	AIBS	Died 25/1/55 Scutari
3040	William Evans	AIBS	Killed 12/4/55
4018	William Evans	—S	Landed in Crimea 26/1/55. Died, Mint 8/3/62
4478	Julian Evarny/ Evamy	—S	Landed in Crimea 13/7/55. Sly/ Wounded 21/8/55 And 4/9/55
4452	James Everitt	—S	Landed in Crimea 22/2/55. Died 14/7/55
3848	William Evershed	—S	Landed in Crimea 26/1/55. Scutari
3722	Matthew Evert/ Evett	AIBS	Died
2964	Samuel Eyres	AIBS	Died
4490	George Farcey	—S	Landed in Crimea 13/7/55
3799	Richard Farey	—S	Landed in Crimea 28/11/54 Scutari
2890	William Fairburn/ Farbourn	A—S	Died 24/10/54 Scutari
3937	Thomas Fall/ Farr	—S	Landed in Crimea 26/1/55. Killed in Trenches 15/5/55
2920	John Fallon	—S	Died 7/12/54
4284	James Farquharson/ Farghamson	—S	Landed in Crimea 12/6/55. Sly/ Wounded 9/8/55
3799	Richard Farley/ Farey	—S	Landed in Crimea 28/11/54
3939	George Farndell	—S	Landed in Crimea 26/1/55
2167/3167	Christopher Farrell	AIBS	Died 13/3/55 Scutari. SA'53
3621	John Farrell	AI–S	KIA Inkerman 5/11/54 England
3543	Michael Farrell	—S	Died
3604	Michael Farrell	AIB—	16/2/55 Crimea
3693	Frederick Faulkner	—S	Landed in Crimea 28/11/54

3080	William Feakins/? Ferkins	AIBS	Sly/Wounded 28/12/54 Died 24/12/?
1619	John Fearn	AIBS	
3725	Edward Fenn	AI–S	Died 30/12/54
3721	Charles Fennell	AIBS	
2781/2787	Joseph Fergy	AIBS	SA'53 Medal
2800	Henry Ferris	AI–S	SA'53 Medal
3072	William Ferris	AIBS	H+R 19/3/?. SA'53 Medal
3625	Edward Fiddeman/Fiddiman	AIBS	Wounded 5/11/54 Inkermann
3281	James Field	AIBS	Sly/Wounded 7/7/55
3832	Joseph Field	——S	Landed in Crimea 28/11/54. Died 30/1/55 Scutari WO 24/9/56
4691	John Finch	——S	Landed in Crimea 17/6/55
4537	William Dean Finch	——S	Sev/Wounded 18/6/55 Redan
3878	Robert Finley	——S	Landed in Crimea 28/11/54 Scutari
4499	Henry Fisher	——S	Landed in Crimea 17/6/55. Died 9/7/55
4330	John Fisher	——S	Landed in Crimea 13/7/55
3260	J. Fisher	AIB–	
4307	Thomas Fisher	——S	Landed in Crimea 13/7/55. Died 12/8/55
3140	William Fisher	A—S	Regt 19/9/56
5210	William Fisher	——S	Landed in Crimea 30/7/55. Regt 20/7/57
2918/4912	Edward Fitzgerald	AIBS	
4413	George Flack	——S	Landed in Crimea 22/2/56
4400	John Flannery	——S	Landed in Crimea 27/1/55. KIA 18/6/55 Redan
2955	J. Flanagan	A——	SA'53 Medal
4190	Patrick/john Flanagan	——S	Landed in Crimea 13/7/55
3457/67	Henry Fleckney/Fleeking	AI–S	Died H+R 13/10/?
4008	Benjamin Fleming	——S	Landed in Crimea 27/1/55. Died 20/5/55 WO 16/3/57
2757	John Floyd	——S	Died
2813/2873	John Floyd	AIB–	4/3/55 Scutari
3513	James Flynn	AIBS	
3479	James Flynn	AIBS	Scutari
2893	John Flynn	AIBS	Sev/Wounded 20/11/54
3414/3514	John Flynn	AI–S	

4216	Henry Foster	—S	Landed in Crimea 17/6/55
3746	Henry Fowler	A—S	
1924	James Fox	AI–S	England. SA'53 Medal
2961	James Fox	AIBS	KIA 20/11/54 WO 16. 3. 57
3976	Edward Foxley	—S	Died 27/2/55 Crimea. Landed in the Crimea 27/11/54
3566	John Francis	AIBS	
4494	John Francis	—S	Landed in Crimea 13/7/55 Died
5191	John Francis	—S	Landed in Crimea 13/7/55
4632	Thomas Francis	—S	Landed in Crimea 13/7/55. Scutari
3633	Edward Freeman	—S	
1544	Simon Frindle	AI–S	England H+R 29/2/?. SA'53
4183	William Frost	—S	Landed in Crimea 17/6/55. Died 16/8/55 Scutari WO 9/4/57
4437/4407	William Fry	—S	Landed in Crimea 17/6/55. Died 4/7/55
4419	Jesse Fryer	—S	Landed in Crimea 22/2/55
4678/4670	Henry Fuller	—S	Landed in Crimea 13/7/55
4633	Edward Fueman	—S	Landed in Crimea 12/6/55
3825	Michael Funnigan	—S	Landed in Crimea 26/1/55
4306	Decimus Fursidale/ Finedale	—S	Landed in Crimea 12/6/55
2834	John Gaffing/ Gaffney	—S	Landed in Crimea 27/1/55
3622	Patrick Garraghan	–IBS	Regt 19/9/56
3556	J. Garraghly	AIB—	
4731	James Geat/ Greet	—S	Landed in Crimea 13/7/55
3633/3733	James George	AIBS	Died
3536	Peter Geraghty	—S	
3593/96	Peter Gerrie/ Gerris	AIBS	
2599	Charles Gibbons	AIBS	Sev/W 22/11/54 Died 10/1/55 Crimea. SA'53
3373	Robert Gibbons/ Gibbins	AIBS	
3022	Alfred Gibbs	AI–S	SA'53 England H+R 22/3/?
3962	William Gibbs	—S	Landed in Crimea 27/1/55
2414	W. Gibson	AI—	
2544	William Gibson	AIBS	
3465/3464	John Gill/gile	AIBS	Died 4/12/54 Mint 31/8/57. WO 20/8/57
3173/3176	James Gillings	AIBS	Died 6/8/55 Scutari
2631/3631	Nathanial Gilpin/ Gilham		A—S Died 4/12/54 Scutari. 10/12?
4540	John Gladwin	—S	Landed in Crimea 22/2/55. England
3498	James Gleeson	AIBS	

2123	Michael Gleeson	AI–S	SA'53
3606	Patrick Glynn	AIBS	
3002	Charles Goad	AI–S	SA'53 19/1/55 Scutari
4027	Richard Goodeve	——S	Landed in Crimea 27/1/55
3501/3581	James Godfrey	A——S	Died 15/1/55 Crimea
3768	Edward Golder	——S	Landed in Crimea 28/11/54. Died 26/2/55
3284	George Goldey/ Gooley	A——S	
3398	Alexander Goodbody	AIBS	
4202	Edward Goodenough	——S	Landed in Crimea 12/6/55. 1/1/56
3048	Robert Goodfellow	–IBS	Wounded 13–17/10/54 Died Scutari 21/3/55
4027	Richard Goodeve	——S	
3916	Obed Goodman	——S	Landed in Crimea 17/6/55
4575/4515	William Goodyear	——S	Landed in Crimea 17/6/55
3998	George Gorden/ Goodeve	——S	Landed in Crimea 26/1/55. Not recorded in Muster Rolls
3240	William Gordon	A——	
1533	William Gore	AI–S	SA'53 Medal
2910	George Goring	AIBS	SA'53 Medal
2873	Charles Gorten/ Gorton	AI–S	SA'53 Medal 29/1/55 Crimea
3991	James Gough	——S	England So 25/11/56. Landed in Crimea 26/1/55
3026	George Gould	AIBS	11/12/54 Died 10/12/?? SA'53
4041	George Gould	——S	Landed in Crimea 13/7/55
3991	James Gough	——S	Landed in Crimea 26/1/55. England SO 21/11/56
3401/3601	Patrick Grady	A——S	Died 9/12/54
1302	George Graham/ Gorham	AIBS	England. SA'53 Medal
1940	James Graham	AIBS	Killed 5/1/55 Crimea. SA'53
3409	William Graham	AIBS	SA'53 Medal
3227	John Green 1st	AIBS	Died 5/3/55 Crimea
3562	John Green 2nd	AIBS	Regt 19/9/56
4569	John Green	——S	Landed in Crimea 13/7/55. Sly/Wounded 11/8/55. England H+R 6/8/?
4692	Joseph Green	——S	Landed in Crimea 13/7/55. Died 13/8/55

3030	Mark Green	A—S	Scutari. SA'53
2906	James Grey/ Green	—S	
3533	John Grey/ Gray	AIBS	
3522/32	John Grey	AIBS	
3608/3096	Robert Grieve	AIBS	
3935	Thomas Griffiths	—S	Landed in Crimea 27/1/55. England
3086	James Griffiths	AIBS	Sly/Wounded 20/11/54 Died
3787	Thomas Griffiths	–I–S	Landed in Crimea 28/11/54. Inkerman Clasp?. Killed 20/1/55 Scutari
2763	Abraham Grigg	AIBS	Died 25/1/55. SA'53
4453	Henry Griggs	—S	Landed in Crimea 22/2/55
3397	William Griggs	AI–S	England
3444/3544	Henry Groom	—S	
3185	Robert Groom	AIBS	Died 1/2/55 WO 16/3/57
4199	William Groom	—S	Landed in Crimea 22/2/55
3116	John Gullett/ Gullit	AIBS	
4114	James Gunning	—S	Died 10/7/55 Crimea
4432	Jesse Guy	—S	Landed in Crimea 17/6/55
4045	John Gwens	—S	
1756	Thomas Gyngell	AIBS	Scutari (2/3/55 Corfu)
1790/96	George Haines	AIBS	Died 9/2/55 Crimea. SA'53
2496	William Hailwood	—S	
3360	Henry Haddon	A—S	Died 30/9/54 Crimea
3223	Joseph Haddon	AI–S	Scutari
3135	Thomas Hadway	A–BS	
2877	Charles Haggeity	—S	Landed in Crimea 28/11/54
3729	J. Haines	AIB–	
3418	Charles Hale/ Hall	—S	Landed in Crimea 13/7/55
2805	Robert Hale/ Hall	AIBS	England H+R 8/12/56. SA'53
4435	John Halfit	—S	Scutari
3302/05 3303	James Hall	AI–S	Died 23/2/55 Crimea
3949	Richard Hall/ Hale	—S	Landed in Crimea 22/2/55
2232/2233	William Hales/ Hall	AIBS	Sly/Wounded 23/11/54 Died Scutari. WO 8/2/55
2612	W. Hall	AI—	SA'53
2432	George Halliwell	AIBS	SA'53
1518	Edward Hallows	AIBS	Died 29/1/55 Crimea. SA'53
3575/3375	Joseph Hallum/ Hullum	AI–S	England WO 29/1/55 Scutari
3499/3699	Henry Ham	—S	Landed in Crimea 26/1/55
4348/4343	John Ham	—S	Landed in Crimea 17/6/55
1668	John Hamblin	AIBS	

3335	Charles Hamilton	AIBS	England H+R 20?/2/56. Turkish Medal Issued
2996	George Hammond	AIBS	Sly/W 4/12/54. SA'53 England
4457	Thomas Hammond	—S	Landed in Crimea 22/2/55
2838	Michael Hanify/ Hanfry	AIBS	W 5/11/54 Inkerman. SA'53
4780	George Hann	—S	Landed in Crimea 17/6/55 Died
2613	Robert Hannan/ Harman	AIBS	Died WO 24/9/57
3463/3643	William Hannell/ Hannill	—BS	
4601	William Hanson	—S	Landed in Crimea 13/7/55
3327/3527	William Hardie/ Hardy	A—S	Wounded 5/11/54 Inkerman Died WO 24/9/56
3045	J. Harding	A—	SA'53
3465	John Harding	—S	Died
4411	Henry Harding	—S	Landed in Crimea 22/2/55. Sev/ Wounded 4/9/55 Died 11/9/55
3505	William Hardy	AIBS	England
4435	John Harfin	—S	Landed in Crimea 17/6/55. Scutari
4631	Thomas Harfelt/ Harfin	—S	Landed in Crimea 17/6/55 Scutari
1775	William Hargreaves	A—	22/9/54 Crimea
3118	James Harman	AIBS	Died
3158/3458	[...]		
3450	John Harman	A—S	Died 1/10/54
3289/3489	Robert Harman/ Harmmer	AIBS	Wounded 5/11/54 Inkerman. Died 5/2/55 Crimea
2774	Edward Harrington/ Hampton	AIBS	Died. SA'53
4538	William Harrington	—S	Landed in Crimea 22/2/55
3670	Emanual/ Edward Harris	AI–S	KIA Inkerman 5/11/54
3413	G. Harris	A—	
3126	John Harris	AIBS	Died 14/2/55 Scutari WO 17/11/56
4427	John Harris	—S	Landed in Crimea 22/2/55
2563	William Harris	AIBS	Scutari WO +SA'53
3129	Henry Harrison	AIBS	

4120	Thomas Harrison	—S	Landed in Crimea 22/2/55. Sev/W 18/6/55 Redan. Scutari Regt 19/9/56
4501	William Harrison	—S	
3334	E. Hart	A—	
3382	Charles Hart	—S	
3223/3230	Dymoke Hart	—S	Landed in Crimea 22/2/55
3701	Frederick Hart	AIBS	Sl/Wounded 18/10/54
3238	F. William Hart	AIBS	
3245	Joseph Hart	AIBS	England
4542	Nathan Hart	—S	Landed in Crimea 22/2/56
2496	W. Harward	AIB—	
3266	George Hassell/ Hassele	AIBS	England
1588	George Hatcher	AI–S	Died 18/8/55. SA'53
4413	George Hawk	—S	
3964	Joseph Hawklebury/ Hartlebury	—S	Landed in Crimea 27/1/55
3683/6	Cornelius Hawkins	AIBS	
3362	Edward Hawkins	AIBS	Sev/Wounded 20/11/54
3147	James Hawkinsford/ Haswkford	AIBS	
4262	William Hayden	—S	
4283/4288	Charles Hayes	—S	Landed in Crimea 13/7/55
4038	John Hayes	—S	Landed in Crimea 26/1/55
4474	John Hayes/ Haynes	—S	Landed in Crimea 13/7/55
3309	J. Hayes	AI—	
3210	William Hayes	A—	18/1/55 Scutari
4676	William Hayes	—S	Landed in Crimea 13/7/55
3286	Henry Hayhoe	AIBS	Wounded/5/11/54 Inkerman. England H+R 17/2/56
3510	Robert Haylett	AI–S	England 4/1/55 Crimea
3241	Charles Hayman	AI–S	England H+R 2/11/?
3617	John Haymes	—S	England
2270	Robert Head	AIBS	W/ 5/11/54 Inkerman. England. SA'53 Medal
3541	David Healy	AIBS	Wounded 5/11/54 Inkerman
1837	James Hedges	AIBS	Died. SA'53 8/12/54
4209/4309	Patrick Hefferman	—S	Landed in Crimea 17/6/55
5207	Robert/ Richard Heggate/ Heggett	—S	Landed in Crimea 13/7/55
2488	Daniel Heimsath	AIBS	Died 5/3/55 Crimea. SA'53
4597/4479	John Hennicks	—S	Landed in Crimea 17/6/55
4100	Edward Henry	—S	Landed in Crimea 17/6/55

3877	Henry Herbert	—S	Landed in Crimea 28/11/54
2055	William Hermitage	AI–S	England. SA'53 Medal
2902	James Herring	AIBS	Died 2/1/55 Crimea WO. SA'53
4080	Alfred Hersey/ Hensey	—S	Landed in Crimea 13/7/55
2621	William He[...]thwaith	—S	
3280	Thomas Hickey/ Hickley	AIBS	Died 5/11/54 Inkerman WO 24/9/56
3879	Thomas Hickinbottom	AI—	Landed in Crimea 16/1/55
3650/2650	John Hicks/ Hinks	–IBS	12/1/55 Scutari. SA'53
3553	C. Hill	AI—	
4165	Edward Hile/ Hill	—S	Landed in Crimea 22/2/55
1172	Richard Hile/ Hill	AI–S	SA'53 Medal
3780	Robert Hill	—S	Landed in Crimea 28/11/54. Died 12/12/54
3480	Thomas Hills	AI—	22/9/54 Crimea
3931	George Hinson	—S	Landed in Crimea 26/1/55
3217	John Hodge	AIBS	
3219	William Hodge	AIBS	Wounded 5/11/54 Inkerman England
3367	George Hodges	AIBS	
4262	James Hogan	—S	Landed in Crimea 12/6/55
2398	William Hodges	AIBS	Wounded 5/11/54 Inkerman
1407	Edward Hogan	AIBS	
4503	John Hogan	—S	Landed in Crimea 17/6/55
3991	David Holden	—S	Died
4635/4638	Hugh Holden	—S	Landed in Crimea 12/6/55. Sly/Wound 10/8/55 Died 24/8/55
4060	Samuel Holden	—S	Landed in Crimea 17/6/55. Sev/Wounded 27/7/55
3911	William Holden	—S	Landed in Crimea 28/11/54. Died 12/2/55
4567	Thomas Holland	—S	Landed in Crimea 22/2/55. Sev/Wound 12/4/55 England Mint 7/3/59
3028	Henry Hollingsworth	–IBS	SA'53 Medal. Mutiny 79th Regt.
4822	George Holloway	—S	Landed in Crimea 13/7/55
4562/4502	William Holloway	—S	Landed in Crimea 17/6/55
3724	John Holmes	AIBS	
4387	Henry Holmes	—S	Landed in Crimea 13/7/55
4256	John Holt	—S	Landed in Crimea 12/6/55

4491	John Holton/ Haltham	—S	Landed in Crimea 13/7/55
3370	T. Holwell	A—	
2208	Thomas Holyland	AIBS	Died 8/9/55 Died 24/9/56
4637	Isaac Honeyball	—S	Landed in Crimea 22/2/55. Sev/ Wounded 10/7/55. Sent to Mint 25/1/60
3141	William Hookey	AIBS	
1419	Charles Hooper	AIBS	England
4196	George Hoper/ Hope	—S	Landed in Crimea 17/6/55
3449/3469	George Hopkins	AIBS	
3273	James Hopkins	AI–S	Sly/Wounded 22/11/54
4469	John/ James Hopkins	—S	Landed in Crimea 12/6/55 Scutari
1330	Thomas Horan	AIBS	Wounded 5/11/54 Inkerman DOW 13/12/54 WO 1/9/56
3820/2820	John Horkley/ Hockley	—S	Landed in Crimea 18/11/54. Scutari 6/2/55. WO 16/3/57
3090	Thomas Horne/ Home	AI–S	Wounded 5/11/54 Died 4/12/54. 17/11/56
4124	Michael Horrigan	—S	Landed in Crimea 12/6/55
3344	Ingram Hortan/ Horton	AIBS	
3739	John Hoskinson	AI–S	Died Crimea 1/2/55 WO 16/3/57
3001	Arthur Howard	AIBS	Sly/Wounded 20/11/54 Died 19/1/55. Scutari WO 16/8/57
3291	Francis Howard	—S	Landed in Crimea 28/11/54. Died 18/2/55 Crimea
3292	John Howe	AIBS	
1850	James Howshaw	—S	A 2050 James Howshaw was Servant to Brigadier Buller during the Crimea and Is entitled to a 3-Clasp Medal; also SA'53.
3486	J. Hubbard	A—	
3618	J. Huckle	AIB–	5/1/55 Scutari
2743	Edwin Hudson	AI–S	Sev/Wounded 2/12/54 Died 21/4/55. Scutari or Smyrna
2434	John Hudson	AI–S	Wounded 5/11/54 Inkerman Died

3680	William Hughban(d)	AIBS	
2139	Henry Hughes	AIBS	Died 18/2/55 Scutari
4422	John Hughes	—S	Landed in Crimea 17/6/55
3208	Patrick Hughes	AIBS	England Sl/W 22/11/54
3618	John Humble	—S	
4185	John Hunt	—S	Landed in Crimea 13/7/55
4428	Charles Hunt	—S	Landed in Crimea 12/6/55
4030	Charles Hunt	—S	Landed in Crimea 12/6/55. H+R 18/5/57
38?1	George Hunt	—S	
3699	J. Hunt	A—	
3320	William Hunt	AI–S	
3807	George Hurt	—S	Landed in Crimea 27/1/55
2978	James Hussey	AIBS	KIA 20/11/54
3963	Edward Hutchings	—S	Landed in Crimea 26/1/55
4418	Henry Hutchings	—S	Landed in Crimea 22/2/55 Scutari
4278/4272	Richard Hutchings	—S	Landed in Crimea 17/6/55. Sev/Wounded Balaklava H+R 27/5/56
1933	John Hutchinson	AIBS	England
3388	John Hutchinson	AIBS	
3482	Thomas Hutchinson	AI–S	Sev/Wounded 22/1/54. Missing believed dead. Scutari 1856
2621	W. Huthwaite	AIB–	
3170	(Wm.) John Hutton	AIBS	Sev/Wounded 20/11/54. Died WO 16/3/57
4185/4105	James Huxtable/Hurtable	—S	Landed in Crimea 13/7/55
4421	James Inglefield	—S	Landed in Crimea 17/6/55
3590	Henry Ingram	AIBS	
3463	John Ingram	—S	Landed in Crimea 26/1/55. Died 8/2/55
3134	Richard Irons	AI–S	Died 15/11/54
3778	George Ives	—S	Landed in Crimea 28/11/54 Scutari. England
3461	Isaac Ivett	AIBS	
1242/8	James Jackson	AIBS	SA'53 Medal 16/7/55
2933	Thomas Jackson	A–BS	Died. SA'53
1315/4515	William Jackson	—S	Landed in Crimea 22/2/55
3561	J. Jago	A—	

3451	Robert Jacques	—S	Landed in Crimea 26/1/55. Canada Medal. Photo R.B.C. 1911
5156	Edward James	—S	
3352	George James	A–BS	14/1/55 Scutari England D(epot) 24/6/57
4017	William Jeeves	—S	Landed in Crimea 13/7/55
3990	John Jefferys/ Jeffereys		—S Landed in Crimea 27/1/55. Killed 12/8/55 Crimea
3788	John Jenkins	—S	Landed in Crimea 28/11/54 Died
3474	John Jenkins	–IBS	Died 24/12/54
2865	Christopher Jesson	AIBS	Sly/Wounded 20/11/54 Died Scutari 21/1/55. SA'53 Medal
[...]	W. Jesson	AI—	SA'53 Medal
3786	Daniel Johnson	—S	Landed in Crimea 28/11/54. Died 30/11/54
3796	George Jessor	—S	
4564	George Johnson	—S	Landed in Crimea 22/2/55
2720	Henry Johnson	AIBS	Died Scutari 21/1/55. SA'53
1905	John Johnson	—S	England
3313	Richard Johnstone	AIBS	Sev/Wounded 20/11/54 England. H+R L9/2/?
1321	Thomas Johnstone/ Johnson		AI–S England SA'53 Medal
4310	Charles Jones	—S	Landed in Crimea 13/7/55
3687	Edward Jones	A—S	Died 17/11/54. SA'53
3549	George Jones	AIBS	
3661/3061	George Jones	AI–S	DOW 10/11/54
3674	George Jones	AIBS	Sev/Wounded 9/8/55
3672/2672	John Jones	—S	Sev/Wounded 30/1/55. Scutari 30/1/55
2936	R. Jones	AIB—	Wounded 5/11/54 Inkerman
3910/3911	Samuel Jones	—S	Landed in Crimea 26/1/55 Scutari
3076	Samuel Jones	——	Died 19/4/54 Crimea 17/9/?
3239	Thomas Jones	AIBS	Wounded 5/11/54 Inkerman
1848	William Jones	AI–S	Died 3/3/55 Smyrna WO 16/3/57. SA'53 Medal
3888	William Jones	—S	Landed in Crimea 28/11/54. H+R 15/3/?
3863	William Benj. Jones	—S	Landed in Crimea 28/11/54 Scutari. England
3865	James Jordan	—S	Landed in Crimea 28/11/54. Died 13/1/55 Scutari WO 16/3/?

4379	Richard Jordan	—S	Landed in Crimea 13/7/55 Scutari
4673	Thomas Jordan	—S	Landed in Crimea 17/6/55 Scutari. Regt. 19/9/56
2772	Henry Josling	AIBS	England
4978	Charles Juger	—S	Landed in Crimea 22/2/55. Died 15/5/55
4878	Charles [...]ge	—S	Died
3985	Michael Kane/ Caine	—S	Landed in Crimea 27/1/55. KIA 18/6/55 Redan
3573	Francis Kavanagh	AIBS	Wounded 5/11/54 Inkerman
3523	Thomas Kearney	A—S	
3519	W. Kearney	AIB–	
4886	James Keenes	—S	Landed in Crimea 13/7/55
3961	Thomas Keiby	—S	Landed in Crimea 26/1/55. England H+R 13/5/?
3550/3650	David Kellett/ Killate	–I–S	
3515	James Kelly	A–BS	SA'53 Medal
	John Kelly	—S	
1249/4154	W. Kempsharl/ Kempshale	—S	Landed in Crimea 22/2/55. 3rd Bn 60th Foot
2716	Robert Kent	AI–S	Died 5/3/55 Scutari. SA'53
3756	J. Kerr/kern	AI—	Died 5/12/54
3651	L. P. Kerr	AI—	
2871	Robert Kerr	—S	
1687	Henry Kibby	AIBS	England. SA'53 Medal
4254	Richard Kidd	—S	Landed in Crimea 17/6/55 Scutari. England
2226	Charles Kiersey	AIBS	SA'53 Medal
1983	John Kiley/ Kiely	AIBS	SA'53 Medal
2117	John Kilroe	A—S	SA'53 Medal
4193	Charles King	—S	Landed in Crimea 17/6/55
4158/4150	Elias King	—S	Landed in Crimea 22/2/55
2629	John King	AIBS	Wounded 5/11 /54 Inkerman. England H+R 29/7/?. SA'53
3441	John King	AIBS	Wounded 5/11/54 Inkerman. England. SA'53
3646	Richard King	AIBS	Scutari
3856	Samuel King	—S	Landed in Crimea 28/11/54. Died Scutari 5/3/55
1722	William King	AIBS	SA'53 Medal
4398/3498	William King	—S	Landed in Crimea 22/2/55

4316	Edwin Kingham	—S	Landed in Crimea 17/6/55
3380	J. Kirby	—	
3156	David Kislingbury	AIBS	Died 11/2/55 Scutari WO 9/4/57
3262	Charles Knapp	AIBS	Died 19/1/55 Crimea.
3660	George Kneller	AIBS	KIA 5/11/54, WO 29/11/56
1413	Thomas Knight	AIBS	Wounded 5/11/54 Inkerman
3312	Daniel Knowles	—S	Landed in Crimea 28/11/54. Died 17/2/55
2515	Thomas James Lacey	AIBS	Died 21/9/54
3798	Thomas Ladd	—S	Landed in Crimea 26/1/55. England D(epot) 25/6/57
3297	Peter Lafferty	AIBS	Sly/Wounded 18/6/55 Redan
3330	Thomas Lake	AIBS	England H+R 20/12/56
2819	Edward Lamb	AI–S	
3337	James Lamb	AIBS	SA'53 Medal
3013	John Lambert	AIBS	Died 1/2/55 Crimea. SA'53
4532	Simon Lambert	—S	Landed in Crimea 22/2/55. Died 13/5/55 Crimea
3014	Patrick Lamming/ Richard Lanning	AIBS	L/6/55 At Sea
4715/4713	Robert Lanaway	—S	Landed in Crimea 17/6/55. Canada Medal. Photo in R.B.C. 1911
4182	George Lane	—S	Landed in Crimea 17/6/55
4345	Henry Lane	—S	Landed in Crimea 17/6/55
3727	James Lane	AIBS	DOW 15–16/11/54. 16/12/?
5215	Robert Lane	—S	Landed in Crimea 17/6/55
4141	Samuel/James Lane	—S	Landed in Crimea 13/7/55
3771/3791	Stephen Langbridge	—S	Landed in Crimea 26/1/55. Scutari H+R 10/3/57
4897	Charles Langford	—S	
3918	James Larcombe	—S	Landed in Crimea 26/1/55
4406	Charles Larkham	—S	Landed in Crimea 27/1/55. Died 29/7/55
3406	Charles Larkin/ Lockyer	AIBS	
1919	John Latchford	AIBS	Bandsman
3899	George Latham	—S	Landed in Crimea 26/1/55
3979	William Latham	—S	Landed in Crimea 27/1/55
3475	George Law	A—S	England
2704	Richard Law	AIBS	SA'53 Medal
2903	Edward Laws	AIBS	Scutari. SA'53 Medal

4439	Abraham/ William Lawrence	—S	Landed in Crimea 17/6/55. Wounded/Dead 12/8/55
4212	Charles Lawrence	—S	
3322	Charles Laycock	AIBS	England
2923	John Leach/ Leech	AIBS	SA'53 Medal
3236	Thomas Lees	A—	21/9/54 Crimea
3460	William Leach/ Leech/ Leich	AI–S	Died 8/12/54
3487	James Leggett/ Leggate	—BS	Killed 14/1/55 Crimea
1994	Thomas Leighfield	AIBS	Died Smyrna 8/3/55. SA'53
4336	Alfred Lemon	—S	Landed in Crimea 17/6/55
3437	Charles Lewis	AIBS	DOW 31/10/54
3880	Charles Lewis	—S	Landed in Crimea 26/1/55
3167	Joseph Lewis	–IBS	England
3595	Patrick Linch/ Lynch	A—S	Scutari
2859	George Lines	A—S	Died 18/6/55 Crimea Redan. WO 16/3/57
3393	Abraham Linfield	AIBS	Died 24/12/54 Scutari
3750	J. Llewellyn	A—	
3841	Morgan Llewllyn	—S	
4492	R. Lloyd	—S	Landed in Crimea 17/6/55
4507/4567	William Lloyd	—S	Landed in Crimea 12/6/55
4482	Francis Lloyd	—S	Landed in Crimea 13/7/55 Scutari
3741	George Lock	—S	Landed in Crimea 27/1/55
4058/4054	Charles Locke	—S	Landed in Crimea 13/7/55 Scutari. Turkish Medal, Canada Medal. Photo in R.B.C. 1911
3046	Charles Locker/ Larkin	AIBS	
*2222	George Lockton	AI–S	Died 27/11/54. Issued with two medals, one with clasps Alma; Inkerman; both impressed
3085	Henry Lockwood	A–BS	Died Scutari 24/1/55
4626	Thomas Lodge	—S	Landed in Crimea 12/6/55 Died. Scutari
4168/4102	James Lord	—S	Landed in Crimea 22/2/55
3638/3658	Francis Love	AI–S	Scutari Missing/Dead 1856
2204	Alfred Lovell	AI–S	Dead
3686	Joseph Lowle/ Lowe	A—S	Wounded 13–17/10/54 England 7/9/56

3304	John Lucking	A—S	
4259	James Mabe	—S	Landed in Crimea 13/7/55
3897	James Mace	—S	Landed in Crimea 27/1/55 Scutari
3506	John Mack	AIBS	Wounded 5/11/54 Inkerman
3833	James Madauld	—S	Landed in Crimea 26/1/55. Sev/ Wounded 10/7/55
4007	John Maesdale	—S	Landed in Crimea 26/1/55 Scutari
3950	George Maffey	—S	Landed in Crimea 27/1/55
3690	William Mahony/ Maloney	A–BS	Died
3745/3745	Charles Maidment	AIBS	Died 22–23/11/54 Crimea
3390	Samuel Makepeace/ Makepaece	AIBS	Wounded 5/11/54 Inkerman
2557	Thomas Makepiece	AIBS	England. SA'53
3827	John Maloney	—S	Landed in Crimea 26/1/55. Sly/ Wounded 8/9/55 Redan
3410	William Maloney/ Moloney	AIBS	
3196	Charles Mansbridge	—S	
3195	T. Mansbridges	AIB–	
3068	John Mansfield/ Masfield		
3839	John Manning	—S	
4543	James Manson	—S	
3428/3488	George Mapleloft	—BS	Dead
4446	Joseph Mapi[...]er	—S	Landed in Crimea 17/6/55
3776	George Martin	—S	Landed in Crimea 27/1/55. Sly/ Wounded 10/8/55
3829	John Mann[...]ly	—S	Landed in Crimea 27/1/55
3792	William Mansell	—S	Landed in Crimea 27/1/55
3878	Thomas Marriot	—S	Landed in Crimea 16/1/55. Regt 19/9/56
4376	John Marcham	—S	Landed in Crimea 22/2/55
3489	William Marks	AIBS	
2864/2804	William Marley	AIBS	5/11/54 Killed Inkerman. DOW 8/11/54
3878	Thomas Marriot/ Mariott	—S	Landed in Crimea 16/1/55
3447	John Marshall	—S	Dead
4890	Charles Martin	—S	Landed in Crimea 22/2/55. Regt 19/9/56
3060	John Martin	AIBS	DOW 8/11/ Scutari. SA'53. 27/9/ 56

3725	Richard Martin	AIBS	W 5/11/54 Inkerman
2041	Thomas Martin	AIBS	England Regt /57. SA'53
2128	Thomas Martin	AIBS	W 13–17/10/54
2659	William Martin	AIBS	SA'53
	Masefield	AIBS	5/3/55 Died Scutari. SA'53
4464	George Maslin	—S	Landed in the Crimea 12/6/55
4414	Charles Mason	—S	Landed in the Crimea 22/2/1855
5018	Charles Mason	—S	Landed Crimea 13/7/1855
3290	George Mason	—S	Dead 5/2/55 Scutari
3665	Thomas Mason	AIBS	England Regt 20/7/57
4338	William Mason	—S	
3528/3258	John Matson	AIBS	Sly/Wounded 22/11/54
3101	David Matthews	AIBS	Dead 27/9/55
3783	George Matthews	AI–S	Dead 22/3/55
3428	J. Matthews	AIB–	
3446	John Matthews	—S	
3082	Thomas Matthews	AIBS	England
5246	Robert Mathison	—S	Landed in Crimea 17/6/55
5236	Robert Mathison	—S	Sly/Wounded 6/8/55. 5/1/56 Crimea
4034	John May	—S	Landed in Crimea 26/1/1855
2131	John Mayth/ Mathyr	AIBS	Sev/Wounded 15/11/54 H+R 9/3/56
3564	Timothy McAuliffe	AI–S	Sly/Wounded 15/11/54
2656	Patrick McCann	AIBS	SA'53 & FMM
[...]	John McCarty/ McCarty	—S	
2878	Peter McConnell	AIBS	Sly/Wounded 9/6/55 & 6/8/55
3639	James McCormick	—S	Landed in Crimea 17/5/55
1363/3363	John McCullen	AIBS	England
3470	Thomas McDonald	AIBS	
2886	Joseph McGee	AIBS	Wounded 5/11/54 Inkerman. England
2505	Patrick McGough	AIBS	Died 26/2/55 Crimea WO. SA'53
2336	Michael McGrath	AIBS	SA'53
3113	T. McGrath	AIB–	
3603	Hugh McInnery/ McInnerny	AIBS	KIA 5/11/54 Inkerman
3999	John McKinhnie	—S	Landed in Crimea 13/7/55
2884	William McKnight	AIBS	
2355	John McLeod	–IBS	D(epot) 25/6/57
2353	John McLowe	—S	
1904	Bernard McMahon	AIBS	SA'53, FMM (Band)

RIFLE GREEN IN THE CRIMEA

2900	Patrick McManama/ McManana	AIBS	KIA Inkerman 5/11/54
3506/3536	John McNeil/ McNeil	AI–S	SA'53
3200	James Mead	—S	Killed 12/10/54
3374/5	John Meas/meads	AI–S	KIA 13/10/54
2265	John Meadows	A—S	Died 17/10/54
2707/2709	George Melhuish	AI–S	Died 11/12/54 Scutari 10/12/??
3471	Henry Merrill	—S	
3737	Henry Merry	AI–S	
4382	Edward Michell	—S	Landed in Crimea 22/2/1855
3784	William Middleton	—S	Landed in Crimea 26/1/1855 Died
4424	Thomas Milchiner	—S	Landed in Crimea 12/6/1855
3641	Henry Milden	AIBS	9/1/55 Crimea
3612	Henry Mildren	AIBS	Died 9/12/54 Crimea
2346	Joseph Miller	AIBS	SA'53
4496	Thomas Miller	—S	Landed in Crimea 17/6/1855
2851	Philip Millgate	AIBS	
3525	John Mince	AIBS	Died 12/1/55 Crimea
3191	William Minds/ Nindy	—S	Died WO 24/9/56
1803	James Mineham	AIBS	
3753	William Minors	AIBS	Died WO
3984	Joseph Mole	—S	Landed Crimea 13/7/55 Died Scutari. Medal Regt 20/7/57
4407	David Monger	—S	Landed in Crimea 17/6/55 Scutari
2973	Timothy Monger/ Morgan	AIBS	Wounded 5/11/54 Inkerman Died
2136	J. Moon	AI—	
3757	W. Moon	—S	
2183	H. Moonan	AI—	
5221	George Moore	—S	Landed in Crimea 17/6/55 Scutari
3854/50	John Moore	—S	Sly/Wounded 12/4/55
3570/6	Robert Moore	AIBS	
5520	Robert Moore	—S	England
3787	William Moore	—S	Scutari
4761	Robert/ Richard Mooreland	—S	Landed Crimea 17/6/55 Died. Scutari England Mint 25/9/57
2188	Henry Moran	—S	
3850	John More	—S	Landed in Crimea 27/1/55

3636	Henry Morgan	AIBS	
3841	Llenleyn Morgan	—S	Landed in Crimea 26/1/1855. Died Scutari
3726	Samuel Morgan	—S	Landed in Crimea 13/7/55 Scutari
4568	Thomas Morgan	—S	Landed Crimea 22/2/1855 England
4712	William/Jerimiah Moriarty	—S	Landed Crimea 13/7/1855
3456	Charles Morling	AIBS	Died 29/1/55 Crimea
3694	James Morris	—S	Landed Crimea 26/4/1850. Died Scutari 12/3/55
3867	Thomas Morris	—S	Landed in Crimea 28/11/54. 8/12/54 Died WO 27/9/56
2392	G. Morrison	—S	
3560	William Moss	A—S	Died 7–8/10/54
3597	James Moyes	A–BS	
3758/3738	Richard Mickle/Muckle	—S	Landed in Crimea 17/6/55. Sev/Wounded 15/8/55. Died 21/4/55 ?56
3483	George Muffett	AIBS	Died 5/11/54 Scutari
3411	Frederick Mullock	AI–S	
3412	Thomas Mulford	AIBS	KIA 17/12/54
3152	Charles Mulock	AI–S	KIA 17/12/54
2827	John Mulony	—S	
3647	Robert Mullis	A—S	20/3/55 Scutari WO
4184	Alexander Munro	—S	Landed Crimea 13/7/1855
3626	Daniel Murphy	AIBS	
3929	George Murphy	—S	Landed Crimea 13/7/1855
3557	John Murphy	AI–S	
3602	John Murphy	AIBS	
2339	Michael Murphy	AIBS	Scutari WO 16/3/57
2756	Michael Murphy	A—	Aug/Sep 1854 Died date unknown
3526	M. Murphy	AI—	
3593	J. Murphy	AI—	
2326	Robert Murray	—S	Landed in Crimea 27/1/55
2972	John Musgrove	AIBS	Sly/W 26/7/55. Sev/W 30/7/55. H+R 21/2/56
3348	Thomas Mussard	AIBS	
2462	William [...]oyle	—S	Died H+R For WO
3833	James Nadauld	—S	H+R 7/5/56

3079	James Nairey/		
4571	William Nash	—S	Landed in Crimea 22/2/55. England H+R 3/?
	Thomas Neary	—S	Landed in Crimea 26/1/1855
4534	James Negus	—S	Landed Crimea 22/2/1855
4461	Thomas Newman	—S	Landed in Crimea 12/6/55 Dead
4543	James Newman	—S	Landed in Crimea 13/7/55
2159	Charles New	AIBS	
3214	Charles New	AIBS	Sev/Wounded 23/11/54 Died
3353	Henry New	AIBS	
2632	James Newbanks	AIBS	SA'53 W 5/11/54 Inkerman
3342	George Newberry	A—S	DOW 11/10/54
3816	George Newbold	A—S	Landed in Crimea 27/1/1855
3366	George Newland	A—S	
4305	Henry Newton	—S	Landed in Crimea 17/6/55. Died 9/9/55
5196	John Newton	—S	Landed in Crimea 17/6/55. Died 9/9/55
4035	George Nibett/ Niblett	—S	Landed Crimea 22/2/1855
4175	Robert Nicholson	—S	
3692	James Nicolas	—S	Landed in Crimea 5/3/55
4291	Thomas Nicoll/ Nicholls	—S	Landed Crimea 12/6/55
4314	Robert Noble	—S	Landed Crimea 13/7/55
4164	Matthew Norman	—S	
4375	Robert Norris	—S	Landed in Crimea 22/2/1855
4701	Charles North	—S	Landed Crimea 13/7/55
2482	W. Nounile	AIB–	
3575/3579	John Nudds	A—S	Died 17/1/55 Scutari WO 9/4/57
2809/3809	William Oakley	—S	Died 8/12/?? WO 24/9/56
1215	T. Oakman	AIB–	
3598	J. O'Brien	—S	
2537	Joseph Ogden	AIBS	England H+R 9/12/56
3603/5	Michael O'Grady	AIBS	
3197	William O'Hare	A—S	England
3132	George Oliver	A–BS	Sev/Wounded 18/6/55 Redan. Died 9/12/??
4323	George Oliver	—S	Landed Crimea 12/6/55 England H+R 2/5/??
2705	George O'Sullivan	AI–S	Killed 23/11/54
3050	John Owen	AIBS	England Regt 20/7/57
4644	George Owens	—S	Landed Crimea 22/2/55
1858	John Oxley	AIBS	England Regt 20/7/57
3021	Thomas Packer	AIBS	SA'53 Medal

4070	Alfred Page	—S	Landed in Crimea 13/7/55
3124	James Page	AIBS	Died 20/12/54 Scutari
2298	William Page	AIBS	SA'53 Sly/Wounded 23/11/54
3554/2554	Cornelius Palmer	AIBS	Wounded 5/11/54 DOW 4/12/54
3705	George Palmer	AI–S	3/1/55 Scutari England WO 9/4/57
3139	Henry Palmer	AIBS	Sev/Wounded 31/8/55 (Parlar?)
4473	Henry Palmer	—S	Landed in Crimea 13/7/55
1611	William Palmer	AIBS	SA'53 Medal
3890	Stephen Parfitt	—S	Landed in Crimea 22/2/55 Died 30/8/55
4387	George Parker	—S	Landed Crimea 22/2/55 Sev/Wounded 18/6/55 Redan
3455	Henry Parker	AIBS	Scutari WO
4799	Thomas/ James Parkinson	—S	Landed in Crimea 13/7/55
3706	George Parkhouse/ Pickhouse	AIBS	Mint 31/1/57
3213	Frederick Parnell	—S	Landed in Crimea 13/7/55
4149	Henry Parnell	—S	England D(epot) 25/6/57
3162	Thomas Parsone	AIBS	8/2/55 Crimea Died WO
2292	William Pascoe	AIBS	SA'53 Medal
3278	Daniel Palrick/ Patrick	A—	Died 14/11/54
4327	Charles Paton	—S	Landed in Crimea 13/7/1855
3885	William Payne	—S	Landed in Crimea 13/7/55
2594	Holford Pavitt	A—	Aug/Sept Died Date Unknown. SA'53
3259	Joseph Peak/ Peck	AIBS	Died 20/1/55 Crimea
3864	John Pearce	—S	Landed Crimea 26/1/1866
1631	William Pearce/ Pierce	AIBS	
*3370	James Pears	A—	England Regt 20/7/57
4434	Thomas Pedder	—S	Landed in Crimea 17/6/55 Scutari
4694	Edward Peat	—S	Landed in Crimea 17/6/55
3969/3669	John Pegler	—S	Landed Crimea 27/1/55 Died 15/5/55 Crimea
3511	Thomas Peitchley/ Pelchley	AIBS	Wounded 5/11/54 Inkerman. England H+R4/2/??
3507	Thomas Pelham	AI–S	Scutari Regt 20/7/57
3707	John Pender/ Perdue	AIBS	

3154	E. Penny	—	
2624	Alfred Percival	AIBS	KIA 5/11/54. SA'53
3164	Robert Perkins	A–BS	England
2803	E. Perrett	A—	SA'53 Medal
2394	John Phillips	—S	
3747	Thomas Phillips	AIBS	Scutari WO 16/5/57
4455	Thomas Phillips	—S	Landed in Crimea 17/6/55
3497	William Phillips	AIBS	England H+R 3/2/57
3058	Henry Philpot	AIBS	England. SA'53 Medal
3781	Alfred Philpots	—S	Landed in Crimea 26/1/1855
3805	Simon/ Timothy Phoenix	—S	Landed in Crimea 26/1/55 Died. Scutari
1965	Joseph Pickering	AIBS	SA'53 Medal
4638	Henry Pickup/ Pickers	—S	Landed in Crimea 13/7/55
3376	S. Pike	AIB–	
4361	David Pike	—S	Landed Crimea 27/1/1855
4092	Charles Pilgrim	—S	Landed in Crimea 13/7/55 Scutari
4646	Nathaniel Pilgrim	—S	Landed Crimea 22/2/55 Mint 10/8/57
2966	John Pine	AIBS	Died WO 25/1/57. SA'53 Medal
4578/4518	William Pitts/ Pills	—S	1/8/55 Died
2637	Henry Plum/ Pezey	—S	Landed in Crimea 22/4/55
1546	John Plumbridge	AIBS	Died 21/1/55 Crimea. SA'53
4648	Abraham Plumpin	—S	Landed Crimea 22/2/1855. England H+R
3789	Edward Porter	AIB–	Wounded 5/11/54 Inkerman. 1/3/55 Scutari
5213	Frederick Posnet	—S	
3501	George Powell	AI–S	Scutari WO 16/3/57
3490	Joseph Powell	AIBS	Wounded 5/11/54 Inkerman. 1856 Missing supposed dead
4493	Walter Powell	—S	Landed Crimea 12/6/55 Regt 19/9/55
4873	William Poynton	—S	Landed in Crimea 13/7/55
4025	John Price	—S	Landed in Crimea 12/6/55
3147/3174	William Price	A—S	Scutari D(epot) 25/6/57
4879	William Pront	—S	Landed in Crimea 17/6/55
4379	William Prout	—S	
3730	James Pucknell	—S	Landed Crimea 27. 1. 55 Scutari H+R
3716	Thomas Pugh	—S	Scutari
3607	William Pugh	—S	

3671	William Pugh	—S	Landed Crimea 26/1/1855
3246	William Purdey	AIBS	Died Wounded 5/11/54 Inkerman So 19/?/56
4459	Henry Purnell	—S	Landed in Crimea 17/6/55
[…]			
[…]			
2870	Felix Quinn	AIBS	Killed Inkerman 5/11/54
3551	Thomas Quinn	A—S	
3502	J. Quills	A—	
[…]			
[…]			
1705	Thomas Radcliffe	AIBS	England Regt 20/7/57. SA'53
3904/3984	William Radford	—S	Landed in Crimea 26/1/55
3363	Charles Raines/ Rains	AIBS	Wounded 5/11/54 Inkerman. Scutari
3257	Charles Randall	AI–S	
3378	John Randall	AI–S	Killed 2/12/54 WO
4485	Henry Randell	—S	Landed in Crimea 17/6/55. Died Scutari
3886	William H. Randle	—S	Landed in Crimea 17/6/55. Scutari Regt 25/7/57
4073	James Rasion	—S	Landed in Crimea 27/1/55
3244/5244	Alfred Rask	AIBS	Scutari WO 8/12/56
3503	William Raven	AIBS	
2254	John Read	AIBS	Died Scutari 21/7/55. SA'53
2557	John Readhouse	AI–S	
2734	William Reith	AIBS	SA'53 Medal, Served in American Civil War in Confederate Army
1674	Charles Remnant	AIBS	SA'53 Medal
3733	John Reynolds	—S	Landed in Crimea 27/1/55. Regt 19/9/56
4348	Frederick Richards	—S	Landed in Crimea 17/6/55. 24/11/56 Aldershot
2807	Thomas Richardson	AI–S	Died 12/2/55. SA'53
3115	William Richardson	AIBS	
4222	William Richards	—S	Landed in Crimea 12/6/55
4336	Charles Ricketts	—S	Landed in Crimea 13/7/55
1561	William Ricketta	AI–S	England D(epot) 25/6/57. SA'53
3908	Henry Rider	—S	Landed in Crimea 26/1/55
2446	James Ridgeway/ Ridgway	AI–S	Died Crimea 15/1/55. SA'53
3710	George Robbins	AIBS	10/12/54 Scutari

3622/3	John Robbins	AIBS	Sly/Wounded 22/11/54. D Scutari. WO 24/9/56
2801	Joseph Roberts	—S	Landed in Crimea 26/1/55, Died Scutari WO 24/9/56
3161	William Roberts	AIBS	Sly/W 11/4/55
2798	James Roertson	—S	Landed in Crimea 27/1/55. Sly/Wound 25/6/55
3004	George Robinson/ Robesson	AIBS	Wounded 5/11/54 Inkerman England. H+R. SA'53 Medal
4173	Edward Robinson	—S	Landed in Crimea 13/7/55
3231	James Robinson	AIBS	Wounded 5/11/54 Inkerman. England Regt 20/7/57
4397	Joseph Robinson	—S	Landed in Crimea H+R 13/11/?
1706/1707	William Robinson	AI–S	Sev/Wounded 18/6/55 Redan. England H+R 15/4/??. SA'53 Medal
3524	William Robinson/ Roberson	AI–S	Died WO 16/3/57
3578	William Robunson	A—	Died Crimea 21/9/54
3831/3813	James Robson	—S	Landed in Crimea 26/1/1855
4359	William Roby	—S	Landed in Crimea 17/1/55
4244	Francis Roche/ Rouch	—S	Landed in Crimea 12/6/54, Medal to H+R 4/10/?
1895	Bartholomew Rock	AI–S	H+R 15/4/?. SA'53
4653	Samuel Rogers/ Rodgers	—S	Landed in Crimea 17/6/55
3565	Henry Rolfe/ Ralph	AIBS	Died 21/3/55 Crimea
2788	Edward Rooney	AIBS	Died Scutari 27/3/55 WO. SA'53
2794	John Rooney	AIBS	Died Regt 20/7/57. SA'53
3818	John Rooper	—S	Landed in Crimea 27/1/55
3221	Alexander Rose	AIBS	Regt 19/9/56
3243	Richard Rose	A—S	Wounded Alma 20/9/54
3131	S. Rose	—S	Scutari
3521	S. Rose	AIBS	
4520	Robert Ross	—S	Landed in Crimea 22/2/55 Scutari
2939	James Rowe	AIB—	SA'53 Medal 13/1/55 Scutari
4010	William Rowley	—S	Landed in Crimea 13/7/55
3192	Patrick Ruby/ Rielly	AIBS	
3806	Richard Ruckley/ Rackley	—S	Landed in Crimea 26/1/55
4353	Richard Rumary	—S	Landed in Crimea 17/6/55
3549	Henry Rumble	AIBS	

3717	Joseph Russell	AIBS	Sly/Wounded 18/6/55 Redan. England Regt 20/7/57
3719	J. Russell	A—	
3018	Robert Russell	AIBS	Sev/Wounded 20/11/54. SA'53 27/12/54
3329	William Russell	—S	Sev/Wounded 3/8/55
4489	George Rutten/ Rutter	—S	Landed in Crimea 13/7/55. Scutari D(epot) 25/6/57
4451	Frederick Sadler	—S	Landed in Crimea 12/6/55. England Mint 29/9/57
3130	William John Sadlier	AIBS	
4174	William Sandell	—S	England D(epot) 25/6/57
4716	John Saunders	—S	Landed in Crimea 17/6/55
3689	William Saunders	AIBS	Wounded 5/11/54 Inkerman. Died Scutari 4/2/54
3942	James Sayer	—S	Landed in Crimea 26/1/55 Regt 19/9/56 Medal Also
1312	John Scammell/ Scannell	AIBS	England. SA'53
3684	Archibald Scott	AIBS	Killed 5/11/? WO
2952	Henry Scott	AI–S	Sly/Wounded 18/6/55 Redan. SA'53
3834	William Scragg	—S	Landed in Crimea 26/1/55 Scutari
2721	George Sculley	A–BS	Scutari. SA'53 Medal
8652	Job Seabrook	–IBS	Regt 19/9/56
4295/4296	Richard Seddin	—S	Landed in Crimea 13/7/55
2730	Henry Sepping(s)	AIBS	Died Crimea 23/1/55. WO 2/1/57
1357	William Serge	AI–S	23/9/54 Crimea? Has I+S Clasps. WO 9/4/57
4290	Ferderick Sharp	—S	Landed in Crimea 12/6/55
2200	Abraham Shaw	AI–S	Died 3/12/54. SA'53 Scutari
4276	Charles Shaw	—S	Landed in Crimea 12/6/55 Regt 20/7/57 with Medal
3491	James Shaw	AIBS	England H+R 15/5/56
3047	Joseph Shaw	AI–S	Died WO
3011	J. Shean/ Shien	AIBS	Wounded 5/11/54 Inkerman. England H+R 13/3/??
3144	Thomas Shenton	—S	Landed in Crimea 26/1/55
3391	James Shenton	A–BS	
4206	Charles Shewell	—S	Landed in Crimea 17/6/55

3332	William Shepherd	—S	Died Crimea 31/1/55/Wo 9/12/57
3685	John Shirley	—S	Landed in Crimea 26/1/55
3114	John Shooter	—S	Died 12/12/54 Scutari
5199/5190	Isaac Short	—S	Landed in Crimea 17/6/55. 19/6/55 Crimea
4399	Richard Shorten	—S	Landed in Crimea 13/7/55
2153	John Shroeder	AIBS	KIA Inkerman 5/11/54 Band
4346	Henry Simmonds	—S	Landed in Crimea 13/7/55
3355	Cornelius Simmons/Simmonss	AIBS	Sev/Wounded 22/11/54
3702	James Simmons	+—is	
3517	James Simms	—S	
3057	William Simms	AIBS	Wounded 5/11/54 Inkerman
2816	George Simpson	AI–S	
4450	Stephen Singer	—S	Landed in Crimea 17/6/55
3775	Richard Skinner	—S	Landed in Crimea 27/1/55
3988	Francis Skase	—S	
4804/4806	James Slaughter	—S	Landed in Crimea 13/7/55
4247	William Slovold	—S	
3254	Thomas Slyford	AIBS	WO 18/9/56
4392	Edward Smith	—S	Landed in Crimea 22/2/55
3428	(J) Edward Smith	AI–S	Chatham 20/5/57
4372	George Smith	—S	Landed in Crimea 13/7/55 Deceased
3572	George Smith	A—S	Died 13/8/55
4188	George Smith	—S	Landed in Crimea 12/6/55. Scutari D(epot) 28/6/57
4207	George J. Smith	—S	Landed in Crimea 12/6/55
1590	Henry Smith	AIBS	KIA 14/6/55
3188	James Smith	AI–S	11/12/54 Crimea
3704	John Smith	—S	
3894	John Smith	—S	
4169	John Smith	—S	Landed in Crimea 16/1/55
4385	John Smith	—S	Landed in Crimea 22/2/55
3176	John Smith	AIBS	Died 17/12/54
3857	Joseph Smith	—S	Landed in Crimea 13/7/55
2168	Mark Smith	AI–S	
3802	Richard Smith	—S	Landed in Crimea 27/1/55. England H+R 25/12/??
3358	Thomas Smith	—S	England Regt 20/7/57
2006	William Smith	AI–S	
3591	William Smith	AI–S	England
3339	William Smith	—S	Landed in Crimea 26/1/55 England

3838	W. Smith	A—	
4452	William Smith	—S	Landed in Crimea 12/6/55
4471	William Smith	—S	Landed in Crimea 13/7/55
4561	William Smith/ Saville?	—S	Landed in Crimea 22/2/55
2484	Joseph Smith	A—S	Died Scutari 10/12/54
2921	Frederick Soden	A—S	
3994	John Sowter	—S	Landed in Crimea 27/1/55
2806/3806	Peter Sparks	AIBS	Wounded 5/11/54 Inkerman Sutari
3492	William Sparks	AIBS	Died Scutari 17/2/55 WO 8/12/56
3215	George Spencer	AIBS	Died 7/2/55 Scutari
3763	Thomas Spencer/ Sender	AIBS	
3814	Charles Skilton	—S	Landed in Crimea 26/1/55. Regt. C. Medal 20/7/57
3971	Charles Spreadborough	—S	Landed in Crimea 27/1/55. KIA Redan 18/6/55 Medal also. WO 3/9/57
4693/4093	Charles Spriggs	—S	Landed in Crimea 13/7/55
3376	James Stage	AIBS	Died 12/3/55 Sutari
3277	M. Stacey	AI–S	
3766	Thomas Staff	—S	Landed in Crimea 26/1/55
3912	George Stagg	—S	Landed in Crimea 26/1/55
4560/4563	John Staines	—S	Landed in Crimea 22/2/55
3576	Charles Stanbrook	A–BS	
4378	Charles Stanners	—S	Landed in Crimea 27/1/55
3891	Edward Stainer	—S	Landed in Crimea 26/1/55
3854	William Staniland	—S	Landed in Crimea 27/1/55. Scutari. Mint 4/5/57
[...]	W. Stanley	—S	
3640	William Stanley	A–BS	England
1805	James Stanley	AIB–	SA'53 Medal
2810	William Stanton/ Staunton	A—S	Died Crimea 8/10/54
4347	Edward Staples	—S	Landed in Crimea 13/7/55
4203	Samuel Stapleton	—S	Landed in Crimea 17/6/55
3698	James Stead	AI–S	
3401	John Stenhouse	AIBS	SA'53 Medal
[...]	W. Stephens	AIB–	
2261	George Stephenson	A—	SA'53 Aug–Sept 54 Place not recorded

2983/2953	Alfred Stevens	AIBS	Wounded 5/11/54 Inkerman. Died 16/11/54
3459	George Storeley/ Stopley	AIBS	Died
3067	Henry Stokes	–IBS	Wounded 5/11/54 Inkerman
4247	William Stovold	—S	Landed in Crimea 13/7/55
3607/	Patrick Stringer	AI–S	Wounded 5/11/54 Inkerman
3744/3484	John Strivens	AI–S	Died Crimea 27/1/55
3493	John Strother/ Strethen/ Strothan	—S	27/1/55 Landed in Crimea. 18/7/55?
1658	George Stubbs	AIBS	SA'53 Medal
4328	John Stubbs	—S	Landed in Crimea 17/6/66 Scutari
4591	William Stubbs	—S	Landed in Crimea 13/7/55
4034	William Stubbington	—S	Landed in Crimea 22/2/55
3790	William Stubbington	—S	
2746	John Stuckley	AI–S	Died Crimea 19/1/55. SA'53
3385	J. Stuffin/ Staffin	AIBS	Sly/Wounded 18/8/55
3555	Henry Sutherland	AIBS	
3098/9/ 3099	George Sutton	AIBS	Sly/Wounded 22/11/54. Died Scutari 1. 2. 55
3085/88	George Swain(s)	AI–S	Scutari WO 8/12/56. SA'53
2338	John Swanscott	AIBS	SA'53 Medal 20/1/54 Crimea
4721	Robert Sweet	—S	Landed in Crimea 13/7/55
4202/4302	Joseph Swift	—S	Landed in Crimea 13/7/55
2/3732	Thomas Swindell	AIB–	Sly/Wounded 22/11/54. Scutari 22/11/54?
3723	T. Swindell	A——	
4370/4270	Thomas James Sykes	—S	Landed in Crimea 17/6/55
3900	John Tait	—S	Landed in Crimea 27/1/55
4352	Philip Tarrant	—S	Landed in Crimea 12/6/55
2703	Richard Tarrant	AIBS	SA'53 Medal
3535	T. Tarrant	AIBS	
2675	Daniel Taunton	AIBS	SA'53 Medal
2781	W. Taunton	AIBS	SA'53 Medal
3521	E. Taylor	AIBS	
3639/3689	E. Taylor	AIBS	
3237	Henry Taylor	AIBS	Wounded 5/11/54 Inkerman. 7/1/55 Scutari

Number	Name	Clasps	Notes
2594/6	J. Taylor	AIBS	SA'53 Medal
2574	John Taylor	AIBS	
3153	J. Taylor	AIBS	
3611	L. Taylor	A–BS	
2726	W. Taylor	—S	SA'53 Medal
3673	W. Taylor	AI–S	
3331/3336	William Taylor	—S	Landed in Crimea 15/3/55
3732	Charles Taylor	—S	Landed in Crimea 13/7/55
3944	Alexander Taylor	—S	Landed in Crimea 27/1/55
3966	David Taylor	—S	Landed in Crimea 26/1/55
2390	W. Telford	AI—	SA'53 Medal
4639	Joseph Theobald	—S	Landed in Crimea 22/2/55 Died 26/4/55
3443	W. Thitchener	AIBS	10/11/55 Scutari
3495	Henry Thompson	AIBS	Wounded 5/11/54 Inkerman
3338	George Thorn	AIBS	Sev/Wounded 22/11/54
2749	F. Thornhill	A—	SA'53 Medal
4098	Samuel Thompson	—S	Landed in Crimea 17/6/55
4606	Caleb Thomas	—S	Landed in Crimea 13/7/55. Slightly Wounded 9/8/55
4440	James Thompson	—S	Landed in Crimea 17/6/55. WO 25/9/56
3806	William Thurston	—S	Landed in Crimea 26/1/55
3839	[…] Tickner	—S	
3293	M. Tierney	AIBS	
2492	Thomas Tillby/ Tilby/ Tilbey	—BS	18/2/55 Scutari WO 6/4/57. SA'53 Medal
4005	Samuel Tilling	—S	
2390	[…] Till[…]	—S	
3105	W. Tilman	AIBS	
1911	Thomas Timperley	AIBS	Scutari. SA'53 Medal
3655	James Tobin	AIBS	SA'53 Medal (Band)
3620	Abner Tomalin	AIBS	17/1/55 Crimea
3862	Edward Tomkins	—S	Landed in Crimea 27/1/55
3059	Richard Tomlin	AIBS	SA'53 Wounded 5/11/54 Inkerman
3534	W. Topcliffe	AI–S	
3734	Edward Chas. Townsend	—S	Landed in Crimea 27/1/55 Scutari
3751	John T. Trapp	AIBS	KIA Inkerman 5/11/54
3774	[…] Trendle	—S	Landed in Crimea 26/1/55
4513	Gill Trower	—S	Landed in Crimea 12/6/55. Scutari

4210	[...] Truel?	—S	
2827	Charles Tumber	AIBS	SA'53 Medal 13/3/55 Crimea
4511	John Tumblin	—S	Mint 7/?/?
3033	G. Turner	A—S	SA'53 Medal
3453	H. Turner	AIBS	
3316	John Turner	AIBS	Sev/Wounded 20/11/54. 3/2/55 Ab–dos
4386	George Turner	—S	Landed in Crimea 12/6/55. Sev/Wounded 28/6/55
4646	[...] Turner	—S	
3842	Samuel Turner	—S	Landed in Crimea 27/1/55. 13/3/55 Crimea
3247	W. Tyler	AI–S	
4664	[...] T[...]	—S	
2963/2962	Joseph Underwood	AIBS	SA'53 12/3/55 Scutari
3546	William Unwin	A—	Died Aug–sept 1854 Date Unknown
4337	Ebadiah Usher	—S	Landed in Crimea 13/7/55
2383	J. Vanson	AIB–	SA'53 Medal
2737	S. Vast	–I—	SA'53 Medal
3253	John Vincent	A—	12/1/55 Scutari
4337	[...] [...]		
4483	[...] [...]		
2074	W. Wacket	AI—	
3349	A. Wadham	AIB–	
1878	W. Wakeham	AIB–	SA'53
3317	Frederick Wainwright	AIBS	SA'53 Scutari 25/2/55
1688	W. Wainwright	AIB–	SA'53
3440	B. Walker	AI—	
4000	John Walker	—S	Landed in Crimea 26/1/55
3936	John Walker	—S	Landed in Crimea 26/1/55
2522	J. Walker	A—	
4457	Joseph Walker	—S	Landed in Crimea 17/6/55 Deceased
2868	J. Walker	AIB–	SA'53
3473	William Walker	AIB–	Wounded 5/11/54 Inkerman. Scutari Died 17/12/54
3346	W. Wall	AIB–	
3066	G. Wallington	AI—	SA'53
4369	Joseph Watkins	—S	Landed in Crimea 22/2/55
3967	James Waterman	—S	Landed in Crimea 22/2/55
3749	James Watson	—S	Landed in Crimea 26/1/55
2777	John Walsh	–IB–	Died Crimea 26/2/55
4576	Michael Walsh	—S	Landed in Crimea 17/6/55

4581	Richard Walsh	—S	Landed in Crimea 17/6/55
4005	John Ward	—S	Landed in Crimea 27/1/55
4593	Charles Ward	—S	Landed in Crimea 17/6/55
4271	Edward Ward	—S	Landed in Crimea 13/7/55
1918	Samuel Ward	AIB—	SA'53
2552	Thomas Warner	AIB—	SA'53
1126	J. Warren	AI—	SA'53 (Band)
3476	J. Watkins	AIB—	
3417/3442	Edward Watson	AIB—	Wounded 5/11/54 Inkerman
3682/3602	Thomas Watson	AI—	3/2/55 Scutari
4656	James Weaver	—S	Landed in Crimea 13/7/55 Canada Medal. Photo in R.B.C. 1911
3945	James Weares	—S	Landed in Crimea 13/7/55
4380	William Weaver	—S	Landed in Crimea 22/2/55
4248	George Weedon	—S	Landed in Crimea 17/6/55
3600	Jabez Weller	—S	Landed in Crimea 26/1/55
4285	John Wells	—S	Landed in Crimea 17/6/55
4333	John Webb	—S	Landed in Crimea 17/6/55
3034	Henry Webb	AIB—	Died Scutari 18/2/55+sa'53
4583	William Webb	—S	Landed Crimea 17/6/55
4677	William Webb	—S	Landed in Crimea 13/7/55. Sly/ Wounded 8/9/55 Redan
3925	Thomas Weedon	—S	Landed in Crimea 26/1/55. 18/3/ 55 Scutari
2998	George Weeks	AIB—	SA'53 8/9/55
3668	Richard Wells	AIB—	Died 17/1/55 Crimea
1885	Henry West	—S	
3318	John Weston	AIB—	Sly/Wounded 22/11/54
1701	Francis Wheatley V.C.	AI—	SA'53, D.C.M., Legion of Honour
2935	T. Whelan	AIB—	SA'53
4057	Thomas Wheeler	—S	Landed in Crimea 17/6/55
3419	F. Whiffin	AI—	
1821	R. K. Whittaker	AIB—	SA'53
3454	A. White	+—	
4229	John Williams	—S	Landed in Crimea 17/6/55
4022	John White	—S	Landed in Crimea 17/6/55 Scutari
3545	Francis White	AIB—	Sly/Wounded 20/11/54
3713	Samuel White	AI—	13/1/55 Scutari
3074	E. Whitehead	AI—	
2925	T. Whitem	—B—	
4634	Henry White	—S	Landed in Crimea 13/7/55 Scutari

2898	John Whiting	AIB–	Sly/Wounded 20/7/55. Wounded Inkerman SA'53
3295	Robert Whitcook	AI–	Sly/Wounded 20/11/54 Died Scutari 5/2/55
2935	[…] Whi[…]		
4321	William White	—S	Landed in Crimea 12/6/55
3507	A. Whybourne	AI–	
3715	A. Whybourn	—B–	
4014	Francis Weeks	—S	Landed in Crimea 26/11/54. KIA Redan 8/9/55
4153	Samuel Wilson	—S	Landed in Crimea 22/2/55
4297	William Wisdom	—S	Landed in Crimea 13/7/55
4602	C. Williams	—S	Landed in Crimea 13/7/55
3504	Martin Wilkinson	AIB–	Killed 8/9/55 Redan
3631	J. Wilkinson	–I–	
3571	Francis Willie/Willey	AIB–	Died Scutari 26/2/55
3341	John Williams	AIB–	Died Scutari 10/2/55
2769	R. Williams	AIB–	SA'53
3589	Robert Williams	AIB–	Wounded 5/11/54 Inkerman. DOW Crimea 25–26/12/54
2263	T. Williams	AI–	SA'53
1335/1355	John Williamson	AIBS	SA'53
3467	Charles Willis	AIB–	Wounded 5/11/52 Inkerman
3630	John Willmot/Wilmot	A—	Sev/Wounded 22/11/54 Crimea Died 7/12/54
3422	William Willoughby	AIB–	Wounded/Dead 8/8/55
4381	George Williams	—S	Landed in Crimea 22/2/55
4068	John Williams	AIBS	Landed in Crimea 27/1/55 Scutari
2769	[…] Wi[…]		
4523	James Wilson	—S	Landed in Crimea 22/2/55
3436	'Cpl' Thomas Wilson	AIB–	13/12/54 Crimea Died 29/1/55
3679	J. Wise	A—	
3142	J. Wishes	AIB–	
4463	Henry Wise	—S	Landed in Crimea 12/6/55
4453	Thomas Wyatt	—S	Landed in Crimea 12/6/55
2359	W[…]	[…]	
4094	[…] W[…]	[…]	
4649	James Wheeler	—S	Landed in Crimea 22/2/55
4702	John Worsfold	—S	Landed in Crimea 17/6/55
4118	Ez[…]la Woodhead	—S	Landed in Crimea 22/2/55
3993	Henry Wood	—S	Landed in Crimea 27/1/55

3359	Charles/ Pope Wills	—S	Landed in Crimea 27/1/55 Scutari
4444	Isaac Wheeler	—S	Landed in Crimea 12/6/55
3730	William Whillingham	—S	Landed in Crimea 27/1/55
3870	William White	—S	Landed in Crimea 27/1/55
3987	William Wells	—S	Landed in Crimea 27/1/55. Sly/Wounded 8/8/55
4043	Ferderick Woods	—S	Landed in Crimea 27/1/55
2981	Thomas Woods	—S	Landed in Crimea 27/1/55
3468	Samuel White	—S	Landed in Crimea 26/1/55
3922	Henry Williams	—S	Landed in Crimea 26/1/55 Scutari
3830	John Wilder	—S	Landed in Crimea 26/1/55. Sly/Wounded 19/8/55
3333	James Wood	A—	26/1/55 Scutari
2679	Josiaa C. Wood	AIB–	Sev/Wounded 2/1/55
2899	William Wood	AIB–	Wounded 5/11/54 Inkerman SA'53. 14/1/55 Scutari
2945	T. Woodall	AIB–	SA'53
3508	J. Woodward	A—	
3500	Abraham Worley	AIB–	22/9/55
3755	Jacob Worley	AIB–	Died 14/1/? 10/3/55 Scutari
2828	W. Wrake	AIB–	SA'53
3496	W. Wren	AIB–	
2989	John Wren	AIB–	SA'53 Sev/Wounded 21/7/55
3071	George Wright	AI—	SA'53 14–15/6/55 KIA
2686	T. Wright	AIB–	SA'53
3785	William Wright	AI—	Landed in Crimea 15/4/55?, Sly/Wounded 25/10/54. Photo in *R.B.C.* 1911 shows clasps Inkerman and Sebastopol
3424	R. Yarley	–IB–	
2359	Esau Yewn	AIB–	Died 19–20/1/55 Crimea

PART SIX

2nd Battalion Rifle Brigade Medal Roll for the Crimea

CAPTAIN THE EARL OF ERROLL'S COMPANY

Captain
The Earl of Erroll A—— Wounded Alma

Lieutenants
Hon. J. Stuart A——
G. S. Wyndham A—S B. Sent to Depot 18/3/??

Sergeant Major
1489 James Singer AI—— H+R

Quarter-Master Sergeant
1912 William Harrington A——

Paymaster Sergeant
1893 Henry Harvey AI—— H+R

Hospital Sergeant
2335 William Jas. Stanley AI——

Armourer Sergeant
2304 John McLennan –I—

Bugle Major
1217 James Cordial AI—— Mutiny

Colour Sergeant
2548 Mowbray R. Skeates A—— Sev/Wounded 8/9/55 Redan

Sergeants
2048 Charles Lowe A——
1751 Charles Marsh A——
2946 Frederick Piper A—— Mutiny
1995 William Smith ——

2213	James Taylor	——	(Colour Sergeant)

Corporals

2087	Patrick Behson	A——	
2623	Thomas Blagburn	A—S	
3425/2426	Joseph Cherry	A——	Cpl/Sgt. Sev/Wounded 5/9/55 Sebastopol. Sent away. Mutiny
3098	John Scott	A—S	
3084	William Scott	A——	Mutiny
3379	Dennis Shea	A—S	Killed 18/8/55 Sebastopol
3308	John Vincent	A——	
3310	John Robinson	A——	Killed Alma

Buglers

3036	Isaac Dyer/Dyre	A——	Wounded Alma
2986	William Hy. Murray	A——	

Riflemen

3651/3657	Charles Ashcroft	A—S	WO 31/12/54 Scutari
3480	Richard Attwood	A—S	
3636/3486	John Baker	A—S	
3650	Thomas Barnes	A——	
3530	Stephen Beak	A—S	Mutiny
3553	John Beasley	AB——	Mutiny
3064	David Beeney	AB——	Scutari 16/6/54
[..]17	Augustus/Aneus Beeton/Beeton	A——	Wounded Alma
3654	James Bennett	——S	5/12/54 Place not shown on roll
2558	John Bennett	A——	Wounded Alma. Sly/Wounded also on 23/4/55
2800	Robert Blake	A—S	Wounded Alma
3655	William Blanchard	AB——	Sly/Wounded 18/6/55. Redan. Mutiny
3343	Henry Blishen	A——	Pte/Cpl. KIA Sebastopol 8/9/55 Redan WO
2724	John Blizard	A——	
4056	Thomas Bloxham	A——	
2531	William Bolton	AB–S	
2072/2172	Edward Bowen	A——	Mutiny
[.]015	Stephen Brighting	A——	
2853	William Brown	AB——	Mutiny
[.]665	Jesse/George Burchill	A——	Wounded Alma
2990	Frederick Carden	A——	Mutiny
4688	Patrick Cavanagh	A——	Sev/Wounded 6/9/55

2248/3248	Henry Chapman	A——	Sly/Wounded 8/9/55 Redan
3950	Henry Coles	A——	Sev/Wounded 10/6/55. Mutiny
3367	Patrick Condon	A——	
3790/3791	Robert Crosbie	A——	Sev/Wounded 8/9/55 Redan
[.]552	Graham David	A——	Wounded in trenches; died
2872/2892	George Dawson	A–I–	Mutiny
1803/[.]808	William Farrar	A——	Wounded Alma 22/9/54 (20th?)
3567	Peter Fenwick	A—S	
3122	John Ferguson	A——	Mutiny
3535	George Finch	A——	Mutiny
3497	James Fisher	A—S	17/1/55 Scutari
2533	Henry Fletcher	A——	23/9/54 not shown on roll
3549	William Fritter	A—S	
[.]457	James Gray	A——	Wounded Alma
2945	Thomas Gunston	A——	
4105	John Hall	A——	Mutiny
3106	William Harris	A——	(Later Corporal)
1666	Richard Hawkins	A——	Wounded Alma 22/9/54
4146	William Heard	A—S	Killed Sebastopol 10/6/55
2267	William Heater	A——	
3008/[.]108	Edward Hexter	A——	Killed Alma 21/9/54
2626/2526	William Hope	AB—	Mutiny
3897/2829	George Holt	A—S	
3869	Alfred Hine	A——	Sly/Wounded 21/5/55
2633	Thomas Hoare/Hore	A—S	9/3/55 Scutari
2493	William Johnson	A—S	Mutiny
1651	David Jones	A——	Wounded Alma
3807	James Kelly	A——	
4055	William Kennedy	A——	KIA Alma 20/9/54
2422	Henry Kentsey	A—S	
2342	John Kilroy	A——	Mutiny
2745/3745	Samuel King	——S	Sev/Wounded 18/6/55 Redan
3695	John Ladd	——	
3509	William Liptrot	A—S	13/2/55 Scutari
3047	George Light	A——	Mutiny
3307/3587	John Little	A——	Sly/Wounded in the hand in the trenches 17/8/55 Sebastopol. Mutiny. Camel Corps
1022	John Loughlin	A——	Sev/Wounded 8/9/55 Redan
3133/3153/3155	Samuel Love	A——	Sly/Wounded 8. 9. 55 Redan. Mutiny
3702	James Mack	A——	Sev/Wounded 8. 9. 55 Redan. Mutiny

4303	John Martin	—S	Mutiny
2947	Richard Martin	A—	
2602	Richard Marton	A—	Wounded Alma
3834	William Milligan/ Mulligan	A—	Wounded Alma. Mutiny
2961	William Mills	A—	Wounded Alma
3050	George Moore	A—	Sev/Wounded 8/9/55 Redan
1616	William Moore	A—	
2550	Thomas Morgan	A—	12/8/49 (1859) Sebastopol. A.S?
2645	James Morman/ Morsman	A—	
1614	John Morris	A—S	
2850	George Mortimer/ Mortimor(e)	AB—	Sev/Wounded 29/7/55
3875	William Mountjoy	A—S	
3711	Christopher Murphy	A—	
3292	Morris/Maurice Nailan/Nailon	A—S	Wounded Alma
2757/2759	Thomas Nally	A—	Wounded Alma. Mutiny
3105	Edward Nulty/Nutty	—S	Sev/Wounded 7/6/55 assault on Quarries
2844/3844	Patrick O'Hallerghan/ Hallerhan/ O'Halloran	A—	
2440	Benjamin Osmond	AI–S	4/1/55 Scutari
1649	John Parkinson	A—	Wounded/DOW 16/9/55
3042	Robert Penney/ Penny	A—	Mutiny
3636	Michael Pratt	A—	(24/6/1855 Renkioi)
3306	Henry Quainton/ Quenton	—	
3519	Jacob Reed	A—	Mutiny
3834	William Robertson	A—	
2615	Samuel Rook(e)	A—	
3137/2139/ 3139	Isaac Russell	A—S	Died 15/10/1854
2744	William Saberton	A—S	Died at Sea
3856	Edward Sheen	A—	
3377	Timothy Sheehan	A—	
1385	Richard Short	A–I–	
3570	John Soper	—S	27/12/54
3597	William Stephens	A—	16/12/54 Balaklava. Mutiny
2688/3688	Benjamin Stocker	A—S	
3633	Charles Stone	A—S	Mutiny

2872	Thomas Stacey/Stracey	A—S	
1673	James Stubbles	A–IS	
3171	Richard Summers	A—	Wounded Alma
3726	Peter Sutton	—	
3571	Francis Tero	—	
2499	Alfred/Alex Thornhill	A—	Killed 8/9/55 Redan. WO Oct
4143	George Tucker	A—	Mutiny
2567	James Tyrrell	A—	Mutiny
3485	Thomas Vince	A—	Sly/Wounded 18/6/55, Killed 8/9/55 Sebastopol Redan
3575	Charles Ward	A—	
3732/3735	Henry Warren	A—S	Sly/Wounded 27/6/55
3065	John/James Warren	A—	Sly/Wounded 18/6/55 Redan. Mutiny
2002	Henry West	A—	
3771	Henry Williams	A—	Mutiny
3482	Joseph Williams	A—	Mutiny
3736	William Williams(on)	A—	Sly/Wounded 8/9/55 Redan
3737	Joseph Wilson	A—	Mutiny
3748	John Wines	A—S	
3520/3530	Daniel Wright	—S	Sev/Wounded 8/9/55 Redan

Drafts from England and transfers from other companies posted to Captain Erroll's Company and entitled to Medal and Clasp Sebastopol

Paymaster Sergeant

3877	Alfred Powell	—S	

Sergeants

3507	Joseph Ashford	A–IS	On Main List
3841	John Macnamara	—S	Alma as Cpl. Markham's Coy
2959	William Wiffin	—S	Sev/Wounded 8/9/55 Redan. D 8/6/56

Corporals

3106	William Harris	—S	Sly/Wounded 8/9/55 Redan
4068	Richard Martin	—S	
3777	William Phipps	—S	
3939	James Porter	—S	
2922	Richard Ronan	—S	
3099	George. F. Smith	—S	

3728	James Tiernay	—S	A Cpl Turney. Sly/Wounded 20/8/55 Sebastopol
3801	William Welsh	—S	

Riflemen

4378	John Andrews	—S	
4524	William Boucher	—S	
4426/4486	Francis Chadwick	—S	Dead 27/9/55
3662	Richard Chapman	—S	Sly/Wounded 8/9/55 Redan; also Sev/Wounded 25/7/55 Sebastopol on Main List
4335	William Clarke	—S	
4232	John Cloaver	—S	
4496	John Cosgrove	—S	Medal. Sent away 3/9/?
4394	Thomas Coton	—S	
4316	James Davies	—S	
3920	Richard Day	—S	Sev/Wounded 8/9/55 Redan
1428	John Dolan	—S	Sly/Wounded Redan 18/6/55. Died on 12/7/55
4615	Andrew Draper	—S	
4504	John Evenden	—S	
4025	Arthur French	—S	Sly/Wounded 6/5/55. Sev/Wounded 14/8/55 Sebastopol; sent away. Died 24/9/56
3535	George French	—S	
3761	John Gayman	—S	Medal also? Mint?
4586	Thomas Gimbert	—S	
3552	David Graham	A—S	29/10/54 WO Wounded (on Main List)
4036	Richard Harding	—S	Sly/Wounded 8/9/55 Redan
4432	George Harvey	—S	
4483	John Harvey	—S	
2762	Henry Haywood	A—S	D. On Main List
4197	William Hicks	—S	W/Dead 8/9/55 Redan (DOW 17/9/55?)
4443/33	James Holston	—S	(D 6/6/56)
1369	John Jackson	A—S	Sly/Wounded 7/6/55 assault on Quarries. SO 19/11/57
3153	Samuel Lane	A—S	
4206	Samuel Leatherland	—S	D
4340/8	John Leonard	—S	
4340	Thomas Lennard	—S	Sly/Wounded 17/8/55 Sebastopol
4490/09	James McCann	—S	Killed 2/9/55. WO 19/3/57
3781	Patrick Maclellan	—S	

4109	Henry Madgewick	—S	Sev/Wounded 8/9/55 Redan (Mint 2/4/57)
4329	Thomas Mears	—S	
1561	Henry Moore	—S	(DOW)
4470	Henry Moseley	—S	
4430	Thomas Powell	—S	
4629	James Pratt	—S	
4568	John Rankin	—S	
3944	John Rees	—S	Scutari 21/8/1855
4360	William Richards	—S	
3883	Joseph Richardson	—S	
4597	William Riley	—S	
4541	George Rockingham	—S	
2472	James Rouch(e)	—S	
4275	James Sanders	—S	
4366	William Shaw	—S	
4638	Benjamin Shelton	—S	
4557	Joseph Steth	—S	
4388	Thomas Taylor	—S	13/8/55 Scutari
4534/5534	William Turbutt	—S	
4256	John Twiggs/Twiffs	—S	Sly/Wounded Sebastopol 21/4/55; Killed 8/9/55 Redan
4501	Thomas Vearns	—S	
4467	Alexander Walkinshaw	—S	Sev/Wounded 30/7/55 Sebastopol. WO 2/8/55
4435	Samuel Warwick	—S	
4285	William White	—S	
4512	John Williams	—S	
3733	Robert Wilson	—S	(Killed Oct)
3748	John Wenis	—S	(H+R 21/2/?)
4642	John Wood	—S	
4465	Thomas Young	—S	Killed 6/10/55

Captain W. J. Colville's Company

Captain

Hon. W. J. Colville A——

Lieutenants

A. Nixon	A–IS	Regt 18/7/57
P. C. B. Egerton	A—S	H+R 17/3

Colour Sergeant

2788	George Round	A——	

Sergeants

2886	Thomas Austen/Austin	A—S	H+R 28/12. Mutiny
2888	William G. Bourne	A——	
2582	Samuel Smith	A——	Mutiny

Corporals

1693	Thomas Burge	A—S	(Sgt later) also FMM. Mutiny
2664	Thomas Carter	A——	
2375	Henry Donaldson	A——	
2257/2357	William Edmonds	A——	Sev/Wounded 15/11/55, Magazine explosion French Siege
2664	Thomas Carter	A——	

Buglers

2590	George Ebelthite/Ebethorte	A——	Wounded Alma; Died 27/1/54 Scutari. WO
3491	Edward Hough	A——	Mutiny

Riflemen

3794	James Anderson	A—S	Died 20/11/54 Balaklava. (WO)
2752	John Austen/Austin	A——	Mutiny
1892	Thomas Baker	A—S	H+R
1513	James Bennett	A—S	D
3095	Richard Bird	A—S	Killed 8/9/55 Marching to trenches
3470	William Bolton	A——	Mutiny
4079	Septimus Bland	AB–S	Sly/Wounded 16/6/55; Sly/Wounded 30/6/55. Wounded dangerously 17/8/55.? 28/8/55; WO 25/9/56
4095	Nicholas Buckley	A——	
2808/3808	James Burke	——	Sly/Wounded 8/9/55 Redan
3383	George Cable	—S	Sev/Wounded 16/6/55
3817	John Carroll	A——	Sly/Wounded 6/9/55. Mutiny
3229	William Carter	A—S	Died at Scutari
2748	Isaac Cates	A——	Sly/Wounded 1/9/55. Mutiny
1993	Henry Christmas	A——	Mutiny

1225/1865	Henry Calton/Colton	A——	DOW Alma 21 Sept 54 WO 25/9/56
3792/5322	John Conroy	——S	Mutiny
3664/3669	Horace Cornelius	A—S	(WO) Died 25/6/55
4276	Thomas Crown	——	
3876	George Davis	A——	KIA 18/6/55 Redan
1902	Thomas Davison	A——	
3010	Charles Dodd	A—S	
2556/3556	Thomas Dowling	A—S	
2220	Henry Downer	A——	Died 11/10/54 Balaklava
2600	Thomas Edwards	A–IS	7/1/55 Scutari. WO 15?-?/56
2606	David Ellis	A–IS	H+R
3500	John Exton	A—S	7/3/55 Scutari. WO
2673	Henry Fancourt	——	Sev/Wounded 8/9/55 Redan
3560	David Farrelly	A——	
2585	John Foot	A——	Mutiny
1417/1676	Robert Garner	A——	Sev/Wounded 8/9/55 Redan
1679/3699	Charles Garvay	A——	Mint 12/7/57
3479	Frederick C. George	A——	H+R
3833/3853	Thomas Gray	A—S	
3539	James John Green	——	Sly/Wounded 6/8/55 Sebastopol
3899	George Gregory	AB—	
3336	Thomas Grundy	A—S	Mint 20/9/57. Mutiny
3221	John Gunston	——	Mutiny
3607	Thomas Harrison	A——	Sly/Wounded 1/9/55
3837/3857	William Henderson	A——	
2516/2576	John/Joseph Heritage	A—S	Killed 16–17/6/55 Sebastopol WO
1868	George. T. Hurst	A—S	Died 15/11/54 Balaklava
3508	William Ives	——	
2772	James Johnston	——	
3533	John Jones	——	KIA 14/6/55 Sebastopol WO
3291/3294	Henry Kent	A—S	Wounded when sharp shooting 18–19/10/54; DOW. Mint 4/12/68
3693/3695	Thomas Killeen	AB-S	Wounded 28/6/1855
3606	James Lee	A——	(WO) D. Mutiny
3762	Matthew Maloney	A——	
3880	John Mansbridge	—I—	
1406	Henry Mansfield	A——	Died
2461/3461	James McDonald	A——	Killed 8/9/55 Redan

3703	Patrick McKeowne/ McKewin	A——	Mutiny
3312	Joseph Miduinter	——	
2049	William Milligan	A——	Mutiny
3916	Thomas Minton	A—S	
3709/3708	George Mitchell	——S	18/8/54 Monastre
1854	William Mooney	A——	Mutiny
3474	John Murphy	——S	5/2/55 Scutari. WO
3300	Samuel Nicholls	——	H+R + Sebastopol Clasp; Sev/Wounded 8/9/55 Redan
4517	James Newland	——	Sebastopol Clasp
2156	John O'Neil/O'Niel	A—S	Died
2805	John Owen	A——	Wounded Alma
2726	Peter Palled/ Pallett	A——	Sly/Wounded 9/8/55; H+R 2/1/56
4169	John Paine/Payne	A——	Sev/Wounded 15/11/55 Magazine explosion French siege train
3475	Thomas Phillips	——S	WO 24/10
3908	Luke Ratican	——	Sly/Wounded 18/6/55 Redan. Mutiny
3721	Martin Regan	A—S	Mint 28/6/64
3804	Thomas Riley	A——	
3527	John Roberts	——S	Died 14/11/55
[...]	Richard Ronan	A——	
3735	John Scott	AB——	H+R
4026	Samuel Sewell	A——	Sly/Wounded 18/6/55 Redan
2400/2408	Thomas Shakespear	A—S	Mutiny
2506	George Singer	A—S	H+R 26/12
2114	Henry Smith	A—S	
3391/2891	William Smith	A—S	Killed 5/11/54 Inkerman. WO 17/3
1948	Thomas Snape	A——	
3503	Joseph Sparks	A——	Mutiny
4000	Alfred Stanton	A—S	
3313	William Stork	——	C
3774	William Sudders	A——	Corporal
2434	William Summers	A—S	8/4/55 Scutari
2230/3330	David/Daniel Sutton	A—S	Killed Marching to trenches. WO 19/3/57
2116	William Thomas	A—S	25/10/54
3835	Alexander Thompson	A—S	

4085	Alfred Thompson	A——	
3349	Austin Tong	A—S	Killed 2/10/54 Marching to trenches. (WO)
3972	George Tunnecliffe	A——	
2017	Isaac Underwood	A——	Mutiny
3508/3580	William Underwood	A—S	6/1/55 Scutari. WO 17/3/57
3731	Aaron Walker	A—S	
3852/3858	Robert Walsh	A—S	23/5/55
2622	William Warren	A——	Mutiny
2332	David Webster	A—S	Killed marching to trenches Sebastopol. WO 2/11/56
4147	John C. Weeles	A——	Sly/Wounded 25/5/55
3028/3928	Samuel Wells	A—S	WO 13/11/56
3371	John Wheeler	A—S	Died 13/12/1854 Balaklava. WO
3994	William Whitley	AB——	
2456	John Williams	A—S	Mutiny
3799	Robert Williams	A——	30/9/54. WO 14/2/61.
2626	James Wilkinson	A——	
3738	William Wilson	A——	Sly/Wounded 8/9/55 Redan
3884	Thomas Woods	A——	Sly/Wounded 16/7/55 & Sly/Wounded 28/8/55 Sebastopol
3740	Samuel Woolf	A——	Wounded Alma. Muntiny
[..]91	Joseph Wright	A——	
[.]513	William Wyatt	A——	

Drafts from England and transfers from other companies posted to Captain Colvilles Company entitled to a Medal and Clasp Sebastopol.

Sergeants

2793	George Baker
2668	George Palmer
2525	Thomas Wallace

Corporals

3795	Joseph Bradshaw V.C.	And FMM.
4226	William Brooks	
1902	Thomas Dawson	Sev/Wounded 18/6/55 Redan
3685	Hugh Hannan	D.C.M.
3559	Samuel Lockett	
4120	Robert Winder	

Buglers.

4006	Charles Spencer
3630	George Storey

Riflemen

4948	William Adwick	
4348	James Bailey	
3493	Frederick Baker	KIA Before Sebastopol 25/7/55
4031/4531	John Baker	
3877	Henry Baker	
4322	Henry Banks	S/Wounded 8/9/55 Redan
4561	George Beadle	Sev/Wounded 8/9/55 Redan. H+R 19/11/?
4357	William Beardwell	20/?/??
4463	William Beck	Sev/Wounded 28/8/55. Sebastopol 20/9/55
3905	John Bidgood	
4094	Joseph Blackmore	
2660	James Bow	
4267	Thomas Boyle	Sly/Wounded 23/8/55 Sebastopol
3995	George Bradley	4/4/55
4374	Alfred Brooks	Sent away. H+R 29/8/56
4361/4361	Thomas Brooks	Died 20/6/55
4418	Edward Bryant	Sev/Wounded 8/9/55 Redan. Dead
4298	Thomas Bunting	
4286	John Burdett	
4676	George Burleigh	Died 23/2/56, Place not shown
4446	John Cartwright	
3924	Amos Catling	Dead 22/9/54. As part of draft, the date should possibly be 1855. WO 24/9/?? WO
4294	William Chapman	
4164	James Childs	Sly/Wounded 3/7/55 & Sev/Wounded 23/8/55 Sebastopol
4395	Thomas Cook	Sly/Wounded 8/9/55. KIA 8/9/55 Sebastopol. WO 25/9/?
4221	William Cook	
4511	William Cooper	
4333	William Crockford	KIA Sebastopol 30/6/55. WO 19/11/56
4666	Thomas Daly	Sev/Wounded 28/8/55 Sebastopol
4585	Samuel Daniels	

4482	William Dawson		H+R 16/3/57
2220	Edward Downey		
4393	John Downey		
2257	William Edmonds		
4626	John Ettridge		
4127	Joseph Francis		
4390	George French		
4080/8	Joseph Gunter		Sly/Wounded 21/7/55 Sebastopol & Sev/Wounded 8/9/55 Redan. SO 20/12/56
4112	John Hanbury		Specially Ordered 23/4/57
2446	Henry Herbert	A——	Sly/Wounded 11/6/55 & Sev/Wounded 14/8/55 Sebastopol
4402	Philip Herity		Sev/Wounded 8/9/55 Redan
4219	Edward Hockley		D
3964	James Howlett		KIA Sebastopol 18/6/55. WO Regt 15/7/57
4566	John Hulme		
4635	Samuel Johnson		Sly/Wounded 17/8/55; Sev/Wounded 8/9/55 Redan. Sent away. D
4100	George Kent		
4521	Charles Lewis		Wounded/Dead 12/8/55 Sebastopol
4516	Martin Macks		
4104	Thomas Macmillian		
4418/3946	James Martin		Killed 3/7/55. (WO 1/4/57)
3861	Frederick Meades		Not shown?
4210	William Mellor		
4261	John Mills		
4408	Charles Millson		
4016/4816	William Nicolls		Sev/Wounded 18/6/55 Redan. (4012) Died 19/8/54 Monastre)
3976	James Packer		KIA Sebastopol 7/9/55
4165	James Pack		
4356	James Perks		18/6/55
3511	Stephen/Joseph Philips	A——	Sly/Wounded 5/9/55 Sebastopol
4542	George Priest/Preece		
4048	John Quantrill/Quainhill		
4002	William Rage		Died 4/8/55
4231/4231	James A. Reed		4/8/1855

3919	James/Charles Rigby		Wounded/Dead 10/6/55 Sebastopol. H+R
3984	Robert Rivers		
4106	Oliver Simpson	D	
4618	James/Charles Skerrett		
4433	George Smith		
3955	James Staff		
4494	Walter Staff		
4481	Daniel Turnstall/ Tuostall		Wounded/Dead 8/9/55 Redan
4266	Peter Walsh		

Captain Elrington's Company

Captain

	F. R. Elrington	AI–S

Lieutenants

	J. Rowles	AI–S	
	H. R. L. Newdigate	A——	Wounded at Inkerman
	[…] […]	AI—	
	[…] […]	AI—	
	[…] […]	A——	

Colour Sergeant

1133	Thomas Wilkinson	AI–S	28/6/55 Sebastopol

Sergeants

2471	William Adams	–I—	
2658	William Johnson	AI—	
2069	William Mills/Wills?	AI—	
1815	William Richards	AI—	Mutiny
2250	James Smith	AI—	
2359/2389	William Thorogate	A–B–	Wounded/Dead 8/9/55 Redan

Corporals

3181	Richard Beach/ Beech	A–BS	Sev/Wounded 18/6/55 Redan. KIA Sebastopol 2/7/55
3232	William Campbell	A—S	Killed 13/10/54. WO 28/11/56
3388	William Garratt	A—S	WO
2304	John Lee	AI—	

2549	Samuel Poundall/ Pounhall	AI–S	22/2/55 Scutari. WO 1/4/57
1272	William Trull	AI–S	Wounded 5/11/54. WO 17/11/56

Buglers

3483	James Gates	AI—	
2747	Daniel/David McCarthy	AI—	Wounded 13–17/10/54; Wounded 5/11/54; Died

Riflemen

4236	Henry Adams	——	
4160	Henry Arnett	AI–S	Mutiny
1456	John Asher	AI—	Sev/Wounded 8/9/55 Redan
2507/3507	Joseph D. Ashford	AI—	Mutiny
3809/3869	William Barlow	AI–S	Died 7/7/55. WO
3827	William Barr	AI–S	KIA 18/6/55 Redan
2653"	Charles Barratt	——	KIA 18/6/55 Sebastopol
3653	Patrick Barratt	AI—	Sly/Wounded 8/9/55 Redan. Mutiny
2165/3115	Henry Beckingham	AI–S	H+R 20/12/56
2014	Henry Bendall	AI—	Sev/Wounded 22/6/55
2738	James Bendall	AI–S	Wounded 13–17/10/54. Mutiny. Mint 30/1/57
3755	William Berry	AI—	
3755	William Bethery/ Bethrey	AI—	
3641	John Bishop	A—S	Killed 13–17/10/54 (WO)
2050/2052	Thomas Boyd	A—B	Mutiny
1725	James Bristow	AI—	
3107/3707	Andrew Brown	AI—	Sev/Wounded 8/9/55 Redan
2771	Henry Bryan	A—	
2319/3319	Andrew Byrne/ Byrnie	AI—	Died 20/6/55
3815	William Buchanan	A–B–	Wounded/Dead Redan. H+R 19/11/56
3813	William Buchby/ Bushby	AI—	
2943	George Cann	A—S	Wounded 13–17/10/54
3793	Joseph Cara/Carey	AI–S	Killed 5/11/54 Inkerman. WO 19/3/57
4069/4569/ [.]899	John Callow	A—S	Killed 13–17/10/54
3663	Thomas Clary	AI—	Sev/Wounded 8/9/55 Redan

3878	Simon Cockbill	A—S	(3848 Died 10/2/1855)
3254	Patrick Collins	A—S	Sly/Wounded 17/8/55 Sebastopol
[...]	Samuel [...]	–I—	
[...]	[...] [...]	A—	Mint 15/2/59. D
[...]	[...] [...]	AI—	
[...]9	[...] [...]	AI—	H+R 4/12
4317	John Cooper	—S	Dead (4217 7/12/54)
3665	John Cowan	—S	Died 19/8/55
[.]162	Abraham Cullough	—	WO 25/9/56
4081	William Day	–I-S	15/3/55 Scutari
1039	William Dea[...]	—	
2846/3846?	Henry Dodd	AI-S	Wounded 9/1/1855. WO 15/4/56
3669	Thomas Doolan	AI-S	WO
2842/3842	Patrick Drummond	—	
2838/3838	John Ferguson	AI—	Mutiny
3129	Horace Finn	AI—	Sev/Wounded 8/9/55 Redan
3364/868	Cornelius Finnucane	A—	Killed Alma, 20/9/54 WO 19/3/57
2902/3902	Charles Freeman	AI—	Wounded 5/11/54 Inkerman
4059	Joseph George	—S	31/1/55 Scutari. WO
1875	Alfred Green	A—S	Wounded 13–17/10/54. WO
3684	Charles Groves/ Grooves	AI-S	Wounded 5/11/54 Inkerman. Mutiny
3907	William Gullock/ Gulluck	AI—	Mutiny
2643	Richard Harris	—	
3365	John Hawker/ Hawkes	—S	WO Mint?
3648	Frederick Hillier	AI—	Sly/Wounded 7/6/55. Sev/Wounded 23/8/55. Mutiny
1844/1944	Samuel Hogger	AI—	Mutiny
3389	Charles Hough	AI—	
3473	Charles Howell	A—	Wounded Alma 20/9/54 (WO)
2790	Patrick Howley	A—	Wounded Alma. Sent Mint 1/8/63
2819	Robert J. Hudson	A—	
2968	Edward James	A—	
3620	Thomas Jee	–I-S	KIA 5/11/54 Inkerman. (WO)
3909	Evan Jenkins	AI-S	
2817	John Jones	A–B–	Mutiny
4195	John Johnson	—	

2629	Thomas Johnson	AI—	H+R 21/12
1721	John Kelliher	AI—	Mutiny
4245/8	Job Lacey	——	Sly/Wounded 16/5/55; Sev/Wounded 8/9/55 Redan
2330	Alfred Lane	AI–S	Died 21/12/54. WO 10/7/56
3819	James Lanrie	AI–S	Dead. WO 19/3/1857
3699	James Light	——	Died 13/9/55
2089/2829/ 2889	John Lloyd	A–BS	10/3/55 Scutari. (WO)
3594	William Long	AI—	
2751	James Lovelock	A–B–	Mutiny
3369	Daniel McGarry/ McGrury	AI–S	H+R. D. Mutiny
2046	Patrick McGuire	A——	C. Sev/Wounded 22/3/55
[...]	[...] [...]	A——	
3704	Anthony McNulty	A–B–	
[...]	[...] [...]	AI—	
[...]	[...] [...]	——	WO
[...]	[...] [...]	AI—	
[...]	[...] [...]	AI—	H+R 17/10
2773	William Monk	AI–S	Wounded 5/11/54 Inkerman. Mutiny
1881	James Moore	AI–S	
2785	Joseph Moore	AI–S	
3031	James Murray	AI–S	Wounded 5/11/54 Inkerman. Killed 18/6/55 Redan
1806	John Nelson/Nilson	AI—	KIA 5/11/54 Inkerman
3048	Henry Nevill	AI—	
3716	Thomas Palmer	AI–S	Wounded 5/11/54 Inkerman
4173	John Patterson	——	Sev/Wounded 8/9/55 Redan. Sebastopol Clasp. H+R 24/1/56
3872	John Payne	AI–S	KIA 5/11/54 Inkerman
3277	James Pedder	AI—	Mutiny
1862	John Hampton Penton	——	Mutiny
1829	Edward Geo. Phipps	AI—	Mutiny
3249	Emanuel Price	AI—	Sev/Wounded 18/6/55 Redan. H+R. Mutiny
4114	John Ranson	——	Sev/Wounded 28/3/55. Mutiny
2642	Charles Rason	A——	KIA 20/9/54 Alma
2065	John Rhodes	A–BS	13/3/55 Scutari
2387	Arthur Richman/ Rickman	AI—	Transferred to Newdigate's Company. Mutiny

3/2/437	James Robertson	AI—	Mutiny
3514	Thomas Robertson	AI—	Sev/Wounded 17/8/55
1346/3346	George Robinson	A—	Killed 20/9/54 Alma
4211	Peter Rooney	—	
2783	Joseph Rowe	AI—	
1863	Henry Scott	AI–S	C
3870	Charles Stephen Sheather	AI–S	Killed 5/11/54. (WO) (Medal in Regimental Museum with 4 Clasps)
1707	Henry Smith	AI—	Mutiny
3118	Robert Smith	AI—	
2871	William Oliver Smith	AI—	Promoted from Captain Erroll's Company. Killed 5/11/54 Inkerman
3224	John Stanton	AI–S	H+R 1/9/
3773	Cornelius Sullivan	AI—	
2253	William Sutherland	AI—	Sly/Wounded 18/6/55 Redan. Mutiny
1747	William Taffendon	—S	Mutiny
4162	Charles Tarrant	—S	
2792	William Taylor	A—	Wounded 20/9/54. H+R
4171	James Thornley	AI—	Sly/Wounded 13/3/55; Sly/Wounded 20/7/55 Sebastopol. Mutiny
1883	John Titcomb	AI–S	D
2367	William Trader	A–B—	Mutiny
4046	Richard Trundle	—	
3729	Thomas Turner	—S	KIA 4–5/5/55 Sebastopol
3499	William Tyas	AI–S	14/1/55 Scutari. WO
	Thomas Stivens?	AI—	
2093/2893	David/Dennis Verraker	AI—	Mutiny
4111	John Ward	—S	WO 5/10/57
3631	Thomas Wardle	AI—	
3859/3889	Joseph Wilkinson	A—S	(Dead 8/6/55 Sebastopol)?. Killed 7/6/55 Assault on Quarries
1749	Alexander Wilson	AI—	Sly/Wounded 8/9/55 Redan. Mutiny
3572	Frederick Wingfield	AI–S	Wounded 5/11/54 Inkerman
3739	William Woods	—S	9/7/55 Scutari
2857	Edward Worley	AI–S	14/1/55 Scutari
3321	James Wyness	AI—	

Drafts from England and transfers from other companies posted to Elrington's Company entitled to Medal Clasp Sebastopol

Colour Sergeants

3030	Daniel Fisher	AI—	Also FMM. Mutiny
1736	John Waller	AI—	

Sergeants

2306	Frederick Ansell	AI—	Mutiny
2395	Henry Carley		
3780	William James		
3089	Edward Parnell		

Corporals

4236	Henry Adams	
2941	John Edwards	3941 Corpl. Sev/Wounded 15/11/55, Magazine explosion of French siege train? 17/11/55. WO
2716	Robert Ellis	W/Dead 4/4/55 Sebastopol
3769	Thomas Evans	
3787	George Hickin	
2629	Thomas Johnson	H+R 4/3. Sent away
2891	William O. Smith	Killed 25/5/55 Sebastopol

Riflemen

4188	Thomas Alger	Sev/Wounded 18/6/55 Redan. Mint 8/7/58
4289	John Atkinson	
1362	Charles Ballard	11/8/54 Monastre?
4071	Joseph Balentine	
4940	Edwin Baughan	
4552/3/	William Blick	D
3093	Thomas Buen	
3961	Abraham Bullough	19/6/55 Killed Sebastopol. WO 25/9/??
4250	William Bumpster	
3319	Andrew Byrnie	
2883	Edwin Cave	
4170/4172	Richard Clarke	Sent away. Sev/Wounded 8/9/55 Redan
3362	John Coine	Sly/Wounded 18/6/55 Redan. Sev/Wounded 14/8/55 Sebastopol
3609	Matthew Cooper	H+R. Sent away

3982	Thomas Cooper	29/1/55 Scutari. WO
4536	Thomas Crowdass	
4167	Charles Cullum/Cullem	
3669	William Deacon	(3639) 21/1/55 Scutari
4351	Thomas Dorhaty/Dogerty	
3005	James Dowling	Sly/Wounded 18/6/55 Redan
10[.]6	John Dubson	
4574	Samuel Evans	
4359	William Evans	
4349/4369	William Farr	24/9/56. D
4129	George Finch	C. SO. 12/12/56. Sev/Wounded 13/8/55 Sebastopol
4178	Thomas Franklin	Sev/Wounded 18/3/55 Sebastopol. D
4348	Michael Grogan	
4766	John Hartshorn	D. 5/6/56
4643	William Harris	Sly/Wounded 8/9/55 Redan
3898	James Hawkins	
4218	Richard Hawkins	Died 6/10/55. H+R 11/3/56
4153	Joseph Hodgetts	
4061	Alfred Jones	Killed 10/6/55 Sebastopol
4638	George Key	(4039) Sev/Wounded 8/9/55 Redan
3915	Alfred King	
4422	Thomas Lazenby	
4448	George Leeson	
2304	John Lee	
3783	John Lewis AI—	
4602	Thomas McAvan	
4632	Frederick McEvoy	H+R
4212	George McPherson/McPhesson	KIA 18/6/55 Sebastopol
4406	James Malmsley	Sent away. Mint 20/9/57
4456	Mark Manders	
3586	Edward Marrall/Marratt	Wounded 5/11/54 Inkerman
3973	William Marriott	(3974) KIA 18/6/55 Sebastopol. WO
4129	William Martin	
3705	Frederick Matthews	H+R 2/10/56
4523	William Mellows	
4186	Alex/Alfred Mitchell	Sev/Wounded 18/6/55 Redan. D

3710	Robert Moffatt	H+R 19/10
2550	Thomas Morgan	D
4254	Lewis/Louis O'Dowd	
[.]401	Robert [...]	
4354/2454	William Picken	Sev/Wounded 8/9/55 Redan
3954	John Rice	
1815	Matthew Richards	
4421	William Richardson	
4518	Daniel Riorden	Sly/Wounded 8/9/55 Redan
4183	Edward/Edmond Saunders	Sev/Wounded 8/9/55 Redan. Sent away
4471	John Senior	
3913	John Sinton	
4273	Robert Skinner	Sly/Wounded 8/9/55
4327	George Smith	
4241	John Smith	
4110	Joseph Spick/Spink	Sly/Wounded 8/9/55 Redan
3546	Frederick Starkey	4/6/55 Scutari
3938	Thomas Stevens	
4739	Richard Strickland	
4519	James Sullivan	Sev/Wounded 6/9/55 Sebastopol
4513	Joseph Taylor	
4040	David Tucker	
4341/21	Henry Twigg	KIA 8/9/55 Redan
4735	Herbert Uphall/Upshall	WO 15. Medal also 9/11/55
3927	William Vose	
3621/2621	Thomas Ward	Sev/Wounded 8/9/55 Redan
4598	John/James Walkinson	
4469	Thomas Webster	Sent away. H+R. Medal 20/11/56
3930	William Werrdle/Wevell	
1292/4292	John Wild	
2062/4062	Thomas Wild	Sev/Wounded 18/6/55 Redan. D
3739	Henry Wilson	Sly/Wounded 17/8/55 Sebastopol

Captain Forman's Company

Captain
	E. R. Forman	AI–S	Killed 18/6/55 Redan. WO 21/8/56

Colour Sergeant
1283	William Dawson	AI—	Killed 8/9/55 Redan

Sergeants
[...]	John [...]	A—	(WO)
3317	Joseph Lassad	A–S	W/Dead 3/11/54. C
2884	John Mills	AI–S	KIA 4/4/1855 Before Sebastopol
[...]	[...] [...]	—	
3259	Henry Plumridge	—	Died 16th Sept 1854
1253	George Voke/Yoke/Noke	AI—	Sev/Wounded 27/1/55

Corporals
2253	Stephen Ballard	AI–S	3/3/1855 Scutari. WO 19/3/57
2830	Thomas Bennett	AI—	Sly/Wounded 18/6/55 Redan. WO
477	Edward Fox	A—	
2475/2474	George Hodgkinson	AI–S	Wounded 11/5/?? Dead 28/11/54 Scutari. WO 19/3/57
1340/3484	John McQueen	A–BS	H+R
668	George Palmer	AI—	

Buglers
3414	Samuel Hitchman	AI–S	D. 5/6/56
3286	Christopher Whair/Wheir	AI—	Mutiny

Riflemen
2697	John Almorth/Almouth	AI—	Mutiny
[...]	Thomas Arnold	A—	Since dead 31st December. WO 19/3/57
2235/4335	Frederick Barford	AI–S	Pte/Cpl. H+R 2/2/55? Sly/Wounded 18/6/55 Redan
2940	Charles Bateman	AI–S	Sev/Wounded 23/8/55
2712/3912	Elijah Bennett	AI–S	Sly/Wounded 29/6/55
2837	William Berkely	–I–S	Wounded 9th Nov 54; Since dead

[...]	Joseph Bolton	AI—	
2660	James Bone/Bore/Boor	—S	Sly/Wounded 6/9/55
3795	Joseph Bradshaw V.C.	AI—	Sly/Wounded 21/7/55. Mutiny
687/3657	Henry Brown	A—	Since dead 28th Dec
1796	John Brown	——	Dead 20/3/55
3134	William Brown	AI–S	Wounded (dead) Redan 18/6/55. WO 15/10. Mutiny
3372/3382	John Bryan/Bryant	AI–S	Sev/Wounded 18/6/55 Redan
4246	William Bruntell	—S	WO
3605	William Budd	A—S	
3840	James Campbell	AI–S	Sev/Wounded 18/6/55 Redan. M+C specially prepared
[...]	John Cave	A—	
4182	Henry Clark	——	(Mutiny)
[...]	Thomas Cunningham	AI–S	Since dead 6th Jan 1855
3948	Charles J. Davies	AI—	
4253/4255	John Day	——	Mutiny?
1710	Charles Dean	AI–S	
498	Robert Dean	——	
3085	Nathaniel Dennison	AI–S	(3055) 6/2/55 Scutari WO
[...]	[...] [...]	——	
[...]	[...] [...]	——	
[...]	[...] [...]	——	
3394	Joseph Dyer	—BS	
[...]	[...] [...]	——	
3934	James Elliott	—S	Sev/Wounded Redan 18/6/55
[...]	[...] [...]	——	
[...]	James Farmer	AI—	H+R 2/8/56
2822	Patrick Finnigan	—S	18/12/54 Scutari. WO 19/3/57
3581	William Ford	AI–S	Dead 18/11/54
[...]	Henry Gardner	——	(4194 Gardiner) 7/2/55 Scutari. WO 19/3/57
4095	Charles Goldsby	——	Sly/Wounded Redan. Mutiny
[...]	[...] Grant	AI—	A+I Clasps Regt 19/7/57
3785	John Harragan/Harrigan	AI—	
3957	Henry Hayward	AI–S	Sev/Wounded 15/6/55
3005	Frederick Haywood	A—S	
3826	Robert Heard	AI—	
4142	Joseph Hicks/Hocks	AI–S	Wounded Alma 11/12/54, not shown on muster. WO 19/3/57
[...]	Robert Hinley	——	

3365	John Holdsworth	AI–S	25/1/55 Scutari. WO 19/3/57
3687	Philip Hooton/ Horton	AI–S	D
3688	Robert Humpston V.C.	A—	Pte/Cpl. Sly/Wounded 22/4/55 Sebastopol. Mutiny
2005	William Hurst	A—	Mutiny
18[..]	George Izzard	A—	
4205	Alfred Jackson	—	(3/4/1855)
2770	Charles Jeal	A—S	(16/11/1854)
2445	John Johnson	AI—	Sly/Wounded 8/9/55 Redan
3863	Robert Jones	A—	
2281	Edward Jupp	A—	Mutiny
4199	Robert King	A—	Sly/Wounded 7/6/55 assault on Quarries
3275	Edward/William Lawrence	–I–S	WO
2231	Alfred Lee	AI–S	22/2/55 Scutari. WO 15/11/56
3626	Thomas Lee	AI–S	Since dead 16th Nov. WO
2232	Walter Lee	A—S	15/11/56, place not recorded. WO
3543	David Lenton	AI—	Sev/Wounded 18/6/55 Redan; Sly/Wounded 8/9/55 Redan. Mutiny
2617	John Lloyd	A—	H+R 23/8/56. Mutiny
3768/3786	William Lynch	AI—	Wounded 18–21/10/54
3117	Daniel McCarthy	AI—	Sly/Wounded 17/8/55 Sebastopol. Mutiny
31[.]9	James McCarthy	A—	4300 J. McCarthy Killed 5/4/55
3079	John McCarthy	AI–S	Since dead 19/1/55. WO 11/6/57
2138/3138	Thomas McDonnell/ Macdonald	A—	W/Dead 8/9/55 Redan
2752/3752	Jos./James McDonough	A—S	Wounded 15th Oct; Sly/ Wounded 18/6/55 Redan
2074/37[..]	Patrick McGee	AI—	Sly/Wounded 8/9/55 Redan
3[..]8	Alexander M'Lean	A—	Since dead 7th Oct. WO 1/4/57
4022	William Maggs	—S	W/Dead 30/6/55 Sebastopol. C
3[.]31	John Martin	A—	
3[.]69	John Miller	AI–S	Since dead 17/1/55
3717	Robert Miller	AI—	
3830	Robert Muir	AI–S	DOW 10/6/55 Scutari. WO
3814	William Noble	A—	
2502	Christopher Norris	A—	

[...]	Joseph Norris	——	
2663/5	Joseph Nugent	—B—	Sly/Wounded 18/6/55 Redan; Sly/Wounded 23/8/55. Mutiny
3351	Henry Padgham	——	Sly/Wounded 18/6/55 Redan
3996	Thomas Parkinson	——	W/Dead 28/4/55 Sebastopol. H+R
4151	Charles Parks	A——	
[...]	[...] Pearce	AI—	
3558	William Peak/Peete	A——	
3557	Frederick Powell	A——	Mutiny
3583	Edward Preston	AI—	Sly/Wounded 18/6/55 Redan. Mutiny
[...]	[...] [...]	AI—	
4168	William Quay	AI–S	5/4/55 Scutari
3767	Patrick Rafter	AI—	
2490	John Rawlings	AI—	WO 19/3/57 (24/3/55 Scutari)
2621	James Reeves	AI—	
3138	Robert Reynolds	A——	Wounded 26/10/54. WO 19/3/57
2767	Charles Rhodes	A——	Wounded Alma. Mutiny
2513	John Riggett	A—S	Killed 26/10/54 whilst engaged as a sharp shooter
3887	Robert Rivers	——	22/9/1854
2765	John/Thomas Ruffle	AI–S	(2/1/54 Scutari). WO
3723	Joseph Rutson	A—S	Woumded 3/11/54. (14/11/54 Scutari Since dead)
3840	Robert Sandy	A–B—	
3775	John H. Sawyer	A——	Sly/Wounded 8/9/55 Redan
4367	James Sladden	A—S	WO
3643	Charles Smith	A——	Wounded 3/11/54 (7/11/54)
2027	William Stammers	AI—	Regt 18/7/57. Mutiny
2786	Samuel Stephens/ Stevens	AI—	Sly/Wounded 18/6/55 Redan
2842	William Stickland	–I–S	WO 1/12/57
3128	William Henry Story	A—S	Mutiny
758	Martin Sweeny	AI—	
3727	Edward Tench/ Tainsh	AI—	Sly/Wounded 7/6/55 Assault on Quarries. Killed 8/9/55 Redan
35	James Theale	——	D
2701	Thomas Theobald	A——	
3857	Joseph Thomas	A—S	WO 10/1/57

1758	Frederick Verender/ Verinder	AI–S	WO Died at Sea
3183	Thomas Waldron	AI–S	Regt 18/7/57. Mutiny
4152	Abraham Walker	AI—	
2064	John Walker	—	
[…]	William Walsh	—	
1531	James Warrener	AI—	Mutiny
3933	George Warren	A—	Wounded Alma. Mutiny
3733	John Webb	—S	1/2/55 Scutari. WO
3947	George Wellerq	A—	Sly/Wounded 1/9/55 Sebastopol
4091	James White	A—S	Wounded 3/11/54
3126	John White	AI—	A+I Clasps Regt 18/7/57. Mutiny
3974	Charles Willett	AI–S	H+R
2144	Joseph Williams	AI—	
4091	John Wilson	AI—	Killed 3/11/54
4052	Henry/Harry Wright	—	Sly/Wounded 15/4/55 Sebastopol
2880	James Younger	—	Died 14th September 1854

Drafts from England and transfers from other companies posted to Captain Forman's Company entitled to Medal & Clasp Sebastopol

Colour Sergeant

2211	William Swarbrick	WO

Sergeants

2618	John Brambleby	Sev/Wounded 18/6/55 Redan. H+R 31/1
3078	H. Cartwright	
3517	George Hart	Killed 3/6/55 Sebastopol
4187	Adam/Andrew Hinchcliffe	H+R
4244	Joseph Seaford	Sev/Wounded 8/9/55 Redan

Corporals

4400/4416	Joseph Cawlishaw/ Cowlishaw	Sly/Wounded 8/9/55 Redan
4176	Joseph Lizzard	
3767	Patrick Rafter	
2701	Thomas Theobald	
[…]	Christopher […]	
4312	John Weller	
[…]	[…] […]	

Riflemen

[...]	[...] [...]	
[...]	[...] [...]	
3830	Thomas Bennett	23/6/55 Sebastopol
4339	William Bowers	
4407	James Campbell	
4252	Charles Christian	
4263	Thomas Clapham	
4283	George Clark	
4373	Joseph Clark	
4001	Joseph Cotterill	
4282	Robert Cox	
4343	George Day	Sly/Wounded 29/6/55 Sebastopol
[.]777	Henry J. Dolton	
4249	William Drury	
2394	John Eite	H+R 1/3
4545	John Elcombe	
4665	Henry Everard	
[.]597	William Everard	
3097	Robert Finley	Died at Sea. WO
3678	James Freeman	H+R 2/8
3714	Josh. [...]	Mint 10/11/57
[...]	Charles [...]aree	
3959	Robert Garbett	
4096	Richard Grantham	
3794	Sidney Grout	
4362	John Hadley	Sly/Wounded 18/6/55 Redan
3826	Robert Heard	
4655	John Hilton	
4097/8	William Hobden	Sly/Wounded 18/6/55 Redan
1094	William Jamieson	
4603	George Jervis	Sent away. 18/7/57 Regt
2020	Edward Kent	
4424	John King	
[..]49	David [...]	
[...]	Peter [...]	
[...]	[...] [...]	
[...]	[...] [...]	
[...]	[...] [...]	
[...]	[...] [...]	
4464	James Plant	No 4364 Sly/Wounded 8/9/55 Redan
4352	Charles Rogers	

3911	Thomas Seawood/Seaward	Sly/Wounded 8/9/55 Redan
4335	James Sheeney	No 4235
4603	Edward Sheffield	No 4403
4035	William Shor[...]	
4640	Charles Smith	
4375	Francis Smith	
4222	Henry Smith	D
3917	John Smith	
4314	William Smith	Sly/Wounded 18/6/55 Redan
3056	Henry Tarrant	
4399	John Warrener	
4410/4401	John We[...]sin	
4201	Benjamin Whitmore	Sly/Wounded 8/9/55 Redan
[.]363	[...] Wil[...]	Regt 18/7/57
4441	William Wilkinson	Sev/Wounded 8/9/55 Redan
3603	Robert Wreatham	Medal. Also Regt 18/7/57
4653	William Yorke	

Captain W. Fyers's Company

Captain

W. Fyers   A——

Lieutenants

[...] [...]
[...] [...]
[...] [...]

Sergeants

3524	Robert Bridgland	A——	(No 1709) Wounded 18–21/10/54. Killed 18/6/55 Redan
2077	Joseph Cook	A——	Wounded 4/6/55 assault on Quarries Sly/Wounded 26/8/55
2192	John Davis/Davies	A——	
2964	Andrew Holdaway	A——	D
2521	William Kemp	A——	
1866	George Lusignia/Lussignia/Lusiger	A——	(14/11/1854 Scutari). WO
2280	James Swallow	A——	Killed at Alma. WO 22/9/57

Corporals

[..]90	Charles Dancer/Dencer	A—	D. A
2758	George Hart	A—	KIA 4/6/55 Sebastopol. WO 2/1/57
1448	John Newham	A—	Sly/Wounded 18/6/55 Redan
2190	Richard Trundell	A—	19/7/1855 Scutari

Buglers

3547	Joseph Eite	A—	Sly/Wounded 17/8/55 Sebastopol
3026	John Davis	A—	Wounded at Alma

Riflemen

3650	Daniel Andrews	A—	
3099	William Atkins	A—	
3140	Thomas Baldry	—	
3910	Charles/Thomas Barrett	A—	H+R
5325	John Bates	—	KIA 3/7/55 Sebastopol
3052	Mark Benn	A—	Sev/Wounded 8/9/55 Redan
3307	William Bennett	A—	Mutiny
3797	Alfred Booth	A—	Mutiny
2127	John Booth	A—	Sly/Wounded 7/6/55 assault on Quarries. Sev/Wounded 8/9/55 Redan
3955	Frederick Brooks	A—	25/4/57
3823	Adam Brown	A—	
2126	Charles Brown	A—	H+R. S Clasp
3114	Daniel Byrnie	A—	
3333	John Canderton	A—	Head Quarters
2679	Patrick Carbury	A—	Regt 18/7/57, Mutiny
3354	Edward Carr	A—	Killed 18/6/55 Redan. WO 25/9/56
3506	William Christolow/Christeloe	A—	(Cpl) No 1567
3260	William Cooper	A—	KIA 16/6/55 Sebastopol. WO
3750	Elijah Coston	A—	Wounded at Alma. D. Mutiny
2614	Jesse Crew(e)	A—	KIA 29/6/55 Sebastopol. WO
3573	James Crockford	A–B–	16/1/55
3891	Theopholus Cross	A—	
[...]	John Cox	A—	
1520	Samuel Davidson	AI—	D
2746	Edward Davis (1st)	A—	22/1/55 Scutari. WO 19/3/57
3848/4848	Edward Davis (2nd)	A—	C. Sev/Wounded 18/6/55 Redan

2004	William Downs	A—	22/2/55 Scutari. WO 19/3/57
2551	William Duthie/ Dutchie	A—	KIA 18/6/55 Redan. WO
3945	Charles Earle	A—	Mutiny
3671	Thomas East	A–B–	Sev/Wounded 18/6/55 Redan
3672	Peter Easton	A—	Died 30–31/12/54 Balaklava
2459	Benjamin Eaton	A—	Sly/Wounded 18/6/55 Redan. Mutiny
3462	William Eite	A—	H+R
2377/3377	John Elliott	A—	H+R
1715	John Everitt/Everad	A—	
2404	James Ewens	A—	
1644	Joseph Ewens	A—	WO
1730	George Faulkner	A–B–	Died 4/11/54 Balaklava. WO. B
2822/3822	William Ferguson	A—	Sly/Wounded 10/8/55 Sebastopol; Sly/Wounded 8/9/55 Redan
3673	Prince Finch	A—	At Headquarters. D
3825/3385	George Gerrard	A—	
3501	John Giles	A–B–	D. Mutiny
1579	James Goodwin	A—	Sly/Wounded 18/6/55 Redan. Mutiny
1394	William Goodwin	A—	C. Mutiny
3293	Charles Gray	A—	Killed 18/6/55. WO
3682	Robert Green	A—	Sev/Wounded 20/9/57 Redan. Mint
2776	Frederick Greenwood	A–B–	Wounded 18. 6. 55 Redan. Mutiny
3685/3686	Hugh Hannan	A—	Sly/Wounded 23/8/55 Sebastopol; Sly/Wounded 8/9/55 Redan. Mutiny
4156	Richard Harris	A—	28/1/55 Scutari
2711	William Harris (1st)	A—	Died 7/10/54 Balaklava. WO
3780/3788	William Harris (2nd)	A—	
3517	George Hart	A—	Mutiny
1701	Samuel Haseman/ Haysman	A—	
3967	William Haynes/ Haines	A–B–	Sev/Wounded 8/9/55 Redan. Mutiny
4159	Joseph Hewitt	A—	Sev/Wounded 18/6/55 Redan
2617	Henry Hill	AI—	H+R. 21/1/56
3495	Joseph/James Hook	A—	25/6/55. WO

4177	Robert Howden	A—	KIA 8/9/55 Sebastopol WO 17/11/56
3585	Thomas Ilsley	A—	
1766	Thomas Jeffery	A–S	D. H+R 21/6/56. Former Medal lost
2876	Thomas Jordon	A—	Sev/Wounded 18/6/55; Sly/Wounded 8/9/55 Redan
3690	Peter Keating/Kealing	A–S	Died 30/9/54
3225	Charles Kennett	A–S	WO
2806/3806	James Kerr	A—	Sly/Wounded 18/6/55 Redan. Mutiny
3694	Thomas King	A–S	Sev/Wounded 18/6/55 Redan. C
2791	Henry Lee	A–S	H+R
33/3572	James Long	A–BS	Sly/Wounded 3/7/55 Sebastopol. 11/7/55
[..]22	William Long	A—	Wounded Alma. C
3706	Michael McCormick	A—	
1932	William Major	A—	
3381	John Mayberry/Maybry	A–S	H+R Sev/Wounded 18/6/55 Redan
1124	William Mexstead	A–S	22/1/55 Scutari
3600	Richard Millership/Milluship	A—	
2832/3832	Henry Milline	A—	Sly/Wounded 20/1/55. Mutiny
2637	William Moss	A—	Mutiny
2859	George Mould	A–S	Sev/Wounded 18/6/55 Redan
3305	Joseph New	A–S	KIA 18/6/55 Sebastopol Redan. WO
3562	William Olive	A–B–	
1433	Thomas Ovey	A—	Sev/Wounded 18/6/55 Redan. Mint 30/1/57
3394	Charles Overall	A—	Mutiny
2044/2644	James Payton/Paton	A–S	Died 3/10/54
3089	Edward Parnell	A—	
3100	William Henry Pence/Pierce	A–S	H+R
2777	William Phipps	A—	
3/5718	Thomas Pine	A—	Killed Alma 20/9/54
2312	Henry Price	A—	Killed Alma
2369	William Robinson	A—	Headquarters. Mutiny
3611	Charles Salter	A–S	Died at Sea 1/4/57. WO
1149	Alexander Scott	A–S	19/3/57. 8/2/55 Scutari. WO

3724	Robert Semple/ Simple	A—S	Sev/Wounded 24/6/55 Sebastopol. 4/7/55. WO
2769	William Small	A—	
3099	George Fred. Smith	A—	
3918	Richard Smith	A—	C
1326	Thomas Smith	A—	
4154	John Sully	A—	Mutiny
2411	Charles Taylor (1st)	A—S	
3587	Charles Taylor (2nd)	A—S	KIA 18/6/55, Redan. WO 17/10/56
2176	John Cox Taylor	A–BS	B. Regt 18/7/57
1634	Edward Thomas	A—S	Alma Clasp 5/6/56. D
3728	James Tirney	A—	Regt 18/7/57. Mutiny
2743	William Trew	A–BS	B. specially Ordered 20/8/57
3932	Richard Turner	A—	KIA 8/9/55 Sebastopol. WO 19/3/57
2368	Henry Voss	A—	Died 7/10/1854 Scutari
2393	John Warsman/ Wareham	A—	
1214/1814	William Webb	—	
3849	Alfred Wheeler	A—	Mutiny
3645	William Williams	A—	8/9/55 Sebastopol
2263	Thomas Willis	AI—	Mutiny
3940	Thomas Witts/Wetts	A—	
2934/2954	Henry Yeats	A—	
3820	James/Joseph Young	A—	Sly/Wounded 21/6/55 Sebastopol

Drafts from England and other companies attached to Fyers Company entitled to Medal and Clasp Sebastopol

Sergeant

2546   Samuel Kirk

Corporals

2335	Frederick Bouford	Line through name?
3817	John Carroll	
3681	William Graham	
3719	James Purcell	
3999	Edward Stretch	
4444	William Sheppherd	

Riflemen

4537	Joseph Alexander	
4925/4952	Alan Alltree/Attree	11/11/55 Sebastopol. WO 17/11/56
4753	James Black	
4048	James Branning	
4425	Henry Brockwell	Dead 15/10/55
4544	Thomas Brook	
4281	Henry Buckley	Sev/Wounded 8/9/55 Redan
4553	James Bumford/Burnford	
4437	Henry Caldicott	
3506	Robert Christie	Regt 18/7/57
4498	Philip Clarke	
4412	Cornelius Crawley	Sev/Wounded 8/9/55 Redan. Dead 12/11/55. WO
4436	John Dakin	
4462	Thomas Dellon	
1890	Charles Dencer	
4064	William Fitch	H+R 2/9
4237	George Ford	
4248/4284	Henry Foulks	D
4565	Henry Graham	
4504	John Green	
4650/4630	Henry Gough	
2879	Henry Hall	H+R
4331	George Harrison	
2275	James Harwood	
4662	William Hebby	
3585	Thomas Hesley	
4637	Henry Hopcroft	1/12/56 Dead. WO
3931	Edward Jeffey?	3431 Edwin Jeffery?
4119	Henry Khons	M. Specially?
4347	William Lyon	Mint 366942. 2/8/1855
2637	William Map	
4567	William Marsden	15/11/56 Dead. WO
4611	William Naish	
4407	James/Joseph Partington	Dead 19/4/55. WO
4338	Richard Phillips	KIA Sebastopol 8/9/55. WO. Medal
4569	James Philpott	
4084	George Pitt	W/Dead 28/5/55 Sebastopol
3864	Edward Pritchard	Entitled to Medal
4238	John Robinson	

4428	[...] [...]		
4671	George Shelton/ Skelton		
4087	William Tandy		
3728	Henry Ternery		
4372	William Thompston (1)		WO 12/9/56
3895	James Wallace		Sly/Wounded 5/9/55 Sebastopol
4453	James Walsh		
4504	William Ward		KIA 8/9/55 Sebastopol
3888	William Warner		Sly/Wounded 8/9/55 Redan. D
4181	William Welfare		
4208	Joseph West		Sly/Wounded 8/9/55 Redan

LIEUTENANT MARKHAM'S COMPANY

Lieutenants

	W. T. Markham	A—S	H+R 10/2
	W. F. Thynne	A—S	

Colour Sergeant

1699	C. F. Munro	A—	

Sergeants

2379	John Andrews	——	
2664	William Everitt/ Everrett	A—	KIA 8/9/55 Redan. WO
2693	Lucas/Lucius Lucas	A—	Wounded Alma 20/9/54. H+R
1169	William Simpson	A—	KIA Alma 20/9/54. WO
2774	Alfred Slade	A—	Died Sebastopol 14/10/54. WO
2353	Henry Steer	A—	Died Sebastopol 9/10/54. WO

Corporals

1587	George Tapley	A—	Died Balaclava 21/10/54
2619	Thomas Farrell	A—	KIA 8/9/55 Redan. WO
2249	John Hazle/Hazel	A—	
3841	John M'Namara	A—	See Erroll's Coy as Sgt
2877	Alfred Powel	A—	
3399	John Shakespear	A—	Sly/Wounded 18/6/55 Redan
1279	James Wallace	A—	
2959	William Charles Wiffen		——

Buglers

3010/2	Robert Goldring/ Golding	A——	(Mutiny)
2973	James Pearce	A——	

Riflemen

3741	John Allen	A——	Mutiny
3649	Thomas Allen	A——	Wounded Alma 20/9/54
2551/2581	William Andrews	A——	22/9/55 Crimea. WO
3088	Frederick Arnold	——S	KIA 18/6/55 Redan. WO 17/11/56
2710	Edward Aspen/ Aspin	A–B–	WO 22/9/56
3652	John Atkins	A——	
1394/1594	Jesse Bailey	A——	Killed 8/9/55 Redan
3640	William Baker	A——	1/2/55 Scutari WO 17/3/57
2670/3670	Joseph Barnard/ Bernard	A——	30/5/54 Scutari. WO
3490	George Bennett	——	
3516/3561	Thomas Berkshire	——	12/12/54 Dead
2570	William Birkett	A——	Wounded Dangerously 8/9/55 Redan. WO 1/4/57
3009	John Bone	A——	25/6/54 Scutari. WO 17/11/56
3642	Thomas Bone	A——	Sly/Wounded 17/8/55. Mutiny
3342	Henry Bourne	A——	Mutiny
3635/3655	Frederick Bowen	——	Sev/Wounded 18/6/55 Redan. WO
2245	John Bowes	A——	Died Balaklava 15/11/54
1979	Richard Brown	A——	Sly/Wounded 18/6/55 Redan. Scutari 29/6/55. WO
3589	William Brown	A——	W/Dead 8/9/55 Redan. C
2218	James Buckell/ Bucknell	A——	H+R 31/7/56
3531	Jacob Burck/ Burch/Birch	A——	
2539	Alexander Carey	AI—	Mutiny
[...]5	Henry Coley	A——	
3344	Patrick Carey	A——	
3661	Francis Cash	A——	Mutiny
2828	Joseph Cave	A——	C
2438	Thomas Challenger	A——	Mutiny
1337	William Chapman	A——	15/11/54
4105	Walter Clarke	A——	
3604	Harry/Henry Cooper	A——	Wounded Alma 20/9/54

[...]	Thomas Cooter	A—	
3338	Daniel Cox	A—	Sev. wound 3/7/55 Sebastopol
2442	George Cox	A—	Sev. wound 8/9/55 Redan
3790	James Crosbie/Crosby	A—	Sl. wound 19/7/55 Sebastopol
[..]75	Henry Crosley	A—	
3667	James/Joseph Crevy/Creevie	A—	Wounded 13–17/10/54. Mutiny
2402/2407	William Crouch	A—	DOW Sebastopol 26–28/10/54
3510	James Cuttle/Crittle	A—	Sev. wound 5/9/55. Mutiny
2933/53	Thomas Dawson	AI—	
2742	George Dench	A—	KIA 14/6/55 Sebastopol. WO
3844	Anthony Doherty	A—	Killed 18/6/55 Redan
[..]43	Michael Donaghy	A—	
1951	Richard Donohoe/Donohue	A–B–	4/11/1854
1613	William Drain(e)	A—	Died Sebastopol 11/10/54
3489	James Dunk/Dank	A—	31/2/1855 Scutari
3874	Richard Duofield/Dudfield	A—	
[.]674	William Flowers	A—	26/11/54 Scutari
3922	Thomas Ford	A—	Wounded Alma 20/9/54. 26/11/54 Scutari. WO 19/3/57
3820	Philip Forsyth	A—	KIA 8/9/55 Redan Sebastopol
4544	Henry Gline/Glint	A—	Mutiny
3681	William Graham	A—	Sev/Wounded 6/9/55 Redan
3753	James Gray	A—	Sly/Wounded 6/9/55. Mutiny
3326	John Gray	—	
3683	John Griffiths	A—	Wounded Alma 20/9/54. Mutiny
3120	Philip Grimes	A—	
2317	John Hagerty	A—	Mutiny
3929	William Hallifax/Halifax	A—	WO
3810/19	James Hendrie/Hendry	A—	19/1/55 Scutari WO 19/3/57
3628	Thomas Henshaw	A—	
502	William Hill	A—	
4086	James Hollem	—	
3289	Charles Jacobs	A—	Sly/Wounded 7/6/55 Assault on Quarries. Sev/Wounded 8/9/55 Redan. Mutiny
2095/3595	James Jones	A—	Mutiny
2676/3676	William Jones	A—	Mutiny
3691	John Kelly	A—	Sly/Wounded 21/6/55; Sly/Wounded 3/7/55

2124	Florence King	A—	Sev/Wounded 14/6/55
[.]486	Henry Lambileu	—	
2692	Edward Ledger	—	
2474	David Lee	A—	
3502	George Lewis	—	
3086/3804	Henry Longmire	A—	Sev. wound 7/6/55 Assault on Quarries
1563	William McQueen/ McQuinn	A—	KIA 16–17/6/55 Sebastopol. WO 8/10/57
3304	William Mason	A–B–	Sly/Wounded 3/9/55
3812	Thomas Maxwell	A—	
3708	John Mimter	[...]	
3460	William Morgan	[...]	1/10/1854
2173	John Morris	[...]	
1556	Thomas Munday	[...]	Mutiny
3843/5484	James Murray	[...]	Mutiny
3780/3786	James O'Donnell	A—	Mutiny
2528	Edward Owens	A—	Mutiny
2051/4051	William Preston	A—	Mutiny
3763	John Pobby/Polly	A—	6/1/1855 Scutari
3250	James Quin	A—	Mutiny
4202	John Quin	[...]	Mutiny
3378	Patrick Quin	AI—	
2889	Robert Rivers	A—	
3536/38	James Roberts	A—	Scutari
1660/1616	Robert Sadler	A—	Died at Balaklava 23/11/54 WO 15/11/56
2789	John Sands	A—	Wounded Alma 20/9/54. H+R
3024	Samuel Sargeant/ Sargent	A—	KIA Sebastopol (3613 S. Sergeant Killed 8/9/55) WO 6/8
1688	James Short	A—	
4093	George Silverthorn	A—	
[..]29	William Simpson	A—	
3615	William Smith	A—	Sly/Wounded 15/11/55 magazine explosion French siege train
3384	John Stean	A—	Mutiny
3835/3825	Alexander Stewart	A—	Wounded Alma 20–22/9/54 WO 4/11/56
3969	George Stone	A—	
2718	Henry Stoutbridge	A—	(Swatheradge?) 22/9/54. WO 17/11/56
3215	Charles Taylor	A—	

3582	Charles Thomas	A——	Mutiny
2222	William Todd	A——	Sly/Wounded 18/6/55 Redan
2372/3	Joseph Tomlinson	A——	31/12/54 Scutari
3747	John Turner		
3730	John Waldron	A——	Sly/Wounded 26/10/54; Sev/ Wounded 8/9/54 Redan. 15/12/54 Scutari
2/3534	James Walsh	A——	
3356	Thomas Ward	A——	
3220/3320	William Watling	A——	D. H+R 21/6/56. Mutiny
3043/43	John West	A——	Mutiny
2599	James West	A——	
3627	John Westley	A——	Sly/Wounded 17/8/55; Sly/ Wounded 6/9/55 Sebastopol. D
3489/3498	George White	A——	Mutiny
2810	Stephen Winter	A——	
3770	Robert Wiseman	A——	Sly/Wounded 7/6/55 assault on Quarries

Drafts from England and transfers from other companies attached to Markhams Company entitled to Medal and Clasp Sebastopol

Sergeant

2628	John Krumbleby	Sent away

Corporals

4622	William Buschell	
3438	Thomas Challenger	
[.]621	Matthew Maloney	
1240	John Quinn	
1688	James Short	
2599	James West	Sly/Wounded 8/9/55 Redan

Riflemen

4646	William Ayers	
[...]	Henry Bassett	
4090	John Bates	
4451	Robert Bean	
4313	George Beaumont	
4473	William Bellinger	
4379	James Birke	
3143	Henry Bishop	
4579	John Bodger/Badger	
4039	Joseph Brand	Died 6/8/1855

3657	Joseph Brown	
4444/4477	Patrick Cahill	Sev/Wounded 8/9/55 Redan
4274	George Carney	
3660	Thomas Carter	Sly/Wounded 8/9/55 Redan
4337	Henry Cheater	
4033	Joseph Clark	WO Died 15/7/1855
4491	Daniel Cleaver	H+R
4571	James Clements	Sev/Wounded 8/9/55 Redan. H+R 31/9/56
3767	Edward Cody	Sly/Wounded 18/6/55 Redan. Medal Mint 25/9/57
4343	Michael Cook	Sev/Wounded 8/9/55 Redan
4138	Thomas Corlis	
4681	James/Dennis Crawley	
4508	John Crompton	
4472	Thomas Crosbie	
3668	Hugh Donnelly	H+R 16/?
4208	James Donnelly	Killed Oct 8/9/55 KIA Sebastopol. WO
4208	A. Dorsworth	
4230	George Dowse	
4272	Edward Dwyer	H+R
4358	John Edwards	
4594	John Elliot	(4584) KIA Sebastopol 18/6/55
4415	George Gatton	
1018	William Goddridge	
3370	William Goodall	Sly/Wounded 8/9/55 Redan. Sent away 1/2/56
1457/4457	George Gray	26/7/55 Scutari
4269	Samuel Green	Sly/Wounded 23/8/55 Sebastopol. H+R sent away. 26/1/56
[...]	William Hallfor	Sent away. WO
4311	Edward Hawkins	Died 10/8/55
3744	Alfred Holden	10/1/55 Scutari
[.]323	John Hollinson	
4419	William Hudson	(4417) Sly/Wounded 23/8/55 Sebastopol
3220	George Jenkins	
4397	Stephen Jennings	
1316	William Jones	
4832	James Kearns	
1721	John Keltcher	
4371	Charles Kent	

4396	James Lomas	
4175	Joseph Lowe	
4140	William Lowe (2nd)	
4389	Andrew McGrath	
1628	Isaac Madley	D (depot)
4533	John Marshall	
4290	Joseph Massey	
3488	John Mills	
3892	George Morgan 1st	Sly/Wounded 17/8/55 Sebastopol
4148	George Morgan 2nd	
4445	John/Thomas O'Dell	
3328	William Perkins	Sly/Wounded 22/4/55 Sebastopol. D (depot)
4648	John Pickett	
4589/4689	Frederick Redfern	
4461	Elijah Revel	
4215	George Slake	
[.]710	Charles Smith (1st)	
4582	William Smith	(4852) Died 1/9/55
4505	Christopher Summer	KIA 8/9/55 Sebastopol. WO 15/11/56
4394	William Taylor	
4685	Charles Thomas (2nd)	
4013	John Torner (2nd)	
4264	Frederick Walton	
4616	Henry Ward	
4570	Thomas Webster	Sent away
3985	Robert Whale	
4384	William Wright	

CAPTAIN NEWDIGATE'S COMPANY

Captain

E. Newdigate   AI–S   Sly/Wounded 5/11/54

Lieutenant

A. F. Warren   AI–S

2nd Lieutenant

L. Malcolm   AI–S   Killed 5/11/54 Inkerman

Colour Sergeant

1029	James Harrywood	AI—	Sev/Wounded 1/9/55 Sebastopol

Sergeants

1700/2700	George Brown	AI–S	Died 11/12/54. WO 25/9/56
429/2929	William Hayes	A–B–	D
[..]16	Joseph Irwin	A–B–	

Corporals

4034	William Blackstock	——	W/Dead? Killed 4/9/55 Redan
2562	Edward Boughton	AI—	30/8/55 KIA Sebastopol
3371	Augustus Clifford	AI–S	
3177	David Cook	AI—	Sev/Wounded 8/9/55 Redan. Sent away. SO 11/11/56
2192	John Davis	AI—	Mutiny
3244	Samuel Hanning/ Hemming	A——	O? Sebastopol. Dead 30/9/54 Varna
[.]371	Moses Paine	AI—	

Buglers

3291/7	John Lower/Lowe	AI—	Mutiny
[.]630	George Storey	AI—	

Riflemen

2107	Robert Arnold	A—S	At Scutari
2508	James Ashley	A——	At Scutari. WO
36/3175	Frederick Austen/ Austel	AI—	
2486	Charles Bannister	AI–S	19/3/55 Smyrna
2552	Henry Bartlett/ Batlett	AI–S	Killed 5/11/54 Inkerman. WO 15/9/56
1259	William Bauldshaw/ Baulkham	A——	Dead 23/9/1855
3884	David Bennett	AI—	
3796	Edward Birch	AI–S	17/1/55 Scutari. WO
[.]622	Thomas Blagburn	A——	(Since Promoted)
4214	Hugh Bolton/ Botton	—S	20/12/1854
2515	John Bowring/ Browning	AI–S	Wounded 5/11/54 Inkerman. WO 25/9/56
3625	Daniel Broad	AI–S	

[.]647	William Brockton	A—	On Command Balaklava. WO
[.]369	William Brookes	AI—	
2416	Charles Butt	AI—	Sev/Wounded 8. 9. 55 Redan
2557	William Careless	AI–S	Wounded 5/11/54 Inkerman
3103	William Castles	A—	Dead 22/9/1854
4141	William Catliff	——	Casliffe On. Mutiny
4075	Thomas Chambers	A—S	Dead 9/10/54. WO 1/4/57
3578	David Chapman	——	At Scutari
2075	Henry Chapman	AI—	
3378	Henry Church	A—	At Scutari. WO 25/9/56
2595/3595	William Church	A—S	Sev/Wounded 5/9/55, at Scutari
3335	Thomas Coakley	AI—	
2712	John Colebourn/ Colborne	AI—	D
3637	George Coombes	A—S	Wounded Alma. at Scutari 14/2/55
3021	Richard Cottrell	AI–S	WO 25/9/56
4037	Henry Cox	——	
3891	Frederick Crutchley	A—S	Dead 12/10/54 Scutari
2470	Frederick Dacker/ Darker	AI—	
[.]680/2350	William Dawson	A—S	At Scutari
[.]331	Robert Dow	A—	At Scutari
1923	Edward Dunn	A—S	Dead 4/10/55 Scutari
[..]58	John Dyer	A—	At Scutari
4174	Arthur Eaton	AI—	
2811	Joseph Evans	AI—	Mutiny
4280	Thomas Evans	—S	
3478	William Fairbrass	AI–S	8/2/55 Scutari. WO
3352	Matthew/Mathias Fairclough	A—	11/3/55 at Scutari. WO 19/3/57
2101	John Fitzpatrick	–I–S	Varna
3675	Thomas Flynn	AI–S	W/Dead 21–22/4/55 Sebastopol. WO 1/12/56
3676	Henry Ford	AI–S	Died 19/11/54
[.]392	Michael Gibbons	AI—	
1756	James Godfrey	A—	On Command at Balaklava . Mutiny
3688	William Gold	AI–S	Varna. D
3786	Cornelius Halpin	A—	Dead 2/10/55
3227	David Harris	A—	At Scutari. Mutiny
4257	Charles Harlock/ Hartlock/Harloch	—S	Died 6/7/55. WO 20/6/57
3686	William Hayward	A—S	KIA Inkerman. WO 5/11/54
2297	William Hepburn	A—S	At Scutari

1765	William Hewitt	A—S	Killed 29 Oct 1854. WO
3472	John Hewitt	AI–S	WO. Mutiny
3348	William Horton	A——	On Command Balaklava. Mutiny
3014	Peter Howden	AI–S	WO 28/1/55
3850/3860	Richard Hurley	AI–S	WO 30/6/58
[.]7[.]7	William Illman	A——	At Scutari, Wounded Alma
1723/1728	Edward Jemmes/ Jenness	AI—	
368[.]9	Edward Jones	AI—	At Scutari. WO
[...]	James Keary	——	
1783	Edward Keenan	AI—	Mutiny
[...]	Samuel Kent	A——	On Command Balaklava
4076	John Langford	A——	At Scutari
3366	James Lawn	AI—	Sev/Wounded 30/1/55 Sebastopol. 3/7/55
3700	Richard Lloyd	A—S	At Scutari. Wounded Alma. WO 14/5/59
2831	Charles Lockett	AI—	Mutiny
1517	James Lucas	A——	7/10/54 Balaklava. Dead. WO 15/11/56
2204	John Lyner	A–BS	At Scutari. 3/2/55 Sebastopol. WO 5/11/56
3782	Michael McBride	A——	KIA 20th Sept 54 Alma
2043	Bernard McCall/ McColl	A——	Wounded 5/11/54 Inkerman . Mutiny
3745	John McCarthy	AI—	Mutiny
3617	Samuel McCracken	A—S	W/Dead 18/6/55 Redan. At Scutari
4139	John McDevitt/ McDivitt	—S	23/12/54 Before Sebastopol
3324	Terance McDonald	AI—	Mutiny
3390	Timothy McDonald	A——	At Scutari. Mutiny
2074	Roderick McGregor V.C.	AI—S	Mutiny
3816	Robert McNabb	AI—	Wounded 5/11/54 Inkerman. Mutiny
2740	George Mansfield	AI–S	
3577	Charles Marsh	A—S	Dead
3859	Robert Mathison	AI—	
4190/4192	John Moriarty	——	Sly/Wounded 7/6/55 assault on Quarries. D
2812	Edward Morley/ Mosley	AI–S	

3830/1	Robert Muir	AI–S	DOW. 10/6/55. Dead 16/7/55 Scutari? WO 15/11/56
3347	John Mullins	AI—	
3712	Joseph Murray	AI—	
4129	Walter Newman	—S	WO 15/11/56
3713	William Nix	AI—	Sev/Wounded 18/6/55 Redan
3845	Hugh O'Donnell	A—S	
3322	Richard Palmer	AI—	Sly/Wounded 8/9/55 Redan. Mutiny
4082	Henry Parish	A—S	At Scutari. Mint 20/10/58
3778	Joseph Phipps	A—S	At Scutari 2/1/55
3468	Thomas Pinfold	A—	Wounded 13–17/10/54. At Scutari. Sev/Wounded 8/9/55 Redan
3863	Charles Porton	—S	Mutiny
1836	William Pratt	AI–S	WO 20/6/1855
2869	Joseph Purcell	AI—	Sly/Wounded 8/9/55 Redan
4246	William Henry Ravenhill	—S	
3776	John Reilly/Rielly	AI–S	Sly/Wounded 26/10/54; Sev/Wounded 7/6/55 Quarries
3212	Edward Roberts	AI—	4/8/55
3847	James Robinson	A—S	30/9/1854
[..]60	John Robinson		
[.]215	William Rogers	AI—	
3853	William Salter	AI—	Sly/Wounded 28/7/55. Sev/Wounded 5/9/55, Mutiny
2719	Frank/Frederick Scott	A—S	Sev/Wounded 1/8/55. At Scutari. Mint 30/1/57
1830	John Sharpe	AI—	
2/3980	Gabriel Sheard/Sheare	—S	Dead 28/1/55
[.]750/2715	William Skinner		WO 15/11/56
3287	Thomas Smith	AI—	Killed 15/4/55. Sebastopol. WO
3886	Charles Sutlow/Sutton	AI–S	Wounded 5/11/54 Inkerman
3873	Eli Thomas		6/2/55 Scutari
4185	James Thompson		
3894/4231	Joseph Thompson	—S	KIA 18/6/55 Redan
4017	George Till		Sev/Wounded 18/6/55 Redan
3802	Edward Tucker	AI—	Wounded 5/11/54 Inkerman
3601	William Tucker	AI—	5/7/56 Died at Sea
4089	John Vaughan	AI—	2/12/54 Sebastopol. WO 15/11/56

RIFLE GREEN IN THE CRIMEA

[...]	Thomas Walland	AI—	
2352	John Westway	AI—	Killed 5/11/54 Inkerman WO 15/11/56
3734	William Witeadon	AI—	Died at Sea. WO 12/2/55
2428	James Wild(e)	AI—	Sev/Wounded 24/6/55 Sebastopol +Mutiny
1639	James Williams	AI—	Killed 18/6/55 Redan
3614	Joseph Winson	——	Sev/Wounded 18/6/55 Redan
3711	George Wright	AI—	Wounded 5/11/54 Inkerman
3428	Henry Wright	[...]	21/12/1854 Scutari
11	James Wright		
2556	Joseph Yardley		19/5/55

Drafts from England and transfers from other companies attached to Newdigate's Company entitled to the Medal and Clasp Sebastopol

Sergeants

1709	William Broad	
3524	William Broad	W/Dead 1/5/55 Sebastopol

Corporals

2387	Arthur Richman	H+R 15/3
3513	William Wyatt	

Riflemen

4288	William Atkinson	
3178	John Austin	
4278	Samuel Barbes	22/6/55 Scutari
4103	George Birch	KIA 2/11/55
2679	William Bracken	WO
4092	Frederick Bristow	26/2/1855 Scutari
2054	William Burns	
4404	Frederick Carey	D
4480	Richard Childs	
4528	Edward Collins	D
4019	William Cooksley	Dead 7/7/1855. WO 25/9
3966	Edward Cox	Sly/Wounded 8/9/55 Redan
4230	William Dean	Dead 18/2/1855
4442	Henry Denton	
4271/4277	John Dove	Sly/Wounded 18/6/55 Redan. D
4588	Henry Dowds/ Dowden	
4074	Richard Duke	
4365	John Edwards	

4005	John Frecknell	
4228	George Fuller	28/8/55 Scutari
4341	Robert Glynn	
4555/4455	George Goldbey	Sly/Wounded 26/8/55 Sebastopol
4236/4336	William Goldstone	
4472	Richard Gough	
3893	James Hallett	
4057	Edward Halloway/ Holloway	D
4195	Thomas Hathaway	Sly/Wounded 5/8/55 Sebastopol
3880	John Harkin	
3896	Frederick Hewlett	Dead 7/10/54. WO 2/1/57
2620	John Hillier	
3937	George Hill	
4253	William Hollis	
4947	Frederick Hooper	
3868/3638	James Ingham	W/Dead 18/6/55 Redan. For M + Clasp 11/2
3923	Joseph Jones	Sev/Wounded 8/9/55 Redan
4330	James Kemp	
4515	Thomas Lake	
4030	Charles Lawrence	Mint 4/3/69
4191	Robert Lawrence	D
4133	Maurice Ling	(Entitled to Medal)
4300	John McCarthy (2nd)	5/4/55 KIA Sebastopol. WO 17/4/56
4595	Samuel Malpass	
3936	John Maloney	
4183	William Meredith	
4500	Henry Mildew	
4070	John Mitchell	
*3608	William Mitchell	Dead 19/1/1855 Scutari
4520	George Monk	Sev/Wounded 20/1/55 Sebastopol. M+ S Clasp. Sent away. H+R 3/4/57
4887	Richard Moorman	
4620	James Morris	Dead 27/9/55. WO 19/3/57
4490	James Murphy	
4166	Christopher Norwood	Sent away. Regt. 16/11/57
3157/4157	William Owens	
3971	John Paice/Price	

3071	Moses Paine/Payne	Sev/Wounded 25/7/55 Sebastopol
4574	Joseph Parkinson	Sev/Wounded 8/9/66 Redan
3914	William Pope	
4466	William Powell	Killed 15/11/55 magazine explosion at the French siege train. WO
2215	William Ragan	
4170	Alfred Rason	
4399	Joseph Rawbone/Rawline	
3760	George Robinson	
3990	Frederick Rumsby	
3395	John Shakespere	
4549	Henry Shapter	DOW 9/9/55
4192	Alfred Shaw	Died 3/6/55 Scutari. WO 15/11/56
4216	William Slow	
4315	James Smith	
4312	John Smith	Entitled To Medal. Sev/Wounded 12/7/55 Sebastopol
3986	Samuel Smith	
3503	Joseph Sparks	
4440	John Souell	
4158	William Sweetman	
4094/4099	William/Frederick Thompson	Sev/Wounded 10/6/55 Sebastopol
4390	Edward Tool/Toul	KIA 8/9/55 Sebastopol
4293	Edward Tool	Sly/Wounded 8/6/55
4325	George Ward	
2241	John White	Sly/Wounded 17/8/55 Sebastopol

Captain Ingliss's Company

Captain
I. C. Ingliss   A–BS

2nd Lieutenant
H. R. L. Newgate   A—— (In Elrington's Coy?)

Colour Sergeants

1090	Joseph Nutt	——	Joshua on medal. His service in the Crimea from 31/9/54 to 24/2/55 would entitle him to Sebastopol
1133	Thomas Wilkinson	AI—	WO

Sergeants

2356	John Connor	AI—	KIA 8/9/55 Redan. WO
2826	Frederick Edson	AI–S	
3030	Daniel Fisher	AI—	

Corporals

1873	William Burrows	A——	WO
2695	John Cook	AI—	WO 12/?/57
2165	James Crippin	A–S	Wounded 5/11/54
2808/3808	John Hilands	AI–S	D
3058	James Lee	A——	Sly/Wounded 10/6/55 Redan
2179	James Nutt	A——	Mutiny
2861/3297	James Varney	AI–S	(3297 Died at Sea)

Buglers

3127	Thomas O'Dea	AI—	
1390	William Golding	AI—	(Mutiny)

Riflemen

2757	Francis Allen	AI—	KIA 27/6/55 Sebastopol. WO 22/9/56
2309	William Allen	AI—	Wounded 5/11/54. Mutiny
4038	Thomas Archer	——S	Died at Camp 27/12/54 Sebastopol
3121	George Arnold	AI—	Mutiny
1578	James Baker	AI—	KIA 18/6/55 Redan. WO
3858	James Barnes	AI–S	Wounded 5/11/54. Mint 9/8/1861
2191	Thomas Battle	AI–S	Sev/Wounded 12/4/55. Died 27/4/55
2691	Joseph Bennett	AI–S	Died at Scutari 23 Jan? 23/6/55? WO 19/3/57
2191	Benjamin Bowyer	A——	
3023	John Brasher	A—S	Died 5/2/55 Scutari
3956	Frederick Brent	AI—	
3320	John Brent	——	W/Dead 13/8/55 Sebastopol. Mutiny

2616	George Bridgewater	AI—	Mutiny
2261	Henry Brine	AI–S	D
3658/3858	Michael Cagney	AI—	
4306	James Campbell	—	Sly/Wounded 24/7/55
3359	John Chapman	A–B—	Mutiny
2733	Samuel Cheel	A—	
3741/3742	William Bird Clerke/Clarke	AI—	Sev/Wounded 18/6/55 Redan
4023	Enoch Coates	—	
1193	George Collins	AI—	KIA 18/6/55 Redan
3528	John Cook	AI–S	Wounded 5/11/54 Inkerman
4138	Thomas Corlis	—	KIA 18/6/54 Redan
3230	Timothy Couch	AI–S	Mutiny
2848 2258/3558/ 2358	James/Henry/ William Joseph Dawkins?	—S	16/2/55 Scutari. WO 25/9/57
2358	Charles Day	AI–S	Died at Scutari 18 Jan 55
2650	William Deasley	AI—	Sev/Wounded 16/6/55 Sebastopol. C
3668	Hugh Donnelly	AI—	Sly/Wounded 18/6/55 Redan. C
3613	Thomas Downton	—S	H+R
3942	James Dunlevy	AI–S	Died at Camp 19/Jan
1716	Robert Ellis	AI—	C
[.]769	Thomas C. Evans	AI—	
1035	John Eyres	A–BS	Died at Scutari 18/11/?? WO 19/3/57
3610	John Field	AI–S	
3341/5341	John Fitgerald	AI—	Mutiny
2501/2661	George Franklin	AI—	Sev/Wounded 18/6/55 Redan. H+R 30/9/56. C
[.]671/3677	Robert Frary	AI–S	Wounded in trenches. H+R
4107	John Gabbitass	A–BS	Died at Camp 7/12/54. WO 30/9/58
3745/3747	James Gardner	AI–S	
2364	John Gibbins/ Gibbons	AI—	Sev/Wounded 18/6/55 Redan. C
3789	John Glover	A—S	Died 30/10/54 Varna. WO 19/3/57
4083	William Godridge	—	D. Mutiny
3392	Miles Haley	A—S	Mutiny
1154/4155	James Hannagan/ Hannigan	AI–S	

3504	George Harvey	AI–S	Wounded 5/11/54 Inkerman. H+R
2223/2323	Samuel Hembling	AI–S	
3858	John Herring	AI–S	Wounded 5/11/54 Inkerman. Mutiny
3599	John Hill	AI–S	9/4/55 Scutari. WO
3903	Samuel Hill	AI—	W/Dead 5/4/55–11/4/55. WO
3588	George Hiscock	A—S	Died at Scutari 13/Jan. WO 1/4/57
3744	Cecil Hitchcock	A—S	Mutiny
3150	William Holland	AI—	Mint 20/9/57
3150	William Holden		
3963	George John Holmes	AI–S	
2195	James Hubbard	AI—	Mutiny
3487	John Huxstep	–I–S	Died 5/1/55. WO 17/3/57
2882	William Jackson	A—S	DOW 24/10/54 received in trenches. WO
4279	Thomas Jones	——	KIA 18/6/55 Redan
2937	Richard Kent	—S	Sly/Wounded 14/6/55 Sebastopol
2692	Edward Kosswell/ Korswell	A—S	Wounded 18–21/10/54. C
3337/3537	Henry King	AI–S	Sev/Wounded 18/6/55 Redan. Mutiny
3315	Joseph Lacey	A—S	
4032	Patrick Lacey	–I—	Mutiny
1398	William Lawrence	AI—	
3696	Patrick Lewis	AI—	KIA 18/6/55 Redan. WO 5/11/56
3697	Timothy Lewis	AI–S	W/Dead. 8–9/9/55 Redan
3975	John Long	—S	Sly/Wounded 24/7/55. Mutiny
3393/3398	William Lowe	AI—	
1577	James Lucas	A—	Died at Balaklava 7/Sept
1028/1628	Isaac Madley	AI—	Sev/Wounded 18/6/55 Redan
1292	Henry Martin	AI–S	Died at Scutari 15/1/55. WO 19/3/57
1356	William Masters	AI–S	C
2803/3805/3803	Henry Mather	—S	
1424	George Midgeley	AI–S	Wounded 5/11/54 Inkerman
2324/3234	John Morris	AI—	Sly/Wounded 18/6/55 Redan. Dead 27/8/55?
3498/3499	William Muggerridge	AI–S	Wounded 5/11/54 Inkerman
[.]881	George Norton	AI—	H+R

3715	Frederick Nurse	AI–S	Mutiny
3746	Thomas Okey	AI—	
3360	Arthur B. O'Leary	AI–S	Deserted from Balaklava
3779	Edward Parkinson	A—S	Deceased 15/10/54
1401	John Parsons	A—S	Wounded 18–21/10/54
3239	George Partridge	—S	
3081/3181	William Pepper	A–BS	Died at Scutari 18/12/54
[.]232	William Perkins	AI—	H+R
3111/3121	William Pester	AI–S	WO
3953	Thomas Pinches	——	Sly/Wounded 18/6/55–31/8/55
1450/1414/ 4850	William Pope	A—S	Deceased 2/10/54
3108/4108	John Priestley	A—S	Died In Camp 2nd Oct ?KIA
3188	Thomas Randle	A—S	
1740	John Read/Reid	A—S	Mutiny
2007/3067	John Redman/ Redmond	AI—	(Sgt.) Sly/Wounded 18/6/55 Redan
2868	Joseph Reid/Reed	AI–S	Died at Scutari 16/Jan/55
3626	Henry Reeves	——	Sev/Wounded 3/7/55. or Sly/ Wounded 3/9/55
3616	Robert Reynoldson	AI—	
3865	Samuel Roulston	—S	
4101/4104	Abraham Russell	—S	D. Mutiny
3631	George Saunders	A–BS	B
1129	Edward Seath	AI–S	D
2787	Thomas Stacey	AI-	
3309	James Alex Simpson	AI—	
2950	Aaron/Aron Sheldrick	AI–S	WO
1397/3197	Henry Slamaker/ Slaymaker	AI–S	(Died 22/1/55 Scutari)
3110	Charles Smith (1st)	AI—	Died 15/11/56. WO 15/11/56
3327	Charles Smith (2nd)	AI—	Wounded 5/11/54 Inkerman. DOW 19/11/54 Scutari
3590	Henry Smith	A——	Died at Camp 15/11/54
3598	Samuel Smith	A–BS	Died 3/1/55 Scutari. WO 15/11/56
3991	Henry Strock	AI—	
3265	James Chas. Taylor	A——	
3638	Henry Taylor	AI–S	H+R
4227	William Taylor	—S	Died at Camp Sebastopol 17/1/55

3323	John Thomas	AI–S	Sev/Wounded 1/4/55 Sebastopol
1515	William Thurgood	AI–S	Mutiny
2861	William Verney	A—S	H+R 23/8/56. Bandsman. +Mutiny
4283	John Thomas Venables	——	Sly/Wounded 1/9/55
2448	George Wakefield	A—S	Died at Scutari or Balakalva 2/10/54
3540/3546	James Waters	AI–S	
2640	Thomas Watkins	AI–S	Mutiny
3542	Thomas Watts	A–B–	B. C
3735/25	Henry White	A——	Sev/Wounded 12/6/55 Redan. C
3303	John White	A—S	Mutiny
3471/4	James Winchone	AI—	3071 Cpl James Winchcombe Sl/W 8/9/55
3282	George Woods	AI–S	Died 1/2/55 Scutari. WO 19/3/57
4116	William Wood	——	WO 15/11/56

Drafts from England and transfers from other companies attached to Inglis's Company entitled to Medal and Clasp Sebastopol

Sergeants

1042	William [...]later?	
2958	John Dyer	
3477	Edward Fox	
1279	James Wallis	
3862	Walter Willyhill	
3471	James Winchcombe	Wounded/Sly 8/9/55 Redan (see above)

Corporals

2396	John Coote	(2696) 1/5/55 Died Scutari WO 18/1/57
367[.]	James Flowers	
4318	George Houghton	
1916	Joseph Irwin	
4115	Patrick Kilroy	
3393	William Lowe	
3065	James Warren	Sly/Wounded 8/9/55 Redan

Riflemen

4251	Henry Armitage
4196	Charles Badman

4137	William Barker	
4503	James Bellingham	
4240	Charles Bignall	
4029	James Blandford	Sly/Wounded 8/9/55 Redan. Sent away
2050	Thomas Boyde	
4317	Thomas Bridger	(4367)
4578	John Bryant?	(4570 John Bryant killed Sebastopol 8/9/55)
36[..]	Charles Cam[...]	
4477	David Capper	
2990	John Carden	
4423	David Cotter	(Colter 4493)
4242	John Dedward	
43[.]2	Charles Duckett	
4270	Thomas Edwards	
4262	John Everndin?	(George William Evernden 4262)
4304	John Fisher (1)	Sly/Wounded 29/6/55 Sebastopol
4439	John Fisher (2)	
4878	James Gardner	
4495	Samuel Goddard	Sev/Wounded 23/8/55 Sebastopol
4543	Robert Hall	
4060	George Handcock	
4645	Joseph Howard	
3979	Charles Howe	
1656	Evan Howell	
[...]	Edward Hughes	
4018	George Hutching	
1254	John Ives	
4204/5	William Jenning	Sly/Wounded 24/7/55 Sebastopol
4669	Henry Langridge	
1577	James Leekes	
4044	Alfred Lodge	
4123	Daniel/James MacCarthy	
4468	George Mathews	
3887	George Milton	H+R
4116	William Mood	WO 15/11/56
4305	James Morgan	Regt 18/7/57
4385	Peter Mulhern	

4198	Robert Nasmyth	Sly/Wounded 8/9/55 Redan. H+R 20/5
4243	Peter Nicklan/ Nickles	
4492	Dennis O'Connel	
3977	Henry Perry	Sev/Wounded 24/7/55 Sebastopol
3988	William Phillips	
4452	Robert Ride	
4172	Thomas Robertson	H+R 20/6/. (4072)
4181	Charles Robinson	(4684)
4684	James Robinson	(4481)
3882	George Smith	
3632	Lewis Soper	
4426	John Strachan	Sly/Wounded 1/9/55 Sebastopol
4028	Alfred Straight	Sent away. Regt 18/7/57
4450	James Tanner	
4547/87	John Walton	Sev/Wounded 8/9/55 Redan. Sent away. H+R 7/4
4319	Walter Wallbanks/ Walbank?	(4295 William Wallbank)?
4193	Jesse Webb	
4235	George Webster	
3727	John Weedon	
4591	William White	4391 Sev/Wounded 8/9/55 Redan
[.]639	Joseph Williams	
	Joseph C. Wilson	
4624	John Woodhouse	D

Supplementery Return of Men of the 2nd Battalion Rifle Brigade Entitled to the Crimea Medal

2690	Benjamin Bartlett	——	
4163	Edward Cook	——	Killed 8/9/55 Sebastopol Redan
3078	John Jones	——	Died 17/11/56
4287	Thomas Watson	——	
4042	Alexander Webster	——	Killed 8/9/55 Redan
[...]	Robert Witham	——	

Roll of Officers 2nd Battalion Rifle Brigade entitled to Medal for the Crimea

Colonel

A. J. Lawrence	AI–S	

Lieutenant Colonel

A. Macdonell C.B.	—S	

Majors

W. M, Bradford	A—S	
The Earl of Erroll	A—	Wounded at Alma
F. R. Elrington	AI—	
W. S. R. Norcott	A—	
A. P. Cooper	—S	
C. Woodford	—S	Sly/Wounded 8/9/55 Redan

Brevet Major

J. Stuart	A—S	Regt 18/7//57

Captains

T. W. Balfour	—S	
E. Blackett	—S	W/Dead 18/6/55 Redan
Hon. W. C. Campbell	AI–S	ADC to Lt. Gen. Codrington. In Staff Return
H. Colville	—S	ADC to Gen. Simpson. In Staff Return. Line through Name
W. J. Cunningham	—S	V.C
W. A. Fyers	—S	H+R 8/5/56
M. M. Hammond	—S	KIA 8/9/55. Medal Sebastopol
G. B. Legge	—S	
Hon. [...] Pellew	—S	Sly/Wounded 8/9/55 Redan
A. H. Stephens	—S	
C. A. Talbot	—S	

Lieutenants

A. P. Baileau	—S	D
H. W. Ballis	—S	
R. Borough	—S	Sly/Wounded 8/9/55 Redan Died 13/11/55
L. S. T. M. Carey	—S	Dead 10/11/55 Malta. WO
A. M. Drummond	—S	H+R 4/2/??
P. H. Dyke	—S	Died 19/4/55 Balaklava. WO 2/4/??

W. H. Eccles	—S	Sly/Wounded 8/9/55 Redan; Sly/Wounded 15/11/55 magazine explosion French siege train
F. Fremantle	—S	Sev/Wounded 18/6/55 Redan. H+R 1/2/56
S. C. Glynn	—S	
G. A. Grey	—S	
J. S. Knox, V.C.	—S	Wounded 18/6/55 Redan. Delivered to Major Newdigate
F. C. Playne	—S	Sev/Wounded 31/5/55 Sebastopol; Sly/Wounded 8/9/55 Redan
F. A. Riley	—S	Sl/Wounded 8/9/55 Redan
J. Ross	AI–S	
H. J. Ryder	—S	KIA Sebastopol 8/9/55
H. A. Scriven	—S	
James Singer	—S	Delivered to Major Newdagate 22/8
F. E. Southby	—S	
E. S. G. Woodford	—S	DOW 30/6/55. Medal + Clasp Sebastopol. WO

Ensign

H. A. Mildmay —S

Lieutenant & Adjutant

A. Haywood —S

Quarter Masters

T. Gough	AI–S	Sent to Depot 18/5
G. Rogers	—S	

Paymasters

M. Coast —S
[…] […]

Surgeon

J. Fraser AI–S

Assistant Surgeons

J. L. Brown	—S	Sly/Wounded magazine explosion of French siege train
J. B. C. Reade	AI–S	Attached Staff Surgeon
G. Young	—S	Attached 60th Rifles

Drafts from England entitled to Crimea Medal and Clasp Sebastopol for 2nd Battalion Rifle Brigade and Company not known

Lieutenants

Henry David Bailie
Christopher R. H. Nicholl

Sergeants

3241	Henry Murch	KIA Sebastopol 18/6/55
2[.]44	Joseph Traford	
[.]862	Walr. Willsher	

Acting Sergeants

4195	Thomas Hathway	(Pte.) Sly/Wounded 5/8/55 bombardment of Sebastopol
3974	John Reade	

Corporals

4623	George [...]
3559	James C[...]ch
3890	William James
4514	Joseph Parkinson

Riflemen

4434	Thomas Akers	
4378	John Andrews	
[...]	John Banford	
3921	Riley Bateman	Died 3/4/1924 Wingrove, Bucks Age 96 Yrs
4054	William Beared	Sev/Wounded 5/9/55 final bombardment Sebastopol
[.]4[.]3	William Beer	
4513	George Beaumont	30/7/55 Scutari
[...]	William Blien	
4041	Thomas Bottomley	
4617	John B[...]g	
3093	Thomas Breen/Brenn	Sly/Wounded final bombardment Sebastopol
4250	William Brewster	Sev/Wounded 8/9/55 Redan
4978/4179	Adam Brockbridge	Sly/Wounded twice 12/7/55 and 17/8/55 bombardment Sebastopol
4226	William Brook	
3866	Richard Brown	
2589	Thomas Brown	Sly/Wounded 8/9/55 Redan

[...]	Joseph Bunford	
3951	George Burge	
[...]	Thomas Carnes	
[...]	Samuel Cavanagh	
4071/7	Thomas Clark	Died 27/5/55
[...]	George Clark	
[...]	William [...]	
3681	Thomas Cooper	Died 25/9/1854 Varna
3926	Patrick Collings	
4427	Edward Crosby	
4[..]7	Allen Dinsworth	
4[.]49	William Dring	
4157	William English	(4187) W/Dead 18/6/55 Redan
4242	John Edwards	
4661	John Fisher	
41[.]7	Joseph Francis	
4020	Emanuel Gillard	Sly/Wounded 17/3/55 Sebastopol
4364	John Green	
3104	James/Joseph Grier	Sly/Wounded 29/6/55 bombardment of Sebastopol
4457	[...] [...]	
4415	George Gritton	
3962	George Harper	
4053	George Hounsell	
4074	William Jamieson	
4119	Henry Johnson	
4516	William Jones	
4501	Thomas Kearin	
4662	William Kelly	
3987	Edward Kent	Sly/Wounded 17/8/55 Sebastopol
4122	Walter Kenyon	Died 14/2/55 Before Sebastopol
3915	William King	Died 30/6/55
4223	John Leatherday	
[..]06	Patrick Lee	
3952	Richard Lyne	
4176	Peter McGregah	
4104	Thomas McMullen	
4068	Richard Martin	
4339	Thomas Mason	Sev/Wounded 8/9/55 Redan
[.]3[.]5	Henry Meldan	
[...]5	Edward Morton	
4299	Brien Murray	Sev/Wounded 18/6/55 Redan

389244	William Nash	(3892) Sev/Wounded 8/9/55 Redan
[...]7	James Newland	
[...]	[...] [...]	
3944	Robert Norman	
3488	Daniel/James Nutt	Sly/Wounded 8/9/55 Redan
1493	Daniel O'Connell	
4458	Henry Piery	
4829	Joseph Petts	
4334	William Pisking?	
4447	Howel Price	
4271	Thomas Price	
[.]648	John Printh?	
4189	David Pye	Medal + clasp Sebastopol issued to man 7/5/1908
4010	Robert Rayner	
3989	Benjamin Rix	Died date not known
4073	John Rodger	KIA Sebastopol 22/7/55. WO 15/11/56
40[.]7	William Sands	
4428	Barry Saunders	Sly/Wounded 8/9/55 Redan
4275	Joseph Saunders	
4486	Francis Shadwick	
4260/8	Frederick Shaw	
4330	James Smith	
4215	George Stark	
4557	James Steel	
4494	Walter Steft	
4235	Samuel Stiggles	
3958	James Stott	
4216	William Stow	
4426	John Stricker	
4469	William [...]	
4262	Frederick Walker	
4469	Thomas Walker	
3985	Robert Wall	Sev/Wounded 24/5/55 Sebastopol
4310	John Waller	
4406	James Walmoleg?	
3993	Nicholas Walsh	
4548	William Walin	
4296	Robert Ward	
4504	John Warnes	
4302	William Waterman	
4447	John Wattis	

4355	Henry [...]	
4590	William [...]	
4644	Thomas Wilk	
4063	George Wilson	Sly/Wounded 19/7/55 final bombardment Sebastopol
4136	Robert Wilson	Killed 8/8/55 Sebastopol

Notes on the Illustrations

Plate 1   Death of Lieutenant Tryon, 1st Bn. Rifle Brigade, taken from a water colour painting by Harry Payne. Some points of note on the detail in this painting; the badge on Tryon's pouch belt is for the 60th Rifles, the rank badge on the collar are for a Field Officer, Captain or Major. Lieutenant Tryon was killed while defending the captured Russian rifle-pits using a discarded rifle and not when advancing as illustrated. *(d)*

Plate 2   Lt-Colonel Alfred Horsford, 1st Bn. Rifle Brigade, later General Sir Alfred Horsford, G.C.B. *(c,h)*

Plate 2   Lt-Colonel Edward Somerset, 1st Bn. Rifle Brigade, later General Edward Somerset, C.B. *(j)*

Plate 2   Major Lord Alexander Russell, 1st Bn. Rifle Brigade, later General Lord Alexander Russell, K.C.B. *(h,c)*

Plate 2   Captain Henry Clifford, V.C., 1st Bn. Rifle Brigade. Served on the Brigade Staff as Brigadier Buller's A.D.C. Later Major General the Hon. Sir Henry Clifford, V.C. *(h,c)*

Plate 3   Captain John P. C. Glyn, 1st Bn. Rifle Brigade, later Lieutenant General John P. C. Glyn. *(h,c)*

Plate 3   Captain Frederick Morgan, 1st Bn. Rifle Brigade. *(j)*

Plate 3   Captain Hercules Walker, 1st Bn. Rifle Brigade, later Major. *(j)*

Plate 3   Lieutenant Hore Ruthven, 1st Bn. Rifle Brigade, later Captain Lord Walter J. Hore-Ruthven. Besides the Crimea medals he also qualified for the British War and Victory medals, WWI, a unique combination. *(j)*

Plate 4 Lieutenant William J. M. Cuninghame, V.C., 1st Bn. Rifle Brigade, later Major Sir William J. M. Cuninghame, V.C. *(h,c,j)*

Plate 4 Lieutenant Claude Thomas Bourchier, V.C., 1st Bn. Rifle Brigade, later Colonel. *(h,c,j)*

Plate 4 Lieutenant H. Tryon, 1st Bn. Rifle Brigade. *(h,i)*

Plate 4 Lieutenant George R. Saunders, 1st Bn. Rifle Brigade, later Captain. *(j)*

Plate 5 Colour-Sergeant John Fisher, 1st Bn. Rifle Brigade. *(h,i)*

Plate 5 Rifleman James Hawksford, D.C.M., 1st Bn. Rifle Brigade. *(h,c)*

Plate 5 Bugle-Major David Peachey, 1st Bn. Rifle Brigade. *(h,j)*

Plate 6 Rifleman Francis Wheatley, V.C., D.C.M., 1st Bn. Rifle Brigade. *(h,j)*

Plate 6 Rifleman William Reith, 1st Bn. Rifle Brigade, served in the Kaffir War 1853, Crimean War and on discharge went to America, where he took part in the Civil War on the side of the Confederacy. He was captured and made a prisoner of war. *(e,f)*

Plate 6 1st Bn. Rifle Brigade officers in various forms of dress, taken after their return from the Crimea. left to right:—
R. E. Somerset, A. Somerset, A. Brewster, P. Glyn. On steps behind, L. V. Williams. E. Palmer. C. Slade. G. Saunders and Ruthven.

Plate 7 Record of Service of William Reith, 1st Bn. Rifle Brigade. *(e,f)*

Plate 8 Officers and other ranks of 'K' company 1st Bn. Rifle Brigade. The three men on the left of the photograph are sergeants, the officers in the centre being Captain Brewster, Lieutenants Ruthven and Slade. To the right of the photograph are four Crimean veterans, one of whom wears the French Médaille Militaire. *(j)*

Plate 8 Colour-Sergeant, Sergeant and Rifleman. *(g)*

Plate 9   Riflemen Hannan and Ferguson, the affair in the trenches. This painting by Hayes illustrates the action in which Hannan took on, in single combat, a powerful Russian soldier. Some points of note: the Riflemen would not have been carrying their knapsacks on trench duty; Hannan wore his greatcoat horse collar fashion over his shoulder and round his body. The forage cap replaced the shako for most of the service in the Crimea, which numerous photographs and illustrations confirm, so it is highly unlikely that the shako would have been worn in this incident. The figure of Ferguson firing as he climbs over the wall is not a natural position for a right-handed firer, who would have led with his left leg for better balance. *(n)*

Plate 10   General Sir George Brown, commander of the Light Division. Engraving by C. Hobbs. *(d)*

Plate 10   Colonel A. J. Lawrence, commanding officer of the 2nd Bn. Rifle Brigade at the Battle of the Alma and through the beginning of the Crimean War. Later General Sir Arthur J. Lawrence, K.C.B. *(h)*

Plate 10   Lieutenant Colonel A. MacDonell, 2nd Bn. Rifle Brigade, later General Sir Alexander MacDonell, K.C.B. *(h,c)*

Plate 10   Major William Norcott, 2nd Bn. Rifle Brigade, later General Sir William S. R. Norcott, K.C.B. *(h,c)*

Plate 11   Captain and Adjutant John Ross, 2nd. Bn. Rifle Brigade, commanding officer of the Camel Corps in the Indian Mutiny and later the 3rd Bn. Rifle Brigade. Later General Sir John Ross, G.C.B. *(h,c)*

Plate 11   Assistant Surgeon J. B. C. Reade, 2nd Bn. Rifle Brigade, later Surgeon General Sir John B. C. Reade, K.C.B. *(h,c)*

Plate 11   Captain H. Colville,. 2nd Bn Rifle Brigade, later Brevet Colonel the Hon. Sir William Colville, K.C.V.O., C.B. *(h,c)*

Plate 11   Captain F. R. Elrington, 2nd Bn. Rifle Brigade, later Lieutenant General F. R. Elrington. *(h,c)*

Plate 12   Captain. (William) The Earl of Erroll, 2nd Bn. Rifle Brigade, later Major. *(e,f)*

Plate 12 Captain W. A. Fyers, 2nd Bn. Rifle Brigade, later Major General Sir William A. Fyers, K.C.B. *(h,c)*

Plate 12 Captain E. Newdigate, 2nd Bn. Rifle Brigade, later Lieutenant General Sir Edward Newdigate, K.C.B. *(h,c)*

Plate 12 Lieutenant John Knox, V.C., 2nd Bn. Rifle Brigade, Promoted to 2nd Lieutenant in the Rifle Brigade, from Sergeant in the Scots Fusilier Guards, for his gallantry at the Alma. Later Brevet Major. *(j)*

Plate 13 Major J. R. Glyn, 2nd Bn Rifle Brigade, Later Lieutenant General Sir Julius Richard Glyn, K.C.B. *On the Staff in the Crimea. (h,c)*

Plate 13 Lieutenant C. R. Nicholl, 2nd Bn. Rifle Brigade, later Major General Christopher R.H. Nicholl. *(h,c)*

Plate 13 Lieutenant Frederick E. Sotheby, 2nd Bn. Rifle Brigade, later Lieutenant Colonel. *(k)*

Plate 13 2nd Lieutenant Henry Newdigate, 2nd Bn Rifle Brigade, later Lieutenant General Sir Henry R. L. Newdigate, K.C.B. *(k)*

Plate 14 Rifleman Joseph Bradshaw, V.C., 2nd Bn. Rifle Brigade. *(h,j)*

Plate 14 Rifleman Robert Humpston, V.C., 2nd Bn Rifle Brigade. *(m)*

Plate 14 Rifleman Roderick MacGregor, V.C., 2nd Bn. Rifle Brigade. *(m)*

Plate 14 Colour-Sergeant James Winchcombe, 2nd Bn. Rifle Brigade, Winchcombe led the attack on the rifle-pits which distinguished three of his comrades for the award of the Victoria Cross. Winchcombe for ever afterwards maintained that he should also have been honoured with the cross!. *(h,c,j)*

Plate 15 Colour-Sergeant Daniel Fisher, F.M.M., 2nd Bn. Rifle Brigade. From an original daguerrotype. *(e,f)*

Plate 15 Provost Sergeant Mills, 2nd Bn. Rifle Brigade. *(j)*

RIFLE GREEN IN THE CRIMEA 341

Plate 15 Rifleman/Colour-Sergeant George Evernden, 2nd Bn. Rifle Brigade. This shows Evernden as a Staff Sergeant in a Volunteer Rifle Corps or Militia Unit. *(e,f)*

Plate 15 Rifleman William Salter, 2nd Bn. Rifle Brigade. *(b,c)*

Plate 16 Corporal Edward Morley, 2nd Bn. Rifle Brigade, taken from a watercolour painting by his father Ebenezar Morley. *(g)*

Plate 16 Bugler Tobin, Rifleman Hill and Corporal Robert Wiseman, D.C.M. *(b,c,j)*

Plate 16 Crimean veterans, 2nd Bn. Rifle Brigade, taken at Sabutho in India 1862. Most of the men appear to be Private Riflemen. Only the tallest man sitting in the front to the right has any rank distinction, with the pouch belt badge, whistle and chain of a senior N.C.O. It is interesting to note that the Turkish Crimean Medals have had the original ring suspension replaced by the one used on the Indian Mutiny Medal. *(b,j)*

Plate 17 Crimean War Medal 1854, showing an unofficial clasp for 'Balaclava' in addition to the official clasps Alma and Sebastopol. *(a)*

Plate 17 Turkish Crimean Medal with unofficial fixing suspension. *(a)*

Plate 18 Medals of Rifleman Francis Wheatley, V.C., D.C.M. 1st Bn. Rifle Brigade. *(h,b,j)*

Plate 18 Medals of Captain the Earl of Erroll, 2nd Bn. Rifle Brigade. *(e,f)*

Plate 19 Medals of Colour-Sergeant George Evernden, 2nd Bn. Rifle Brigade, Evernden transferred into the newly-raised 3rd Battalion and went on active service with them to India, later seeing further service on the North West Frontier in 1863. The medal for this latter campaign was not issued until twelve years after the event. *(e,f)*

Plate 19 Medals of Colour-Sergeant Daniel Fisher 2nd Bn. Rifle Brigade. *(e,f)*

Plate 20 Other Ranks' shako badge for the Crimea period. *(e,f)*

Plate 20 Part of the Bugle-Major's cloth rank badge, 1st Bn. Rifle Brigade. This is attributed to Bandmaster William Miller when he served as Bugle-Major before promotion to Bandmaster. Having been acquired with a number of known artifacts belonging to Mr. Miller, it seems very likely that it was his, or his brother Alexander's, who served in that rank throughout the Crimean War in charge of the Band and Buglers. However, it is the earliest example of the badge we have seen and is approximately two and three quarter inches wide by one and three quarters in height, silver wire on a black background. *(e,f)*

Plate 21 Cloth Minié Rifle shooting badge. This badge was worn by Colour-Sergeant George Evernden and the crossed rifles appear to be the Minié Rifle of 1851. Whether this was another ranks' badge or that of a senior N.C.O. is not known at this point. The crown above the rifles would suggest a senior N.C.O. Again, the background of the crown is red, with the remaining detail in silver wire on a black background. Approximate height three and a quarter inches by three and a quarter inches wide. *(e,f)*

Plate 21 Short Enfield cloth shooting badge. This badge belonged to George Evernden. Height three and a half inches by three and a quarter wide, red in the crown with silver wire on a black background. The crossed rifles look to be of the two band Short Enfield pattern for 1860. *(e,f)*

Plate 21 Colour-Sergeant Daniel Fisher's cloth rank badge for the coatee or tunic jackets. This badge is earlier than that of Evernden's. The height of this badge from the top to the point of the stripes is six and a half inches, the extreme width at the stripes being five and a half inches with the oval shape, four and three quarter inches wide. The crown has red in the back ground as the previous badge, but all the wire is of silver on a Rifle Green cloth background. *(e,f)*

Plate 21 George Evernden's cloth Colour-Sergeant's rank badge, worn on the greatcoat. The overall height of the badge from the top to the point of the stripes is eight and a quarter inches, with a width of six inches. The wire that encloses the outer edge is of a light brown, the back ground inside the crown is red, while the whole of the remaining detail is in silver wire on a Rifle Green cloth background. *(e,f)*

Plate 22 Enfield Rifle. Detail of Lock. Crown with V.R. underneath, 1856 date and Government stamp. *(a)*

Plate 22 Enfield Rifle muzzle and ram rod, showing front band and sling fastener. *(a)*

Plate 23 Nipple wrench combination tool for Enfield Rifle. *(a)*

Plate 23 Russian Bass drum Plaque, from the captured drum taken at Inkerman by the 1st Bn. Rifle Brigade. The drum was used in the battalion band until it fell in to disrepair and before being destroyed the badge was removed by a member of the band. It is now in a private collection. *(e,f)*

Plate 24 Albert Shako 1844-1855,. *(h,i)*

Plate 24 Officer's Crimean Bugle Horn Badge. Note the ornate filigree pattern design in comparison with the Other Ranks version. *(j)*

Plate 24 The Marshal and a Rifleman, from a painting about 1857-1860. This is the earliest illustration we have seen which shows the other ranks' marksman cloth shooting badge of crossed rifles. As there is no crown above it as in the Evernden badges, it could well be that Evernden's badges are those for a Sergeant or instructor of Musketry. Another item of extreme interest is shown on the Rifleman's left hip. At first it would appear to be the man's haversack, but the ridged shape and what seems to be a badge on the outer flap would dismiss this. The Rifleman was probably only added to give some extra composition to the main figure in the painting of the horse. However, he does seem to be in charge of the animal which, from the horse furnishings, belongs to a field officer or the Colonel of the battalion. If this is the case, then he is more than likely to be the officer's servant or orderly. We have been unable to find the true identity of the item at the Rifleman's hip. Some suggestions have been a form of regimental map-case or an unrecorded type of haversack of a private nature. The Marshal is a fine example of a Rifle Brigade Field Officer's horse, all the horse leathers are in black, with all the buckles in white metal, the bridle black leather with white metal buckles, bent branch bit, pads and plain bent bar link and tee bridoon, plain leather head collar and bridoon rein sewn on. Regimental bosses on bit and face piece. Throat ornament green, 18 inches long, white metal ball and socket. Dress lamb skin; Black Ukraine lamb skin, lined with moleskin trimmed green. Undress lamb skin; Black Ukraine lamb skin but with leather seat and large flap for access to holsters or wallets also trimmed with green. Breast plate black leather, heart-shaped backing to regimental device. Shabraque would be in regimental colours and of the same design as Foot Regiments. *(j)*

Page 31 Two Private Riflemen, Rifle Brigade *c.*1850 watercolour. *(g)*

Page 36 Scutari hospital and cemetery. Engraving after W. Simpson. *(d)*

Page 37 Lady Erroll's tent, Monastere. Sketch by Captain Clifford V.C. *(b,c)*

Page 49 The Alma. Print after Dupray. *(d)*

Page 61 The transport for the Light Division. Sketch by Captain Clifford V.C. *(b,c)*

Page 67 Sebastopol being viewed by the British General Staff. Sketch by Captain H. Clifford V.C. *(b,c)*

Page 68 In the trenches before Sebastopol. Lithograph by E, Walker after W. Simpson. *(d)*

Page 69 Sebastopol: view from the sea. Unsigned engraving. *(d)*

Page 75 Battle of Inkerman, Print after Dupray. *(d)*

Page 76 Old sentry on guard before Sevastopol. Sketch by Captain Clifford V.C. *(b,c)*

Page 76 Young sentry on guard before Sevastopol. Sketch by Captain Clifford V.C. *(b,c)*

Page 78 On sentry duty in the trenches, Sevastopol. Print after Colonel the Hon. W. J. Colville from *The Crimea in 1854 and 1894*, General Sir Evelyn Wood. *(d)*

Page 79   All that remains of the transport for the Light Division December 1854. Sketch by Clifford. *(b,c)*

Page 83   Balaclava town. Lithograph by R. K. Thomas after W. Simpson. *(d)*

Page 85   The French conveying the British sick to Balaclava. Sketch by Captain Clifford V.C. *(b,c)*

Page 87   The trenches at night. Sketch by Captain Clifford V.C. *(b,c)*

Page 88   Rifle Brigade guarding the advanced trench. Sketch by Captain Clifford V.C. *(b,c)*.

Page 99   Storming of the Redan. Engraving after W. Paley. *(d)*

Page 102   Camp of the Light Division, about July 1855. The 2nd Bn. Rifle Brigade are shown drawn up in two lines in front of their tents, extreme left background. Lithograph by Day after W. Simpson. *(d)*

Page 109   The attack on the Redan. Sketch by Captain Clifford V.C. *(b,c)*

Page 110   The trench in front of the Redan the morning after the attack, 9th September 1855. Sketch by Captain Clifford V.C. *(b,c)*

Page 113   Balaclava harbour. Unsigned engraving. *(d)*

Page 119   Encampment of the 1st Battalion Rifle Brigade at Constantinople 1854, from a Daguerrotype by I. Roberts. Engraving from the *Illustrated London News*. *(g)*

Page 129   The Battle of the Alma. Sketch by Captain Clifford V.C. *(b,c)*

Page 134   Balaclava harbour, one or two days after its capture. Unsigned engraving. *(d)*

Page 138   Scutari hospital: in the wards. Note the closeness of the beds. Unsigned engraving. *(d)*

Page 140   Bird's-eye view of Sevastopol, showing Allied siege-lines. Unsigned engraving. *(d)*

Page 146 Lord Raglan conferring with General Canrobert at the Battle of Inkerman. Sketch by Captain Clifford V.C. *(b,c)*

Page 150 Russian attack at the Battle of Inkerman. Sketch made by Captain Henry Clifford V.C. *(b,c)*

Page 152 Battle of Inkerman. Engraving by J. J. Crow. *(d)*

Page 159 Firing from the advanced trench at the Quarries and rifle-pits. Sketch by Captain Clifford. *(b,c)*

Page 165 Transporting supplies from Balaclava. Lithograph by E. Walker after W. Simpson. *(d)*

Page 168 Burying the dead January 1855. Sketch by Captain Clifford V.C. *(b,c)*

Page 170 68-Pounder gun in the 8-Gun Battery with the Redan in the background. Sketch by Captain Clifford V.C. *(b,c)*

Page 172 Bullets brought back from the Crimea by Colour-Sergeant John Fisher, which are attributed to having hit him when in the trenches at Sevastopol without causing any wounds. Shown with a modern one pound coin to illustrate the size of the rounds. *(h,i)*

Page 173 Camp of the 4th Division, 15th July 1855. The wooden hut with the canvas awning over the door, centre left mid-ground, belonged to the 48th Regiment; the tents and huts to the right of that belonged to the 1st Bn. Rifle Brigade. Lithograph by J. Needham after W. Simpson. *(d)*

Page 176 Storming of the Redan. Print after A. Dupray. *(d)*

Page 184 Veterans of the, 1st Bn. Rifle Brigade taken at Hamilton, Canada in 1911, all these men took their discharge in Canada where they settled.
(Front seated left to right) W. Wright*, R. Lannaway*, Band Sergeant William Gardner*, R. Jacques*, J. Hyam
(Middle row left to right) C. Cooper*, W. Burrows*, J. Fletcher, W. Nash, D. Farr, J. Clark, F. Weaver*, J. Johnson
(Back row left to right) C. Blackman, T. Rutter, C. Locke*, R. Fleming, H. Owens, W. Fricker, E. Hodson.
Those marked with an asterisk are Crimean War veterans. *(h,j)*

Page 194 Other Ranks' ammunition pouch viewed from underneath, showing pouch belt fixing buckles, flap strap and stud for securing the pouch. *(a)*

LIST OF THOSE WHO HAVE ALLOWED PHOTOGRAPHS TO BE USED IN THIS PUBLICATION AND OF PHOTOGRAPHERS

(a) By kind permission of Ron Debenham, Australia. Photography Ron Debenham.

(b) By kind permission of N. I. FitzHerbert, Esq., relative of Captain Henry Clifford.

(c) Photography James Cooper.

(d) Photography and kind permission of Philip Haythornthwaite author and military consultant.

(e) By kind permission of Eric Price.

(f) Photography B. Penny.

(g) Photography and kind permission of Michael Barthorp, author and military historian.

(h) By kind permission of the Rifle Brigade Club and Association, the Rifle Brigade Museum Trustees, Royal Green Jackets Museum Winchester.

(i) Photography Andrew Solars.

(j) Photography and kind permission of Derek Haighton.

(k) Photography and kind permission of Michael Haines.

(m) Caldwell collection.

(n) The Royal Collection, copyright 1992. Her Majesty The Queen.

Bibliography

Battles of the Crimean War, by V. Baring Pemberton. Batsford, 1962.
British Army on Campaign, 1816–1902 (3): The Crimea 1854–56, by Michael Barthorpe. Osprey, 1987.
British Battles on Land and Sea. Vol. III, by James Grant.
British Infantry Equipments 1808–1908. Osprey Men-at-Arms series, 1989 edition.
Cadogan's Crimea. Hamish Hamilton. 1979 edition. Book Club Associates.
Charles Ashe Windham, a Norfolk Soldier, by H. O. Mansfield.
Collecting Medals and Decorations, by Alec A. Purves.
Colonel's Lady & Camp Follower, by Piers Compton. Robert Hale, 1970
Crimean War Casualty Roll. Cook, 1976.
Crimean War Research Society quarterly Journals.
Crimean Uniforms British Infantry, by Michael Barthorp. Historical Research Unit Publications, 1974.
Diary of George Everndon 2nd Battalion Rifle Brigade, by kind permission of Eric Price.
Diary of the Crimea—George Palmer Evelyn. Gerald Duckworth & Co Ltd London, 1954.
Extracts from the Diary of Colour Sergeant J. Fisher, 1st Battalion Rifle Brigade. From the Rifle Brigade Chronicles by kind permission of the Royal Green Jackets Trustees and Association.
Extracts from the Diary of Lieutenant A. W. Godfrey 1st Battalion Rifle Brigade. Rifle Brigade Chronicle 1950, by kind permission of the Royal Green Jackets Museum Trustees and Association.
Guns and Cavalry, by E. S. May, 1896.
Heroes of the Crimea: Balaclava and Inkerman, by Michael Barthorp. Blandford, 1991.

History of the Rifle Brigade (95th), by Sir William Cope. Chatto and Windus, 1877

The Invasion of the Crimea. Revised edition, by William Kinglake. Blackwood, 1863–87.

Letter from Rifleman F. W. Hart, 1st Battalion Rifle Brigade, sent from the Crimea Christmas Day 1854. Rifle Brigade Chronicle 1925, by kind permission of the Royal Green Jackets Museum Trustees and Association.

Letter of Rifleman Hills 2nd Battalion Rifle Brigade. Rifle Brigade Journal 1976, by kind permission of the Royal Green Jackets Museum Trustees and Association.

Letters and Sketches from the Crimea, by Henry H. Clifford. Michael Joseph, 1956.

Letters of Lieutenant T. H. Bramston from the Crimea. Rifle Brigade Chronicle, by kind permission of the Royal Green Jackets Museum: Trustees and Association.

Letters of Rifleman John Pine 1st Battalion Rifle Brigade, by the kind permission of Ms. Alice Sheridan, C.B.E.

Lieutenant H. Tryon 1st Battalion Rifle Brigade. Extract from the London Journal—published at the time of the Crimea. Rifle Brigade Chronicle 1954, by kind permission of the Royal Green Jackets Museum Trustees and Association.

Major E. Norcott's Crimea Diary. Rifle Brigade Chronicle. by kind permission Royal Green Jackets Museum Trustees and Association.

Man of Wars (Russell of the Times), by Alan Hankinson. Heinemann, London, 1982.

Medals of the British Army and How they were Won, by Thomas Carter. London, 1861.

Memoir of Captain M. M. Hammond. Sixth edition, 1859. J. Nisbet & Co., London.

Military Illustrated, monthly magazine.

Orders and Medals Research Society Journals.

Redan Windham—The Crimean Diary and Letters of Lieutenant General Sir Charles Ashe Windham K.C.B., edited by Maj. Hugh Pearse. Kegan Paul, London, 1897.

A Soldier's Experience or a Voice from the Ranks, by Sergeant Major T. Gowing 7th The Royal Fusiliers. Published 1886.

Royal Green Jackets Museum

The Royal Green Jackets Museum which is housed in Peninsula Barracks in the heart of Winchester is a must for all those interested in military history. It houses the splendour of uniforms, guns, medals, regimental silver and many more relics and artifacts of three of the most famous Regiments of the British Army. The 43rd and 52nd Light Infantry Regiments (Oxfordshire & Buckinghamshire Light Infantry), 60th Rifles (King's Royal Rifle Corps), The Rifle Brigade (95th Rifles). Its most outstanding feature is the Waterloo diorama of over 20,000 model soldiers with a sound and light display on the battle. For those interested in the Crimea War the Rifle Brigade have many items from this period on display.

It is open Monday to Saturday from 10.00 hrs. to 17.00 hrs. Sunday 12.00 hrs. to 16.00 hrs. Cost of entry at time of writing Adults £2. Children and Senior Citizens £1, Groups of more than ten persons discount of 50 pence per head.

Postal Address for further information:
The Royal Green Jackets,
Peninsula Barracks, Romsey Road,
Winchester, Hampshire, SO23 8TS.

The Crimean War Research Society

If you have enjoyed the contents of this book and would like further information on the Crimea, then contact the secretary of the Crimean War Research Society:

David Cliff,
4 Castle Estate, Castle Lane, Ripponden,
West Yorkshire HX6 4JY.

The aim of the society is to research all aspects of the Campaign including the British and Allied Armies and Russians. Their arms, equipment, uniform, tactics, medals, war games, naval and many other interests are all catered for.

Subscription rates per annum are U.K. £8, Overseas U.S.$18, £12 Sterling or £13 Local Currency. This covers the issue of four quarterly journals with a variety of topics in which the reader can also take part by sending material for publication if they so wish. The society also produces a number of publications which can be bought from the Publications Officer.

The CWRS is a warm, friendly, easy-going society and new members will be most welcome. If you would like further information then contact the secretary at the address above and please mention *Rifle Green in the Crimea*.

The Crimean War has taken on fresh interest over the last couple of years as the country is being opened up to cater for the military historian. Members of the society have already benefited from this by going on organised tours of the area. Future tours are planned.

DESIGNED AND SET
IN 11 POINT GARAMOND LEADED 1½ POINTS
WITH 18 POINT FOR DISPLAY
BY
LANGLANDS EDITION
LOUGHBOROUGH, LEICESTERSHIRE

PRINTED AND BOUND
BY
THE CROMWELL PRESS
BROUGHTON GIFFORD
MELKSHAM, WILTSHIRE